Classics In
Child Development

Classics In
Child Development

CHILDREN ABOVE
1 8 O I Q
STANFORD – BINET
Origin and Development

by

Leta S. Hollingworth

ARNO PRESS
A New York Times Company

New York — 1975

Reprint Edition 1975 by Arno Press Inc.

Reprinted from a copy in
  The Newark Public Library

Classics in Child Development
ISBN for complete set: 0-405-06450-0
See last pages of this volume for titles.

Manufactured in the United States of America

———◆———

Library of Congress Cataloging in Publication Data

Hollingworth, Leta Stetter, 1886-1939.
    Children above 180 I Q.

    (Classics in child development)
    Reprint of the 1942 ed. published by World Book Co.,
Yonkers-on-Hudson, N. Y., which was issued in: Measure-
ment and adjustment series.
    Includes bibliographies and index.
    1. Gifted children. I. Title. II. Series.
III. Series: Measurement and adjustment series.
BF412.H6 1975   155.4'5'5   74-21417
ISBN 0-405-06467-5

MEASUREMENT AND ADJUSTMENT
SERIES
Edited by Lewis M. Terman

CHILDREN ABOVE
1 8 O I Q
STANFORD - BINET
Origin and Development

by

Leta S. Hollingworth

Teachers College
Columbia University

Yonkers-on-Hudson, New York
WORLD BOOK COMPANY

WORLD BOOK COMPANY

THE HOUSE OF APPLIED KNOWLEDGE

Established MCMV by Caspar W. Hodgson

YONKERS-ON-HUDSON, NEW YORK

2126 PRAIRIE AVENUE, CHICAGO

BOSTON: ATLANTA: DALLAS: SAN FRANCISCO: PORTLAND

1

Foreword

SHORTLY after the year 1924 Leta S. Hollingworth prepared a manuscript on "Children above 180 IQ (Stanford Binet)" in which she surveyed the material on the topic available up to that date and added accounts of five cases which she had studied individually.[1] As the years went by she held back the manuscript from publication and one by one found seven more cases to be included in her list. At the time of her death in 1939 she had begun to revise this manuscript, bringing the survey up to date and adding the new cases. The present book gives as much of this revision from her own hand as is available. The Preface and Chapters 1, 2, and 3 are as she wrote them. The accounts of the first five cases are given just as she originally wrote them up, but to them "editorial supplements" have been added in which an endeavor has been made to present for each case such data as have been found in her files, with little in the way of discussion or interpretation.

The seven new cases which the original author had intended to include in the manuscript she had not yet written up. For these, therefore, it has been necessary to study the data she had accumulated for each child, to secure additional data when and where possible, and to present such an ac-

---

[1] Chapter 9 of *Gifted Children*, published in 1926, bears the title "Children Who Test above 180 IQ (Stanford-Binet)." Some of the cases described more fully in the monograph manuscript are also sketched in that chapter.

count of each as she might herself have written, patterned after her reports of the earlier cases.

Much is lost that would have been contributed had the author lived to complete her project. She knew these cases intimately and at first hand. Some of them she had followed for as long as twenty years, taking a personal interest in the individual children and their problems, advising them, assisting them, continuously observing them, and frequently testing and measuring them.

Particularly inadequate must be the accounts of the later development of the individuals herein described, for many of the details well known to the author she had not committed to paper, since she fully expected to complete the manuscript herself. It is to be regretted that a follow-up study of these recent developments could not have been undertaken, and a hope is expressed that this may yet be done.

The chapters summarizing the group of twelve new cases are wholly without Leta S. Hollingworth's touch. It seemed desirable, however, to give such a summary as could be made under the circumstances. Had the original author been able to complete her book, we know that penetrating light would have been thrown on many of the more personal difficulties of these children of rare intelligence. This experience and insight can no longer be recovered. It must suffice to put on record chiefly the factual data now available, leaving it for future workers to follow up, if it should seem desirable, the subsequent career and destiny of the individuals whose early development and background are herein reported. Identification of these children is not made in this book, but the necessary facts for this purpose are on file and identification can be made at any time in the interests of educational research.

The third section of this book as originally outlined by Leta S. Hollingworth was to have dealt with general principles and with the social and educational implications of the study of children of very high intelligence. Up to the time of her death nothing of this character had been written by her explicitly, but throughout the years in which her projected book was developing she wrote a number of papers and reports bearing on the subject, and these were published from time to time in technical journals. It is well known that the content of these papers was dictated by her study of such cases as are herein reported, by her familiarity with the reports of other students in this field, and by her own very concrete and long experience in the organization and conduct of two experimental projects in the education of "rapid learners" among children in the schools of New York City. It is, in fact, likely that the final chapters she had in mind for this book would have been a reorganization of the conclusions set forth in these articles.

Consequently, the last five chapters of this book, instead of being an attempt to guess at what the author might have said in them, are all from her own hand. They are either selections from or complete reproductions of papers she had published on what she considered to be the implications of her observations of children of rare intelligence.

The publication of this book has been made possible by funds granted by the Carnegie Corporation of New York. That Corporation is not, however, the author, owner, publisher, or proprietor of this publication, and it is not to be understood as approving by virtue of its grants any of the statements made or views expressed herein.

Harry L. Hollingworth

Barnard College
Columbia University, New York

Contents

Preface

T HIS study is founded upon the work of Francis Galton, on the one hand, and of Alfred Binet, on the other. It goes back to Galton's *Hereditary Genius*, read as a prescribed reference in the courses of Professor Edward L. Thorndike, in 1912; and to the publication in 1916 of Professor Lewis M. Terman's *Stanford Revision of the Binet-Simon Scale for Measuring Intelligence*. It comprises observations, measurements, and conversations covering a period of twenty-three years, during which acquaintanceships and friendships, every one of them delightful, have been formed and maintained with the twelve exceptional individuals who form the basis of the study.

It was in November, 1916, shortly after taking appointment as instructor in educational psychology at Teachers College, Columbia University, that I saw for the first time a child testing above 180 IQ (S–B). I was teaching a course in the psychology of mentally deficient children, and it seemed to me that my class should if possible observe under test conditions one bright child for the sake of contrast. Accordingly, I asked whether any teacher present could nominate a very intelligent pupil for demonstration.

Miss Charlotte G. Garrison and Miss Agnes Burke, teachers in the Horace Mann School, Teachers College, New York City, thereupon nominated the child who is called E in this monograph. E was presented at the next meeting of the class. It required two full classroom periods to test this child to the limits of the Stanford-Binet Scale, which had just then been published. E exhausted the scale without being fully measured by it, achieving an IQ of *at least* 187. He was on that date 8 years 4 months old.

This IQ of at least 187 placed E in Galton's Class X of able persons; i.e., more than six "grades" removed from mediocrity. Taking 1 PE_{dis} as one "grade," it placed him *at least* plus 11 PE away from the norm; for 1 PE (Probable Error) equals 8 IQ, according to Terman's original distribution of 905 school children.[1] This appeared as sufficiently striking to warrant permanent recording, since it would rate E as one in a million for statistical frequency, assuming "zeal and power of working" to be also abundantly present.

I did not at that time have any expert knowledge of highly intelligent children. I had been working for some years in the hospitals of New York City with persons presented for commitment to reformatories, prisons, and institutions for mental defectives. I had tested thousands of incompetent persons, a majority of them children, with Goddard's Revision of the Binet-Simon Scale, scarcely ever finding anyone with an IQ rating as high as 100. This thoroughgoing experience of the negative aspects of intelligence rendered the performance of E even more impressive to me than it would otherwise have been. I perceived the clear and flawless working of his mind against a contrasting background of thousands of dull and foolish minds. It was an unforgettable observation.

[1] EDITORIAL NOTE. The larger and better sampling of subjects tested for the 1937 Stanford Revision showed a wider variability than the 1916 group and indicates that the true PE of the IQ distribution of unselected children is in the neighborhood of 11 IQ points, according to Terman.

I then began to look for children like E, to observe them with reference to the principles of education. This search has been conducted in a desultory manner, in "odd" moments, ever since 1916. At times, as in 1922–1923 and in 1935–1936, when pupils were being sought for special classes at Public School 165, Manhattan, or at Public School 500, Manhattan, the search has been systematic. Usually, however, the quest has been quite otherwise, for in the course of long searching I have learned that it is nearly useless to *look* for these children, because so few of them exist. In twenty-three years' seeking in New York City and the local metropolitan area, the densest center of population in this country and at the same time a great intellectual center attracting able persons, I have found only twelve children who test at or above 180 IQ (S–B). This number represents the winnowing from thousands of children tested, hundreds of them brought for the testing because of their mental gifts. Of course there were and are others who have not been found, since search has never been exhaustive.

The most interesting part of this research is yet to come, in the form of a record of the mature performances of these gifted persons observed in childhood. However, I propose to make a report now of origin and development; to be followed, if I live so long, by further reports of adult status. Such researches require more than the life span of one investigator, since time is of the essence of the task. Universities should make provision for institutional prosecution of these long-time studies as distinguished from individual prosecution. In any case, I shall try to leave the records to some younger student who will comprehend them, and who will amplify them if I prove unable to do so myself.[2]

[2] All such records have been deposited in the psychological laboratory of Barnard College, Columbia University.

Galton, in his efforts to understand ability, was limited to the study of the eminent adult, dead and gone. The only test he could use was that of reputation, for at the time he was at work on the problem, mental measurement had not yet been developed as a technique. He wished for a more valid method of gauging ability, and he fully realized that it would be of greater advantage to study "the living individual." "Is reputation a fair test of natural ability?" he asked. "It is the only one I can employ . . . am I justified in using it? How much of a man's success is due to his opportunities, and how much to his natural power of intellect?"

Galton's work was finished before Binet's studies made it possible to measure natural ability apart from reputation; and what is most essential of all, to measure *natural ability in childhood*. It was Binet's great and original service that he rendered it possible to determine accurately the permanent intellectual caliber of an undeveloped human being. It has always been possible to appraise the ability of people forty or fifty years old, after they have met "the tests of life," but for the pursuit of education and social science it is not very practically useful to know what a person is like only at the end of his life. It is essential, rather, to know with a high degree of precision and certainty the mental endowment of persons at the beginning of their lives if anything is to be done in the matter of special training for special children.

The facts derived from the study of the twelve exceptional persons herein described, and from the study of others like them, and the principles deduced from these facts, are of that order of importance for social science which Galton ascribed to them. Nevertheless, to hear of the tremendous differences between the dullest and the most intelligent individual, between the average man and the person who falls more than +10 PE away from him in mental ability, is extremely tedious to the typical American listener. This is only too well known to one who has long tried to interest foundations and moneyed persons in the education of gifted children. There is an apparent preference among donors for studying the needs and supporting the welfare of the weak, the vicious, and the incompetent, and a negative disregard of the highly intelligent, leaving them to "shift for themselves."

Perhaps a wider dissemination of facts such as have been adduced in the studies of Professor Lewis M. Terman and other educators, and in this study, may eventually bring about a more constructive point of view, one more conducive to a recognition of national welfare involved in educational plans for the unusual student.

It is desirable in this introduction to make known some of the etiquette and ethics involved in the scientific study of very gifted children. This is a new area in the field of human relationships and the investigator who works within it comes rather frequently upon certain questions of good manners which do not arise in any other field of psychological research.

For instance, persons who test above 180 IQ (S–B) are almost sure to read and recognize in books and articles whatever has been written about them, no matter how anonymously they may have been described. This is true of them even as children. When the book *Gifted Children* was published, in 1926, Child A, who is described therein as well as in these pages, was thirteen years old. He read the book within two weeks of publication; for, as he said in mentioning the matter to the author, "I go every week to the Public Library and look first at the shelf of new books." The problem always in the foreground is how to present the whole truth about such matters as family history, social-economic status, and character, without invading the privacy of those described and without identifying them to the general public or to curious persons.

Those who test above 180 IQ (S–B) are characterized by a strong desire for personal privacy. They seldom volunteer information about themselves. They do not like to have attention called to their families and homes. They are reluctant to impart information concerning their plans, hopes, convictions, and so forth. The question arises, then, how to avoid presumption; for it is by no means easy for a young person politely to evade an older person who can lay claim to having known one "all one's life."

Thus, in this study, in order to preserve the privacy of those concerned, some items have been omitted from the histories which would have been of interest to students of child psychology. Let it be understood at once, however, that the omissions include nothing discreditable to any of the twelve individuals studied; rather, many of these items are highly creditable. There have been acts of moral courage, acts of skill, and acts of self-sustaining heterodoxy that if told at all should be told only by those who performed the actions. Perhaps autobiographies may some day be written by these persons, telling whatever they may wish to tell.

In the matter of the attitude of people in general toward gifted children, there are, of course, a majority who are kindly and understanding and helpful, but it is a melancholy fact that there are also malicious and jealous people who are likely to persecute those who are formally identified as being unusual. It may prove a handicap rather than a help to a gifted youngster to have been identified in book or article or school as extraordinary. Some of the children herein described have suffered considerably from the malice of ill-mannered persons, even their instructors, who have felt the impulse to "take them down a peg." Specific instances of such persecution can be cited from public prints, and reference will be made to them in the course of this monograph.

It would be of interest to present a photograph of each child herein observed, to show how in personal appearance they are diametrically opposite to the popular stereotype of the highly intelligent child; but photographs would tend to identification.

These questions of what is right and what is wrong, what is permissible and what is forbidden, in reporting the origin and development of the gifted cannot be fully determined here. The policies pursued in this study have been discussed from time to time with gifted children and their parents, and I have been guided by their advice. Everything has been presented that is consistent both with scientific interest and with the preservation of personal privacy. The work as it stands has taken hundreds of hours of the time of these children and of their parents and teachers, over a period of twenty years. They are all very busy people, yet they have given time and energy for tests, measurements, and interviews as requested. It is obvious that without this coöperation no study could have been made.

LETA S. HOLLINGWORTH

Teachers College
Columbia University
New York City

PART I

Orientation

Chapter One

THE CONCEPT OF INTELLECTUAL GENIUS

I T WOULD be an ambitious project to find and discuss all the definitions of genius that have ever been offered in writing. To do this is beyond our present purpose, which is, rather, to illustrate the various concepts that have been formulated and to take guidance from them in the consideration of children of great ability. It will perhaps be many years before it will be apparent whether the children studied herein are geniuses or not. Perhaps this can never be determined, as the word "genius" may eventually be found to have no meaning that can be agreed upon. All we know about the status of the subjects of the present study is that they test above 180 IQ (S–B) and are thus more than $+10$ PE removed from mediocrity in general intelligence.[1] It may be possible to arrive at some comparison between their characteristics and performances on the one hand, and the concepts of genius that have been offered on the other.

CONCEPTS OF THE ANCIENTS

The concept of the genius is very ancient. Ovid (12),[2] referring to Caesar and his preparations to complete the con-

---

[1] See footnote on page xii.

[2] Numbers in parentheses refer to correspondingly numbered references in the Bibliography at the end of each chapter.

1

quest of the world, notes the manner in which a genius acts in advance of his years:

> Though he himself is but a boy, he wages a war unsuited to his boyish years. Oh, ye of little faith, vex not your souls about the age of the gods! Genius divine outpaces time, and brooks not the tedium of tardy growth. Hercules was still no more than a child when he crushed the serpent in his baby hands. Even in the cradle, he proved himself a worthy son of Jove.

The Greeks called that a person's "daemon" which directed and inspired his creative work. Dictionaries refer to the Roman concept of genius as "a spirit presiding over the destiny of a person or a place; a familiar spirit or a tutelary." The genie was one of the powerful nature demons of Arabian and Mohammedan lore, believed to interfere in human affairs and to be sometimes subject to magic control.

Thinkers in any and every field, no matter how remote from that of psychology, have confidently discussed the nature of genius. Philosophers, poets, litterateurs, physicians, physiologists, psychiatrists, anthropometrists, lexicographers, encyclopedists — all have offered definitions, each according to his light. It has been deemed a subject on which anyone might legitimately express an opinion. The result is, as might be expected, an interesting miscellany of contradictions.

DICTIONARY DEFINITIONS

By derivation the word "genius" means to beget or to bring forth, coming from *genere, gignere*. Samuel Johnson's Dictionary — from which Galton took his point of departure in choosing the word "genius" for the title of his work on ability — defines a genius as "A man endowed with superior faculties."

Funk and Wagnalls' Dictionary offers the following definition: "Very extraordinary gifts or native powers, especially as displayed in original creation, discovery, expression, or achievement." Webster's New International Dictionary defines "genius" as "Extraordinary mental superiority; esp. unusual power of invention or origination of any kind; as, a man of *genius.*"

The Dictionary of Psychology defines "genius" in part in terms of IQ, but at the same time denies the word any special meaning as a recognized scientific term: "Genius — a very superior mental ability, especially a superior power of invention or origination of any kind, or of execution of some special form, such as music, painting, or mathematics. . . . It has no special technical meaning, but has occasionally been defined as equivalent to an intelligence quotient (IQ) of 140 or above."

Generally speaking, then, dictionaries define genius as a superior or superlative degree of intellectual capacity, and avoid claiming for it any concept of an added, different, or abnormal element in human faculty.

CONCEPTS OF GENIUS

As a manifestation of abnormal psychology. A number of thinkers in fields allied to psychology have laid emphasis upon a supposed connection between genius and nervous instability or insanity. This idea is embodied in the statement by Pascal: "L'extrême esprit est voisin de l'extrême folie." Lamartine refers to "la maladie mentale qu'on appelle génie." Lombroso (*10*) is perhaps the most widely quoted among those who have held or who hold this point of view.

As constituting a different species. The idea has been expressed by thinkers other than professed psychologists — and at times by psychologists themselves — that men of genius are a separate species, partaking of qualities not shared in any degree by persons at large. This concept is at one with that which would regard the idiot and the imbecile as distinct in kind, not in degree only, from the mass of mankind. Genius would thus be not merely more of the same but a different sort altogether. Thus Hirsch (7) specifically declares:

> The genius differs in *kind* from the species, man. Genius can be defined only in terms of its own unique mental and temperamental processes, traits, qualities, and products. Genius is another psychobiological species, differing as much from man, in his mental and temperamental processes, as man differs from the ape.

As a hypertrophied and highly specialized aptitude for specific performance. The thought has been advanced that intellectual genius is a matter of specialization; that the mind of a genius will not, typically, work on all data with superior results, but that it is adapted only or primarily to certain kinds of intellectual performance. In other words, the genius is thought to lack general ability. A recent statement by Carrel (2) seems to express in part at least this theory:

> There is also a class of men who, although as disharmonious as the criminal and the insane, are indispensable to modern society. They are the men of genius. They are characterized by a monstrous growth of some of their psychological activities. A great artist, a great scientist, a great philosopher, is rarely a great man. He is generally a man of common type, with one side over-developed.

As a combination of traits. Galton (6) thought of genius as that which qualifies a person for eminence, and he believed that achieved eminence must be founded on a combination of no less than three essentials. He wrote:

> By natural ability I mean those qualities of intellect and disposition which urge and qualify a man to perform acts that lead to reputation. I do not mean capacity without zeal, nor zeal without capacity, nor even a combination of both of them, without an adequate power of doing a great deal of very laborious work. But I mean a nature which, when left to itself, will, urged by an inherent stimulus, climb the path that leads to eminence, and has strength to reach the summit . . . one which, if hindered or thwarted, will fret and strive until the hindrance is overcome, and it is again free to follow its labour-loving instinct. It is almost a contradiction in terms to doubt that such men will generally become eminent.

Again, Galton says:

> We have seen that a union of three separate qualities — intellect, zeal, and power of work — are necessary to raise men from the ranks.

Lehman (9) has recently expressed this same idea, as a result of a statistical study of the most productive years of intellectual workers:

> Indeed, it is doubtful that genius is solely the fruit of any single trait. It is the belief of the writer that the fruits of genius are, on the contrary, a function of numerous integers, including both the personal traits of the individual worker, environmental conditions that are not too hostile, and the fortunate combination of both personal traits and external conditions.

As quantitative. Galton (6) was the first to place the study of genius on the basis of quantitative statement, so that comparisons might be made and vertifications be effected. Galton formulated the theory that genius (great natural ability) is nothing more nor less than a very extreme degree

Grades of Natural Ability, Separated by Equal Intervals		Numbers of Men Comprised in the Several Grades of Natural Ability, Whether in Respect to Their General Powers or to Special Aptitudes							
Below Average	Above Average	Proportionate; viz., One in	In Each Million of the Same Age	In Total Male Population of the United Kingdom, Say 15 Millions, of the Under-mentioned Ages					
				20-30	30-40	40-50	50-60	60-70	70-80
a	A	4	256,791	651,000	495,000	391,000	268,000	171,000	77,000
b	B	6	161,279	409,000	312,000	246,000	168,000	107,000	48,000
c	C	16	63,563	161,000	123,000	97,000	66,000	42,000	19,000
d	D	64	15,696	39,800	30,300	23,900	16,400	10,400	4,700
e	E	413	2,423	6,100	4,700	3,700	2,520	1,600	729
f	F	4,300	233	590	450	355	243	155	70
g	G	79,000	14	35	27	21	15	9	4
x									
All grades below g	All grades above G	1,000,000	1	3	2	2	2	0	0

6

in the distribution of a combination of traits — "intellect, zeal, and power of working" — which is shared by all in various "grades" or degrees. Reasoning thus, Galton applied for the first time in human thought the mathematical concepts of probability to the definition of genius.

Quetelet (*13*), drawing objects from congeries of known composition, had elaborated the form which the probabilities take of drawing a given combination. This form, with the law of deviation from the average governing it, is now, of course, a commonplace in psychological laboratories, so that it is hard to realize that when Galton made the mental leap from this curve to the abilities of men, no one had ever thought of human minds as "fitting" the curve drawn by Quetelet. Such a "fit" had already been thought of in connection with measurements of physique, and had been demonstrated for measurements of the shrimp (*16*) and for physical traits of persons. But that "natural ability" should be susceptible to the probability curve and "the curious theoretical law of deviation from an average" as length is among shrimps, or as circumference of the chest is among Scottish soldiers (as shown by Quetelet), was not conceived. With the modern methods of mental measurement it is easy enough to perceive the truth of this. But Galton was working in the dark, entirely without instruments of precision; and his table of frequency "for the classification of men according to their natural gifts" must be regarded as one of the most prescient statements in the history of social science.

Working with the tables devised by Quetelet, Galton proposed the tabular "classification of men according to their natural gifts" shown on page 6.

Interpreting this theoretical tabulation, Galton (*6*) wrote:

It will be seen that more than half of each million is contained in the two mediocre classes *a* and A; the four mediocre classes *a*, *b*, A, B, contain more than four fifths, and the six mediocre classes more than nineteen twentieths of the entire population. Thus, the rarity of commanding ability and the vast abundance of mediocrity is no accident, but follows of necessity from the very nature of these things.

On descending the scale, we find by the time we have reached *f* that we are already among the idiots and imbeciles. We have seen that there are 400 idiots and imbeciles to any million of persons living in this country; but that 30 per cent of their number appear to be light cases, to whom the name of idiot is inappropriate. There will remain 280 true idiots and imbeciles to every million of our population. This ratio coincides very closely with the requirements of class *f*. No doubt a certain proportion of them are idiots owing to some fortuitous cause . . . but the proportion of accidental idiots cannot be very large.

Hence we arrive at the undeniable but unexpected conclusion that eminently gifted men are raised as much above mediocrity as idiots are depressed below it; a fact that is calculated to enlarge considerably our ideas of the enormous difference of intellectual gifts between man and man.

MISCELLANEOUS OBSERVATIONS TENDING TO

DEFINE CHARACTERISTICS OF GENIUS

In addition to the formulation of the rather definite concepts of genius which have been discussed, there are to be found in the literature of this topic a large number of general observations ascribing certain characteristics to persons of genius. There are also many remarks as to the conditions of living, of education, of genetics, and so forth, which are alleged to foster or to hinder the development of genius. Many of these observations and remarks emanate from others than professed psychologists, some of the most interesting coming from litterateurs and philosophers.

One of the most penetrating discussions of genius by a litterateur is that of Shaw (*15*) in his Preface to *Saint Joan.* Shaw regards Saint Joan as a young genius, and in introducing his readers to this point of view he says:

> Let us be clear about the meaning of the terms. A genius is a person who, seeing farther and probing deeper than other people, has a different set of ethical values from theirs, and has energy enough to give effect to this extra vision and its valuations in whatever manner best suits his or her specific talents.

Here is brought out the tendency to heterodoxy which characterizes genius and is the source of much of its difficulty. Shaw dwells upon these difficulties in saying:

> But it is not so easy for mental giants who neither hate nor intend to injure their fellows to realize that nevertheless their fellows hate mental giants and would like to destroy them, not only enviously because the juxtaposition of a superior wounds their vanity, but quite honestly because it frightens them. Fear will drive men to any extreme; and the fear inspired by a superior being is a mystery which cannot be reasoned away. Being immeasurable it is unbearable when there is no presumption or guarantee of its benevolence and moral responsibility; in other words, when it has no official status.

This is the same trend of thought which Mill (*11*) follows in his *Essay on Liberty*, noting the originality that characterizes genius and the troubles that result from it, and insisting upon freedom for genius in the interests of the general welfare.

> It would not be denied by anybody that originality is a valuable element in human affairs. There is always need of persons not only to discover new truths, and point out when what were once truths are true no longer, but also to commence new practices, and set the example of more enlightened conduct, and better taste and sense in human life. . . . It is

true that this benefit is not capable of being rendered by everybody alike; there are but few persons in comparison with the whole of mankind, whose experiments, if adopted by others, would be likely to be any improvement on established practice. But these few are the salt of the earth; without them, human life would become a stagnant pool. . . . Persons of genius, it is true, are and are always likely to be, a small minority; but in order to have them, it is necessary to preserve the soil in which they grow. Genius can only breathe freely in an atmosphere of freedom. Persons of genius are, *ex vi termini*, more individual than any other people . . . less capable, consequently, of fitting themselves, without hurtful compression, into any of the small number of moulds which society provides in order to save its members the trouble of forming their own character. If from timidity they consent to be forced into one of these moulds, and to let that part of themselves which cannot expand under the pressure remain unexpanded, society will be little the better for their genius. If they are of strong character, and break their fetters, they become a mark for the society which has not succeeded in reducing them to commonplace, to point out with solemn warning as "wild," "erratic," and the like; much as if one should complain of the Niagara River for not flowing smoothly between its banks like a Dutch canal.

Mill says further:

I insist thus emphatically on the importance of genius, and the necessity of allowing it to unfold itself freely both in thought and in practice, being well aware that no one will deny the position in theory, but knowing also that almost everyone, in reality, is totally indifferent to it.

Mill, indeed, had much to say about the conditions under which the exceptional individual contributes to social change and progress, which bears immediately upon the education of highly exceptional children.

Bearing further upon the persecution to which genius is

often subject as a penalty for nonconformity, Havelock Ellis
(5) after studying a large number of British men of genius
says:

It is practically impossible to estimate the amount of persecution to which this group of preëminent persons has been sub-
jected, for it has shown itself in innumerable forms, and varies
between a mere passive refusal to have anything to do with
them or their work and the active infliction of physical torture
and death. There is, however, at least one form of persecution, very definite in character, which it is easy to estimate,
since the national biographers have probably in few cases passed
over it. I refer to imprisonment. I find that at least 160,
or over 16 per cent, of our 975 eminent men were imprisoned,
once or oftener, for periods of varying length, while many
others only escaped imprisonment by voluntary exile.

This is a conclusion reached by one investigating the condition of genius among what are probably the most liberal
people in the world — the British, a nation of protestants.

Another condition of genius frequently alleged is that of
personal isolation. Shaw makes Saint Joan say, "I was always alone." Schopenhauer (14) says: "It is often the case
that a great mind prefers soliloquy to the dialogue he may
have in the world." Hirsch (7) dwells at some length upon
isolation:

The genius is constantly forced to solitude, for he early
learns from experience that his kind can expect no reciproca-
tion of their generous feelings. . . . Solitude can best be
defined as the state in which friends are lacking or absent,
rather than as the opposite of sociability. . . . Solitude is but
a refuge of genius, not its goal. Time after time one detects,
from the lives or writings of genius, that solitude is not its
destiny but only a retreat; not the normal fruition of its being,
but an empty harbor sheltering it from the tortures, griefs,
and calumnies of the world. . . . It is a grievous error to
credit the genius with an innate inclination to shun men. But

in his youth he learns by experience that solitude is preferable to suffocation, stupefaction, or surrender.

Alger (*1*) sees isolation as a necessary corollary of the insistence upon perfection and accuracy which characterizes genius:

> A passion for perfection will make its subject solitary as nothing else can. At every step he leaves a group behind. And when, at last, he reaches the goal, alas, where are his early comrades?

These references to the *early* experience of the genius in meeting the uncordial response of the world as constituted, with its resultant tendency to isolation, connect themselves with an account found in the Apocryphal New Testament, in a portion called the Hebrew Gospels:

> And Joseph, seeing that the child was vigorous in mind and body, again resolved that he should not remain ignorant of the letters, and took him away, and handed him over to another teacher. And the teacher said to Joseph: I shall teach him the Greek letters, and then Hebrew. He wrote out the alphabet and began to teach him in an imperious tone, saying: Say Alpha. And he gave him his attention for a long time and he made no answer, but was silent. And he said to him: If thou art really a teacher, tell me the power of the Alpha and I will tell thee the power of the Beta. And the teacher was enraged at this, and struck him.

SPECULATION AND COMMENT CONCERNING GENIUS

The *ecology of genius* has evoked speculation and comment. Thus Churchill (*3*) says:

> Mountain regions discourage the budding of genius because they are areas of isolation, confinement, remote from the great currents of men and ideas that move along river valleys. They are regions of much labor and little leisure, of poverty today and anxiety for the morrow, of toil-cramped hands and toil-

dulled brains. In the fertile alluvial plains are wealth, leisure, contact with many minds, large urban centers where commodities and ideas are exchanged.

The *origins of genius* have also engaged the attention of speculative thinkers. For instance, Dixon (*4*) and also Hirsch (*7*) offer the hypothesis that racial mixture is an antecedent of genius. Kretschmer (*8*) would by inference subscribe to this theory, since he holds that genetically genius results from the union of unlike elements, to which he refers as "bastardization":

> The investigation of the family history of highly talented individuals demonstrates very clearly the effect of biological "bastardization," and shows why it may lead to the production of genius. . . . It results in a complicated psychological structure, in which the components of two strongly opposing germs remain in polar tension throughout life. . . . This polar tension acts as an effective and dynamic factor and produces in the genius the labile equilibrium, the effective superpressure, that continuous, restless impulsiveness, which carries him far beyond placid, traditional practice and the simple satisfaction of life. On the other hand, in regard to his intellectual abilities, the polar tension creates in the genius his wide mental horizon, the diverse and complicated wealth of his talent, the all-embracing personality.

Kretschmer also allies himself with those who hold the concept of genius as closely related to insanity, quoting selected cases in proof:

> "Bastardization" produces internal contrasts and conflicts, affects tensions, highly strung and uncompensated passions, and a spiritual lability. It consequently creates a predisposition to genius . . . but also [points] to psycho-pathological complications. Thus the research on "bastardization" becomes closely interwoven with the old, familiar questions, leading us back to the problem: "Genius and Insanity."

BIBLIOGRAPHY

1. ALGER, WILLIAM. *The Genius of Solitude,* page 144.
2. CARREL, ALEXIS. *Man the Unknown.* See pages 140–141. Harper & Brothers, New York; 1935.
3. CHURCHILL, ELLEN SEMPLE. *The Influence of Geographic Environment on the Basis of Ratzel's System of Anthropogeography.* Houghton Mifflin Company, Boston; 1909.
4. DIXON, ROLAND B. *The Racial History of Man.* Charles Scribner's Sons, New York; 1923.
5. ELLIS, HAVELOCK. *A Study of British Genius.* Constable, London; 1927.
6. GALTON, FRANCIS. *Hereditary Genius.* The Macmillan Company, London; 1914.
7. HIRSCH, N. D. M. *Genius and Creative Intelligence.* Sci-Art Publisher, Cambridge, Massachusetts; 1931.
8. KRETSCHMER, E. *The Psychology of Men of Genius.* Translated by R. B. Cattell. Harcourt, Brace & Co., Inc., New York; 1931.
9. LEHMAN, HARVEY C. "The Creative Years in Science and Literature." *Scientific Monthly* (August, 1936).
10. LOMBROSO, C. *The Man of Genius.* Scott, London; 1891.
11. MILL, JOHN STUART. *Essay on Liberty.* See page 76 ff. The Macmillan Company, New York; 1926 Ed.
12. OVIDIUS NASO, PUBLIUS. *Ars Amatoria (The Love Books of Ovid).* Translated by J. Lewis May. Privately printed for the Rarity Press, New York; 1930.
13. QUETELET, M. *Letters on Probability.* Translated by Downes. Layton & Co., London; 1849.
14. SCHOPENHAUER, ARTHUR. "Essay on Genius," in *The Art of Literature,* Essays of Arthur Schopenhauer. Willey Book Company, New York.
15. SHAW, GEORGE BERNARD. *Saint Joan.* Dodd, Mead & Co., Inc., New York; 1924, 1936.
16. WELDON, W. F. R. "Certain Correlated Variations in Crangdon Vulgaris," *Proceedings* of The Royal Society, Vol. 51, page 2 (1892).

Chapter Two

EARLY SCIENTIFIC STUDY OF EMINENT ADULTS [1]

BECAUSE, strictly speaking, the present study is limited in its interest and data to childhood, no attempt will be made to review in detail the somewhat numerous studies of exceptional adults.

ORIGIN OF EMINENT ADULTS

Such studies as those undertaken by Galton (*11, 12*), De Candolle (*9*), Ellis (*10*), Odin (*17*), and Cattell (*4, 5*) show that those who, as adults, become eminent in intellectual work, are in disproportionately great numbers the children of the "upper" (nobler or professional) classes; and that they are usually born either in cities or on large country estates (in France, in the chateaux). Very few eminent adults have originated in the families of laborers, and relatively few have been born in agricultural districts, in countries long settled. Beyond these facts of origin, the investigators of eminence in

---

[1] EDITORIAL NOTE. No revision of this chapter has been found among the author's papers. In the earlier manuscript reporting but five cases, there was a brief section entitled "Inferences from the Study of Adults," and in the incompletely revised manuscript a list of references is given for this chapter which had not yet been written. The earlier sections and the revised bibliography are, therefore, all that is available for this chapter. The bibliography will be sufficient to guide any reader who may be further interested in the details of the scientific study of adults.

adults have not given much information about their subjects of inquiry in respect to childhood.

YODER'S STUDY

We shall begin our detailed reference to previous observations with Yoder's study, published in 1898. Yoder (25) made a systematic attempt to gather data about the boyhood of very eminent men. He thus tracked down certain facts about fifty great persons concerning whom he could find data bearing on their childhood. From these he was able to make the following generalizations:

1. The child who will become a great man may be born at any time, over a very wide range of the productive period in the lives of parents. The mothers of the fifty great persons studied ranged in age from 18 to 44 years, when the great man was born, with a median of 29.8 years. The fathers ranged in age from 23 to 60 years, with a median of 37.7 years.

2. The average number of siblings of these persons was 5 +, not including half brothers and sisters.

3. In families of more than one child, there was found to be a strong tendency (chances of nearly 2 to 1) for the great man to be in the elder half of the siblings.

4. Of those listed, 17 were only sons, either by order of birth or by death of other sons born. (This is not to say that they were only children.)

5. There was found no evidence that the great were sickly or physically weak in childhood, to a more marked extent than average.

6. There appeared a tendency to greater height among them than among persons in general, "though the tendency is not very marked."

7. Play interests were keen among these children, though the play was often of an unusual kind. "Solitary play" is repeatedly described. Of Emerson, his biographer says: "I don't think he ever engaged in boys' plays, not because of any physical disability, but simply because from earliest years he dwelt in a higher sphere." Others are said to have been "disinclined to general intercourse." Instead of joining in the usual childish games, Newton preferred to play with his machines, Darwin with his collections, Shelley to read, Stevenson to make clay engines, and Edison to mix his chemicals. Of Byron it was written: "The love of solitude and of meditation is already traceable in the child. He loves to wander at night among the dark and solitary cloisters of the abbey." To quote Yoder: "Solitude seems to have played a rather striking role in the lives of these great men. Either by nature or by opportunity, they have stayed a great deal alone."

Nevertheless, many of the fifty persons studied by Yoder enjoyed physical activity. Washington loved outdoor sports, Schiller was a leader in athletics, Byron was an enthusiastic swimmer and rider, and Lincoln was the champion wrestler and woodcutter of his neighborhood.

8. The popular idea that great men owe their success to their mothers' influence upon their education does not receive verification from a study of these cases. The mother's place seems very often to have been filled by some other person, frequently an aunt, either because the mother had died, or because there were many other children to care for. "The role of the aunt stands out prominently."

9. These great persons were, in the decided majority of cases, derived from well-to-do families. Most of them were

privately educated, by tutors or in private schools. Very few were "self made."

TERMAN'S INFERENCES FROM BIOGRAPHY

Terman (20) has effected an interesting advance over Yoder's method, in the interpretation of evidence from the biography of adults.[2] By analyzing the data in the biography of Francis Galton, and by relating these data to modern knowledge of mental tests, Terman derives that the IQ of Francis Galton in childhood must have been not far from 200.

As Terman has elsewhere pointed out, these attempts to study genius in childhood by inference from the biography of adults are very unsatisfactory. In the first place, only those whose potentialities have been realized are included in such study. Since factors other than innate intellectual power act also as determinants of eminence, we cannot be sure whether equal capacity for selective thinking may have existed in persons who died before the age of achievement, who were younger sons, who were girls, or who were the children of the poor. Moreover, such evidence as can be gleaned concerning those who have achieved eminence is comparatively unsystematic and unreliable as regards childhood.

Most clearly related to our present study are the previously reported observations of children made directly, during childhood, by trained investigators. The modern development of mental tests has now enabled psychologists to identify young children who deviate from average in the

[2] EDITORIAL NOTE. Had these pages been written at a later date, or revised by the author, of course the more recent work of C. M. Cox (7), inspired by Terman, would have been considered.

direction of superiority as regards selective thinking, and to follow their development for some years. Eventually, therefore, it will be known how to recognize those children who can become "great," and whether extreme deviation in mental tests is a basis of prophecy.

BIBLIOGRAPHY

1. BINET, A. *Psychologie des grandes calculateurs et joieurs d'échecs.* Hachette, Paris; 1894.
2. BRIMHALL, D. "Family Resemblances among American Men of Science," *American Naturalist,* Vol. 56 (1922) and Vol. 57 (1923).
3. CASTLE, C. S. "Statistical Study of Eminent Women." *Archives of Psychology,* Vol. IV, No. 27 (1913).
4. CATTELL, J. McK. "A Statistical Study of Eminent Men." *Popular Science Monthly* (1903).
5. —— "Families of American Men of Science." *Popular Science Monthly,* Vol. 86, pages 504–515 (1915).
6. CLARK, E. L. *American Men of Letters: Their Nature and Nurture.* Columbia University Press, New York; 1916.
7. COX, C. M. *The Early Mental Traits of Three Hundred Geniuses.* Genetic Studies of Genius: Vol. 2. Stanford University Press, Stanford University, California; 1926.
8. DAVIES, G. R. "A Statistical Study of the Influence of the Environment." *Quarterly Journal of the University of North Dakota* (1914).
9. DE CANDOLLE, A. *Histoire des Sciences et des Savants depuis Deux Siècles.* Geneva, Switzerland; 1873.
10. ELLIS, HAVELOCK. *A Study of British Genius.* Hirst and Blackett, London; 1904.
11. GALTON, FRANCIS. *English Men of Science.* The Macmillan Company, London; 1874.
12. —— *Hereditary Genius.* The Macmillan Company, New York, 1914. (Original edition, London; 1869.)

13. LEHMAN, HARVEY C. "The Creative Years in Science and Literature." *Scientific Monthly,* Vol. XLIII, pages 151–162 (1936).
14. LOMBROSO, C. *The Man of Genius.* Scott, London; 1895.
15. MIDDLETON, W. C. "The Propensity of Genius to Solitude." *Journal of Abnormal and Social Psychology,* Vol. 30, pages 325–332 (1935).
16. MITCHELL, F. D. "Mathematical Prodigies." *American Journal of Psychology,* Vol. 18, pages 61–143 (1907).
17. ODIN, A. *Genèse des Grands Hommes des Lettres Français Modernes.* Paris et Lausanne; 1895.
18. RASKIN, E. "Comparison of Scientific and Literary Ability: A Biographical Study of Eminent Scientists and Men of Letters of the Nineteenth Century." *Journal of Abnormal and Social Psychology,* Vol. 31, pages 20–35 (1935).
19. SCHUSTER, E. "The Promise of Youth and the Performance of Manhood." *Eugenics Laboratory Memoirs,* Vol. 3, pages 16 ff., London; 1907.
20. TERMAN, LEWIS M. "The IQ of Francis Galton in Childhood." *American Journal of Psychology,* Vol. 28, pages 209–215 (1917).
21. VISHER, S. S. "A Study of the Type of Place of Birth and of the Occupation of Father of Subjects of Sketches in *Who's Who in America." American Journal of Sociology,* 1925.
22. —— "The Comparative Rank of the American States." *American Journal of Sociology,* Vol. 36, pages 735–757 (March, 1931).
23. WHITE, R. K. "Note on the Psycho-pathology of Genius." *Journal of Social Psychology,* Vol. 1, pages 311–315 (1930).
24. —— "The Versatility of Genius." *Journal of Social Psychology,* Vol. 2, pages 460–489 (1931).
25. YODER, G. E. "A Study of the Boyhood of Great Men." *Pedagogical Seminary,* Vol. 3, pages 134–156 (1894).

Chapter Three

PUBLISHED REPORTS ON TESTED CHILDREN

GALTON and those who built directly upon his pioneer thought about ability were limited to the study of those who had passed the tests of life itself, the study of the old and the dead, upon whom developing theories and processes of education have no bearing. Today one of the principal reasons for obtaining knowledge concerning able persons is that they and others like them may be properly educated for the social functions which they alone can perform. Inferences from study of eminent adults are, therefore, of negligible importance compared to the identification and education of today's gifted children.

MODERN APPROACH TO THE STUDY OF ABILITY

In 1905 Binet and Simon (3), announcing their scale for the measurement of intelligence in children, rendered it possible to know at the beginning of a human being's existence where — within narrow limits of error — he or she, in comparison with all others, grades in caliber of general intelligence. This work, relating itself to work done also by others — notably Spearman (21) and Thorndike (28, 30) — created a new epoch in the study of ability and inaugurated the so-called modern, or present-day, approach to the subject.

BINET'S METHOD

No extended discussion of what "general intelligence" is will be undertaken in these pages, as it would not be germane to the purposes of this monograph. It will be sufficient to refer to the concept which Binet had in mind in standardizing his scale (4): "It seems to us that there is a fundamental faculty, the alteration or the lack of which is of the utmost importance for practical life." It is this "fundamental faculty" which Binet named "judgment" that is the variable upon which rests the extreme position of the children who are to be studied herein.

The quantitative methods which make possible the study of the status of these children when they have reached adulthood are those developed in recent years by Thorndike (30) and his students. As the children identified years ago by Binet's method grew to adulthood, there were developed in the various laboratories of Columbia University methods of measuring the intelligence of superior adults, based on the fundamental principles which are the same for mental measurement at all periods of development. Methods have thus been made available for making quantitative statements of the status of these individuals both during development and at maturity.

THE RANGE OF INTELLECT ABOVE 180 IQ

It is pertinent to inquire what are the limits of variation in terms of standard use in respect to human intelligence. How far superior to the average person are the most highly intelligent individuals currently produced? Galton's (9) X grade of man was defined in terms of incidence as "one in a million." But this X man was not a product of one variable. Galton's X man resulted from an intellect *in combination* with "zeal and power of working." The incidence of this *combination* of traits would probably be less than the incidence of intellect alone in degree sufficient for X.

Our purpose in this chapter will be to consider investigations, made by direct methods, of the origin and development of children of a type extremely rare in occurrence, incidence being based on one variable only; i.e., intelligence measured in terms of IQ (S–B). For this purpose the line might be drawn at any point farther than + 7 PE or + 8 PE from the mean. A choice of 180 IQ (S–B) as a minimum insures a degree of plus deviation very rarely found even in metropolitan cities and their suburbs, as is clear from the reports of mental surveys conducted during the present century. The choice of 180 IQ (S–B), instead of 179 or 181 or some other amount of IQ in the extreme upper range, is obviously arbitrary and is adopted merely for the purpose of defining a point at and above which there are very few children who score.

Frequency of occurrence. Just how often does a child testing above 180 IQ (S–B) appear in the juvenile population of the United States? We cannot tell exactly until we know more about the spread of the distribution of IQ (S–B). In terms of PE (1 PE = ± 8 IQ), according to Terman's original findings (*24*) we should come upon a deviate of + 10 PE only once in more than a million times, provided the distribution of IQ corresponds exactly or even rather closely to Quetelet's (*17*) curve of probability as respects spread; for on this curve cases above or below ± 5 PE approach zero in frequency.

It is certain, however, even from existing data, that the distribution of IQ extends for at least ± 10 PE (even assuming that wider data will define 1 PE as $\pm$ 10 instead of $\pm$ 8 as found by Terman). It is probable that children who test above 180 IQ are actually present in our juvenile population in greater frequency than at the rate of one in a million. This does not mean that intellect when finally measured *in true units* may not conform in variability to the mathematics of chance; it means only that *in terms of IQ* (in terms of ratio and not of absolute units) the conformity is probably not exact, as respects the law of deviation.

There may be one, or two, or three, or more children among every million born in the United States under present conditions who test at or above 180 IQ (S–B). In any case, however, they are extremely rare, and the study of their origin and development is of correspondingly great interest. In the course of discovering about 1000 children testing at or above 140 IQ (S–B) in the state of California, Terman (*26*) found 15 who tested at or above 180 IQ (S–B). Children who test at and above 140 IQ (S–B) are as 1 in 250 of children in large California cities and environs. Thus 140 IQ (S–B) defines a frequency of about 4 in 1000 of urban juvenile population in California. About 1.5 per cent, therefore, of those children who are as 4 in 1000 reach the status of which we are here treating; i.e., 180 IQ (S–B).[1] Nor can we take the children of California urban districts as a true sample of the population of the United States at large, since there is reason to believe that among urban children there is an uncommon proportion of intelligent individuals (*8*). Also it should be conceded that California has

---

[1] It is not absolutely clear from Terman's text whether the 15 children above 180 IQ (S–B) are to be thought of as representing the 643 children statistically treated in *Genetic Studies of Genius:* Vol. I, or whether they rest upon the "nearly one thousand" as a base, who were located. [In a personal communication Professor Terman writes that it was 15 out of 643.]

a total population that is above the average of the United States in general as regards mental ability (*37*). In any case, it may be guessed with some degree of approximation to fact how very few there are among American children who test at or above 180 IQ (S–B.

CHILDREN OBSERVED BEFORE THE ERA OF BINET

Scattered observations of children estimated by more or less competent persons as very unusual are to be found dating from quite early years. In this period the literature of child psychology was still in the state of narrative. The earliest of these narrations bears the date of 1726 (*1*) and concerns the child Heineken.

Christian Heinrich Heineken. Born February 6, 1721, the "little Heineken," of Lübeck, was the son of an artist. When the child was 10 months old, his elders first noticed that he was looking with sustained attention at the figures wrought in gold on a grotesque that decorated the walls of his room and that were also on a white stove that stood therein.

Den 3 Dezember 1721 bemerkte man zuerst, dass das kind diese Figuren hin und her, eine Zeitlang ohne Unterlass ansah und seine Äugelchen auf eine derselben gleichsam anklebte. Man sagte ihm daher die Namen dieser Figuren, das sei eine Katze, das ein Turm, ein Schäfchen, ein Berg. Den andern Tag, den 4 Dezember, fragte man es wieder, wo die Katze, der Berg, das Schäfchen wäre und siehe da, das Kind deutete mit seinen kleinen Fingerchen hin und traf immer das rechte Bild, das man ihm genannt hatte. Noch mehr, nun gab es sich Mühe, die ihm vorgesagten Wörter: Katze, Berg, Turm selbst nachzusprechen: es sah daher mit unverwandten Blicken dem Redenden nach dem Munde, gab auf die Bewegung der Lippen und der Zunge desselben beständig acht, lallte das Wort

nach und wiederholte dies so oft, bis es endlich eine Silbe nach
der andern herauspresste.

By the time this child was 14 months old he had learned
all the stories in the New Testament. At this age he was
still not weaned from the breast of his nurse, and had an
antipathy to other foods. In order to get him accustomed
to other forms of food, the family took him to sit with them
at meals, but instead of eating "he did nothing but learn."
When he saw the various appurtenances he asked persistently
how the dishes were named, where they came from, what
else could be made from the things, and did not rest until he
had discussed every piece of information.

In this mode of life the child remained always happy and
in good humor. He was lovable. Only when at times
he was refused answers to his questions, because it was feared
that he might be injured by too many remembrances, the
child was "sorely grieved." The extent of his learning in
the fourth year of life was as follows:

> Es konnte gedruckte und geschriebene Sachen lateinisch und
> deutsch lesen.
> Schreiben konnte es noch nicht, seine Fingerchen waren zu
> schwach dazu.
> Das Einmaleins konnte es in und ausser der Ordnung her-
> sagen. Auch numerieren, subtrahieren, addieren und multi-
> plizieren vermochte es.
> In Französischen kam es soweit, dass es ganze Historien in
> dieser Sprache erzählen konnte.
> Im Latein lernte es über 1500 gute Sprüche aus lateinischen
> Autoren.
> Plattdeutsch hatte das Kind von seiner Amme, von der es
> nicht lassen wollte, gelernt.
> In der Geographie fuhr es fort, das Merkwürdigste eines
> jeden auf der Landkarte stehenden Ortes zu fassen.

On a journey across the sea to Copenhagen, undertaken for the boy's health, a storm arose and the passengers were badly frightened, all but the child, who said, smiling, "Qui nescit rare, discat navigare." When subsequently the ship came safely to anchor, he remarked, "Anchora navis sistitur; deserit ille suos nunquam, qui cuncta gubernat."

When the boy was brought before the Danish king, he said of the diamond order that the king gave him to hold, "C'est l'Ordre d'Elephant, garni de diamant." And gazing at the diamonds, he added, "Les bijoux sont precieux, mais la vie du Roi est plus precieuse."

The "little Heineken" died at the age of 4 years 4 months, in accordance with the popular superstition that early death awaits the highly intelligent child, "a wonder for all time."

Karl Witte. The father of Karl Witte (*35*) has furnished a somewhat elaborate account of his son's development, from which we learn that the young Karl could read fluently before his fourth birthday. He learned to write soon thereafter. At the age of 7 years 10 months a public demonstration of his ability to read was given, covering Italian, French, Greek, and Latin. He passed tests of preparedness to matriculate at the University of Leipsic when he was 9 years old. In the field of mathematics he pursued analytical geometry at 11 and calculus at 12 years of age. At 14 he achieved the degree of Doctor of Philosophy, and was awarded the degree of Doctor of Laws at 16. At 23 he became full professor of jurisprudence at the University of Breslau. He was then called to Halle, and continued there for the remainder of his life, teaching and writing. At the age of 83, still vigorously engaged in mental tasks, he died, thus outliving the melancholy promise of early death which had often been prophesied to his father.

Pastor Witte, who directed his son's education, did not claim for him extraordinary intelligence. "Any man normally well endowed can become a great man if properly educated," he wrote (*35*). His special method of educating the boy seems to have been simply to afford him companionship. He describes the child as strong, healthy, and playful, without vanity or conceit. From the total record one must conclude that Karl Witte's intelligence quotient in childhood was in excess of 180, comparing his history with those studied in this monograph. His performances in childhood compare favorably with those of the children we have known with IQ (S–B) in the range above 185.

Otto Pöhler. In 1910 Berkhan (*2*) recorded the performance of Otto Pöhler, "the early reading child of Braunschweig," the son of a master butcher (erstes und einziges Kind der Schlachtermeisters), born August 20, 1892. This child learned to walk and talk and his teeth erupted "at the right time." At the age of 1 year 3 months, when his grandmother led him forth on short neighborhood walks, she would read to him from signs on the streets. And at this period she wrote for him his name, "Otto." Soon he could recognize the word "Otto," when he saw it in the newspaper. Then the grandmother explained to him the alphabet, and read him single words. When Otto was taken to Dr. Berkhan, he was 1 year 9 months old, and he could read incidental matter, such as "April 27," written in Latin across the calendar in Dr. Berkhan's office.

Otto Pöhler, geboren den 20 August 1892 zu Braunschweig, erstes und einziges Kind des Schlachtermeisters, bekam zu rechter zeit Zähne und lernte zu rechter Zeit laufen und sprechen. Als er 5/4 Jahre alt war, führte ihn die Grossmutter vor die Tür und in die nächsten Strassen und nannte

ihm dabei die Namen, welche auf den Haus- und Strassen-
schildern standen, auch hatten ihm die Angehörigen mehrfach
seinen Vornamen Otto aufgeschrieben. Als das Kind nun
eine Zeitung in die Hände bekam, zeigte es den mehrfach in
derselben gedruckten Namen Otto. Von da ab erklärte ihm
die Grossmutter die Buchstaben und las ihm einzelne Worte
vor; dabei ergab sich, dass das Kind ein ungeheures Gedächtnis
für Buchstaben, Worte, und Zahlen hatte.
Als mir der kleine Otto zugeführt wurde, war er wie ich
vorhin anführte 1¾ Jahre alt. Er tat sehr vertraut, kletterte
sofort mehrfach auf meine Kniee, zeigte sich überhaupt sehr
beweglich und unruhig. Als er einen neben dem Schreibtisch
hängenden Wandkalender erblickte, las er unaufgefordert laut
die auf demselben lateinisch gross gedruckte Anzeige: April 27
= "April zwei sieben. . . ."
Im Oktober, 1894, stellte ich den jungen Otto im Alter
von 2 Jahren und 2 Monaten dem ärztlichen Landesverein vor.
Als derselbe nach Beendigung meines über ihn gehaltenen
Vortrags in den Sitzungssaal geführt wurde, zog einer der
Ärzte den Börnerschen Medizinal-Kalender hervor mit der
Aufforderung, die lateinische Aufschrift zu lesen. Er las
fliessend: "Re—ichs Medizinal-Kalender. Begründet von Děr
Pa—ul Börněr. Eins acht neun vier."

When Otto was 4 years old, Stumpf reported concerning
him in the *Vossische Zeitung,* of January 10, 1897, describing
him as "not strongly yet not poorly developed, physically."
The back of the skull was said to be conspicuous; the face,
delicate; and the eyes, "wise and alive, taking on a remarkably concentrated expression in thinking." The general impression was that made by a merry, unspoiled youngster,
seeing the world. His great passion was still for reading,
and the most important things in the world to him were
history, biography, and geography.

Er ist körperlich nicht stark, aber auch nicht schlecht entwick-
elt. Auf den ersten Blick fällt der lange Schädel und der

starke Hinterkopf auf. In dem zierlichen Gesicht fesseln kluge, lebhafte Augen, die beim Nachsinnen einen merkwürdig ernsten konzentrierten Ausdruck annehmen. . . . . Im ganzen macht er keineswegs den Eindruck eines ungesunden, abgematteten, sondern eines noch ganz frisch und lustig in die Welt schauenden Jungen. . . .

Seine grösste Leidenschaft ist noch immer das Lesen, und das Wichtigste in der Welt sind ihm historische, biographische und geographische Daten. Er kennt die Geburts- und Todesjahre vieler deutscher Kaiser, auch vieler Feldherren, Dichter, Philosophen, zumeist sogar auch Geburtstag und Geburtsort; ferner die Hauptstädte der meisten Staaten, die Flüsse, an denen sie liegen u. dergl. Er weiss Bescheid vom Anfang und Ende des dreissigjährigen und des siebenjährigen Krieges, von den Hauptschlachten dieser und anderer Kriege. Das alles hat er sich nach Aussage der Mutter ohne fremdes Zutun durch das emsige Studium eines "patriotischen Kalenders" und ähnlicher im Hause vorfindlicher Literatur, auch durch Entzifferung von Denkmalsinschriften in den Städten (wofür er besondere Leidenschaft hat) angeeignet. Als ihm auf zwei verschiedenen Blättern nacheinander 2 zwölfstellige Zahlen gezeigt wurden, die sich nur durch eine der mittleren Ziffern unterschieden, las er sie sogleich als Milliarden und konnte dann, ohne die Blätter wieder anzusehen, mit Sicherheit angeben, worin der Unterschied lag.

Stumpf further said:

. . . Dr. Placzek u.a. die den Knaben früher beobachteten, den bestimmten Eindruck gewannen eines besonders geweckten, rasch und scharf denkenden und zugleich eines gutartigen, durchaus liebenswürdigen Kindes. An den Eltern und zumal an der Mutter hängt er mit der grössten Zärtlichkeit.

When Berkhan saw Pöhler in July, 1907, the boy was an *Obersekundaner* in a gymnasium. In April, 1909, aged 16 years 8 months, he appeared as an intelligent, wonderfully retentive, cultured young man, who oriented himself easily and who, although favored over and above his contemporaries, had kept a modest and lovable nature.

Jetzt, fast 17 Jahre alt, ist er ein intelligenter, mit einem bewunderungswerten Gedächtnis ausgestatteter, kenntnisreicher, sich auffallend leicht orientierender junger Mann, der, obgleich in seiner Weise vor der Mitwelt bevorzugt, sich ein bescheidenes, liebenswürdiges Wesen bewahrt hat.

Pöhler's plan, when seen on this final occasion, April, 1909, was to go at Easter, 1910, to the university, to become a student of German history.

Other cases. General discussions of mental gifts in children which bear interestingly upon the subject here under discussion but fail to present any specific instances of individuals who exemplify extreme status, are those by Dolbear (7) and by Hartlaub (*12*), and the lectures given in 1930 before the Hungarian Society for Child Research and Practical Psychology (*31*). Among the cases cited by Waddle (*33*) there are none that belong to our study. In the research of Cox (*6*), the following eminent persons were rated as having been in childhood at or above 180 IQ (S–B): John Stuart Mill, Johann Wolfgang Goethe, Gottfried Wilhelm Leibnitz, Blaise Pascal, Thomas Babington Macaulay, and Hugo de Groot (Grotius). We would, however, venture to guess, from what we have observed over a long period of the work of persons who in childhood tested from 135 to 200 IQ (S–B), that a large number of the persons included in Cox's study would have tested in childhood at or above 180 IQ (S–B); and that the reasons why they failed of such rating as studied by Cox were two: (1) the data of childhood requisite for the valid rating were lacking; (2) the raters were not sufficiently familiar with what is required in terms of IQ to make possible the evaluation of those studied, because only a few children testing so high could have been seen by any rater, and nothing was as yet known of the performance of tested children at any stage of maturity. Many of the persons studied by the methods of Cox were rated at 140, 150, 155 IQ (S–B), whose performances in early maturity were far in excess of what can be expected of persons who represent nothing better than what the upper quarter of American college students can do (6). It is only when children test at least as high as 170 IQ (S–B) that they render performance in early maturity that suggests anything like the achievements of the persons studied by Cox.

CHILDREN WHO TEST ABOVE 180 IQ
        BY BINET-SIMON TESTS

After the publication of the Binet-Simon tests (3), a few cases of children testing very high by means of them were reported in the literature which resulted from the tests before they were revised by Terman (24). At that time, which was previous to the appearance of the Stanford-Binet tests, the IQ was not used in expressing mental status, but we are able to calculate what this was from the data of Mental Age. These early cases, definitely measured, are as follows:

Bush's daughter, B. In 1914 Bush (5) reported upon the mental examination of his daughter, B, who at the age of 3 years 6 months tested at 6 years by the Binet tests of 1911. Her IQ would thus be proved at about 185, calculated from her father's detailed record of responses. This report was rendered primarily to show that the Binet tests were too easy, as no child could possibly be really so advanced mentally as was B. "B's state is in no wise extra-normal, or beyond what it should be. She represents the norm."

Additional data concerning B are that she "is of a happy

disposition . . . strong and well of body," and that her parents are both teachers. This record clearly reveals a child of surpassing intelligence, contrary to the father's belief that "she represents the norm."

Elizabeth, recorded by Langenbeck. In 1915 Langenbeck (*15*) contributed observations of a 5-year-old girl, Elizabeth, who tested at a mental level of about 11 years by the Binet-Simon tests of 1911, administered in the Psychological Laboratory at Johns Hopkins University. This would yield an IQ of about 220 (assuming the tests of 1911 to be approximately comparable with Stanford-Binet in power to distribute intellect).

Elizabeth is described as an only child. At 16 months she had a speaking vocabulary of 229 words, some English and some German, as she had a German nurse. At 5 years of age she had a speaking vocabulary of 6837 words, which are inscribed in the record. The observer writes of her as follows:

> Her quickness of thought and readiness with an instant and convincing answer were typified one dusty, blustering day when we were out walking. A cloud of dust enveloped us, to her great indignation, and being a very vehement character she exclaimed, "I should like to kill the dust!" In answer to my reproof, "Do not be so foolish. How can anyone kill the dust?" she replied, "Very easily — pour a little water on it." This was at the age of 4 years. . . . She is highly imaginative, and lives largely in a dream world of her own creation. Her games are nearly all pretense that she is someone else, and that she is surrounded by companions, sometimes purely fictitious, though often characters out of books that have been read to her. . . . When being read to, she asks the meaning of every unfamiliar word, and rarely forgets it, using it thereafter in its proper place. . . . Many of her forebears have been distinguished men and women, and on both sides her family

have been people of more than average capacity and cultivation. . . . From an early age she has shown unusual muscular coördination, using her fingers daintily and with precision. From her eighth month she used a paper and pencil, drawing recognizable figures. At 4 years she could illustrate a little story composed by herself. . . . The source of much of her knowledge is a mystery to her parents, and can only be explained by her keen observation and retentive memory, as well as by a power of comprehension much beyond her years. However absorbed she may appear to be in her play, talking vigorously to herself and to imaginary companions all the time, she nevertheless hears everything that is said in her presence, though months will often pass before she alludes to it. . . . She taught herself her letters from street signs and books, and could print them all before she was three, and during the next few months would write letters of several pages, of her own composition, having the words, of course, spelled for her. . . . She has an accurate ear and could sing a tune correctly before her second birthday, and dances in excellent time. . . . Every new thought or impression is at once associated with some previous idea. Hence, doubtless, her marvelous memory. For example, in a country walk she noticed a typical Virginia snake fence and wished to call attention to it, but knew no specific name, having never seen one before. After a single moment's hesitation she said, "You see that M or W fence?" . . . At the age of five years she had coined twenty-three words — e.g., *laten,* to make late; *neaten,* to make neat; *plak,* to pretend; *up-jar,* pitcher.

Rusk's case, from Scotland. In 1917 Rusk (*19*) published an account of a Scottish boy whose IQ, calculated from Rusk's detailed record, was about 166 on first test and about 200 on second test given two and a half years later, the Binet-Simon tests of 1911 being used. This child was the son of a widow in Dundee, who lived and supported her two sons by letting rooms to lodgers. The young brother of this boy was not judged to be remarkably intelligent, but no test was given to substantiate this impression. Details of family history are not recorded.

The boy was brought to attention at the age of 5 years by his teachers, who noted particularly his aptitude for mathematics. The mother was unaware of her son's extraordinary intelligence, but she had noticed that he spent a considerable amount of time on the floor, counting. He would count such objects as cigarette coupons begged from lodgers. Also the mother observed that he "had learned before going to school, or being taught to read, to recognize certain words."

CHILDREN WHO TEST ABOVE 180 IQ

BY STANFORD-BINET TESTS

Beatrice. Terman and Fenton (25) first described Beatrice in 1921 under her own name. In 1930 Terman (27) again described this child, under the name of Beatrice (evidently being then convinced that pseudonyms are to be preferred in designating children studied), adding data about development.

The child's four grandparents were respectively of Swedish, German-French, English, and Scottish descent. "The mother is a woman of more than average intelligence, and of considerable musical ability. The father's line of ancestry includes several notables, among them a Lord Mayor of London. The father is a physician, and the author of the *Ford Stitch*, favorably mentioned in standard texts on surgery. Betty [Beatrice] has no sisters or brothers."

Beatrice was born in San Francisco, January 21, 1912, and was first tested six weeks before her eighth birthday, by Stanford-Binet, yielding then a mental age of 14 years 10 months and an IQ of 188. Her speaking vocabulary was at that time 13,000 words. A variety of mental tests gave nearly the same composite result as that achieved by Stanford-Binet. At the time of testing, the child had never attended school but had been given a little private instruction at home. Her scores on standard tests of scholastic knowledge ranged, nevertheless, from fifth-grade norms (in the four fundamental processes in arithmetic) to second year of college (in tests of poetic appreciation). Her median score in eight scholastic tests was about eighth grade (where the median birthday age of pupils is about 14 years, and where pupils have been in school on an average of eight years).

Ratings for traits of character and for physique gave this child a score much above average in both respects. She weighed 11 pounds and 15 ounces at birth, and at the age of 8 years 2 months corresponded to the standard for 9 years 6 months in weight and for 10 years 6 months in stature. Her hand grip at this time was equal to that of the average 10-year-old. She began to walk at 7 months of age, which is the earliest age of walking recorded for any of the children so far studied, including those who are the special subjects of this monograph. At 19 months she talked clearly and knew the alphabet; at 20 months she could put puzzle-block pictures together; and at the age of 4 years 6 months she was discovered reading *Heidi*, a book of about fourth-grade degree of difficulty. Her parents did not know that she could read, and they have no idea when or how she learned. By her eighth birthday Beatrice had read approximately seven hundred books, many of them twice. At that age it was one of her favorite pastimes to write stories or poems and to illustrate them with original drawings. Her health was said by her parents to be excellent. The measurements given show her to be large and strong for her age.

Beatrice was not entered at school until she was 11 years old, but studied at home under her mother's guidance. There was little formal instruction — as a rule there was arithmetic, from ten to twenty minutes daily. At 11 years of age Beatrice entered the ninth grade of a private school for girls, which she attended for two years. She entered the university when she was 14 years 8 months old, and graduated at 17. In college Beatrice earned A and B grades in English and languages and C's in science. She fell barely short of Phi Beta Kappa election. Throughout her life she has had few playmates and few intimate friends. Her desire is for a literary career.

Root's case, VIII A. In 1921 Root (*18*) described a boy who at the age of 8 years 0 month scored at a Mental Age of 16 years 0 month, with an IQ (S–B) of 200. Other tests agreed in placing this boy near an average adult level in processes of thought. The stature of the child at this time was 4 feet, and the weight 59 pounds.

The ancestry in the case is predominantly English. Father and mother both graduated from high school. The father was a railroad engineer. Two maternal aunts held prominent places in the public schools. The family had "all comforts but few luxuries." "The aunt who has guided the [boy's] education seems a rare combination; her educational ideas are a happy union of radical, common sense, and practical factors." "Nervous temperament" is judged by Root to be characteristic of the family on the mother's side.

This boy was an only child. His mother stated that he had never been ill, but it is to be considered that she was a Christian Scientist. He was educated at home until he was 7 years 6 months old, learning reading and arithmetical processes through multiplication. He had read the *Young*

Folks' Cyclopaedia of Common Things "over and over."
His chief interests were at this time games and reading and,
to a lesser degree, animals and flowers.

The following is a letter from his aunt, describing his
home education:

> At the age of three he learned his letters untaught by anyone
> apparently, and was spelling words. It was felt that this
> would interfere with his learning to read later on, so he was
> taught to read by the phonic method. This was done with no
> more time and personal attention than any first-grade teacher,
> with ordinary numbers of pupils, could give to each one, pro-
> vided she were generously supplied with different books, and
> not limited to one or two sets — state series or otherwise. A
> few months after his fourth birthday he was reading with
> independence and an almost perfect power to recognize new
> words. His only noticed failures were such foreign words as
> "Chevrolet" seen on billboards, and unusual words like "aisle,"
> used without context, which he pronounced "alicie." His
> ease in reading was, of course, made possible, or at least greatly
> facilitated, by the fact that an effort had always been made to
> use an extended vocabulary in talking to him. Even at two,
> he would surprise acquaintances and strangers with expressions
> which meant no greater effort to him than a child's baby-talk;
> such as, "Oh, the spider has *attached* his web to the board."
> This ability to read opened a new world, for he read car-
> signs, billboards, newspapers, magazines, and books. His
> books and magazines were carefully selected. His access to
> newspapers, especially the funny sheets, had the most question-
> able results. But *The Child's Garden of Verses* and others
> proved a veritable dream world — as real as the everyday one.
> He once asked his mother, "Does Robert Louis Stevenson know
> when I'm naughty?" At another time he wrote a letter to
> some of the characters in another book. At the age of six he
> read *Swiss Family Robinson* and *Champlin's Cyclopedia of
> Common Things* — the two books which have been and still
> are his favorites. Other books which he read before entering

school at seven years were: *Overall Boys, Brownie Book,* Kipling's *Just-So Stories* (read over and over for two or three years), Swift's *Gulliver's Travels,* Kingsley's *Heroes,* Aesop's *Fables,* Tolstoy's *Stories for Children,* Grimm's *Fairy Tales, Arabian Nights,* Barrie's *Peter Pan* and *Peter and Wendy.*

He entered school at seven and a half years and was put in the B1 (beginner's) class. In the two days he was kept there, he developed a distinct aversion to school since nobody discovered he could do anything and the class confinement and need for sitting still (coupled with the fact that he did not find the toilet for over a week) made school most disagreeable to him. On the third day a member of the family intervened and the teacher very reluctantly allowed him to enter the second grade. She insisted that he could not do the work, as he did not know his sounds. Of course he did "know his sounds," but perhaps he refused to do such baby-work, although he never expressed his unwillingness at home, and seemed quite afraid of displeasing his teacher. In the second grade he was forced to sit for 20 to 25 minutes, studying a reading book, which he could have read through in that time. At home he was told to take some work to school, but the teacher refused to let him read in school, even the *Cyclopedia of Common Things.* At the end of a week and a half he was in absolute rebellion and was taken out of school.

The family then took this child to a teacher of fourth grade, who was personally acquainted with him, and asked her to examine him for proper placement. This resulted in a more appropriate adjustment. By February of his first year in school he had reached Grade 5A in school placement, and had had thirteen different teachers, including those for special subjects such as music, nature study, and the like. His initial aversion to school lessened, but he found no positive joy in attending. Root describes the temperament of the boy as "somewhat irascible." This case illustrates in extreme degree the maladjustment to school which is characteristic of children testing above 180 IQ (S–B).

Twins A and B. In 1922 Gesell (*10*) reported the case of twin girls, both of IQ 183 (S–B). Gesell was interested but incidentally in the IQ ratings of these girls, his main interest centering in the condition of twinning. Measurements were taken with a view to comparing twins, and therefore many details that would be of interest for our present purpose — for instance, those of family history — are omitted from the report.

A and B were born by Caesarean section, somewhat prematurely, weighing 4.3 pounds and 5.3 pounds, respectively. Notwithstanding their premature birth, in six months A was able to rise spontaneously to a sitting posture in her mother's lap, and very soon thereafter B did likewise. At 11 months both had begun to walk, and to talk in sentences. At the age of 3 years they began the study of French, and in less than a year from that time they were reading elementary English, French, and Esperanto. At the age of 4 they could distinguish parts of speech. They entered the third grade in school at the age of 6 years, and at the time of report they had achieved the seventh grade and were engaged in junior high school work at the age of 9 years.

They are not prigs: they are attractive, animated, sociable children, with a bubbling sense of humor. They are popular with their playmates. They can take charge of a gymnasium class in which most of the members are two to four years their seniors, and preserve excellent attention and discipline. They speak mature but not pedantic English, and they speak French with the fluency of a native. They have read the *Book of Knowledge* in its entirety in French; and a year ago embarked on Russian. They play duets on the piano, but not with rare distinction. They swim; they ride horseback; they write jingles; and they read by the hour. Their school work does not tax them; they do not worry about it; and they are far from fastidious in regard to the form of their written work.

A complete family chart of the twin sisters, A and B, would show evidence of superior endowment in the immediate ancestry on both the maternal sides. Scientific and linguistic ability of high order and physical energy are some of the traits which are found in the two immediate generations. The trait of twinning likewise has a hereditary basis in this instance, for the mother also bore two boys, twins who died in infancy.

Measurements of physique show A and B to be slightly smaller than children of their age in good private schools, but very well nourished. The children have no living brothers or sisters.

Elizabeth, reported by Hirt. Elizabeth was reported from the public schools of Erie, Pennsylvania, in 1922, by Hirt (*13*). She was born January 16, 1914, and was tested June 14, 1921, aged 7 years 5 months. Her Mental Age was found to be 14 years 0 months, yielding an IQ of 189 (S–B).

Elizabeth's mother was a member of a large family of children brought from Germany to America by their parents. The father (Elizabeth's maternal grandfather) died soon after their arrival in America, and the mother (Elizabeth's maternal grandmother) worked hard to keep her family together and to give them all an elementary school education. Elizabeth's father is of Pennsylvania German descent. He has a high school education, and attended a business college. His occupation in 1922 was that of postal mail clerk.

This child weighed 10 pounds at birth, 22 pounds at 6 months, 28½ pounds at 12 months, and at the age of 7 years 5 months she weighed 61 pounds and was 51 inches tall. Superior size was thus consistently maintained from birth to the time of first report, in 1921. Two teeth erupted before she was 5 months old. She was not quite a year old when she began to repeat words. Her first sentence was, "Open the door, Daddy," uttered at the age of 17 months. The parents remembered this sentence as a sudden transition from one-word communications into sentence structure.

The only illness Elizabeth had ever had until she was 7 years 4 months old was mumps, which came on at that age.

Hirt's report continues as follows:

Among Elizabeth's first toys was a set of cubical blocks with letters and numbers on four sides. One of the baby's favorite amusements was to hold up a block and point to one side after the other for her entertainer to tell what was on the side of the block indicated. Gradually the game changed, and the baby held up the block and pointed to the picture called for by the entertainer. At the age of 15 months she made no mistakes in finding the animals called for, and very soon afterwards she could find the letters in the same way.

One of her first books was *The Story of the Naughty Piggies*. The child seemed never to tire of hearing the story read, and by the time she was two and a half years old, when she sat in the lap of the reader, she could turn the page at just the right place in the story. About that time the two leaves in the center of the book loosened and dropped out. The German grandma made a mistake in sewing them in, putting the second first. Elizabeth quickly discovered the mistake and was very unhappy about it. She followed her grandmother about, asking her to fix it. The grandmother could not understand what the child meant, and finally appealed to the child's mother, who discovered what was wrong. Elizabeth was not yet three years old, and they could not believe that the child detected the difference between these two pages of the book. But after the grandmother ripped out the stitches and replaced the leaves in their proper sequence, the little girl showed unmistakable satisfaction and content.

At three and a half years of age, Elizabeth was spelling everything she saw printed and asking what the letters spelled, and she could recognize many words. At four years, she read the advertisements in the streetcars, as well as everything in all the books she possessed. During all this time there was no attempt on the part of the parents to make their daughter precocious. They were pleased with her readiness to learn, but they did not look upon her as an unusual child.

In September, 1920, Elizabeth was enrolled in the first grade, in the public schools of Erie, Pennsylvania. She was then 6 years 8 months old. On her second day in school her teacher discovered that she could read anything that was placed before her. The principal put her in the second grade until she had time to investigate her case. She spent forty-two days in the second grade, during which time the principal observed her closely, and decided to place her in the fourth grade. Elizabeth had no trouble in completing that grade in the remainder of the school year, the principal giving her some special help in spelling and arithmetic. . . . Elizabeth is not a skillful writer, as far as penmanship goes, but she seldom makes a mistake in either spelling or punctuation, and the content of her letters and compositions is superior, even for the advanced grade in which she is now working. . . . Intellectually speaking, this child takes everything to which she is exposed, and she is not satisfied unless she understands the subject fully. Unfamiliar words or terms bring from her the question, "Just what does that mean?" She has a cheery disposition, and laughs often and heartily. She is contented in any environment, because her imagination makes it as she wishes it. . . . When she is reading or studying, she becomes so engrossed that it is hard to attract her attention to anything outside her book. . . . She is slow in her written work, and she is slow and rather awkward in some of her motor coördinations.

After less than a month in the fifth grade, in September, 1921 (age 7 years 8 months), Elizabeth was promoted to the sixth grade, where she is doing superior work. In the examinations at the end of the last semester she ranked about the middle of the class, due to the fact that she is still slow in her written work. But in comprehension she easily leads the class.

Thus far nothing has been done for this exceptional child except to move her along from grade to grade five times as rapidly as the average child can go. When we see her at times very evidently bored while a teacher is trying to make a subject clear to pupils of average ability, we wonder what would have happened if Elizabeth were now in the second or third grade where most eight-year-old children are found.

In 1925 Hirt again reported upon the child, Elizabeth, as follows:

By February, 1923, she had completed the work of the six elementary grades, and she was promoted to the junior high school. Now, at the end of her fifth year in school, she is ready for the second semester's work in the ninth grade. . . . After her promotion to the junior high school, some of her teachers complained that she was lazy; others said that she was very inattentive; and all declared that she was "very silly." The school psychologist had a conference with these teachers, and it was decided that Elizabeth should be given a heavier schedule, and Latin was added to her program. She has been enthusiastic over this subject from the very first. . . . During the past year there has been a steady improvement in Elizabeth's attitude toward her school work as well as in her behavior in general. Though some of her teachers still consider her "silly," they all recognize her unusual mental ability. While they give her B and C grades in most of her subjects, they realize that she could easily do A work in every subject if she cared to. They say that she wastes much time, though her mind seems always to be busy. Her mother says that when she is at home "she writes, and writes, and writes, covering reams of paper." Elizabeth has told her mother that she is writing a book and a play.

In the spring of 1925, when a friend asked Elizabeth where she was going to spend her summer vacation, the child replied, "Why, I expect to take a trip around the world." Then seeing the surprise in her friend's face, she explained, "Of course, it is not probable that I shall go far from our porch swing, but I find the swing a very satisfactory conveyance; it is perfectly safe, and it always takes me exactly where I want to go."

When Elizabeth entered the tenth grade, in senior high School, in 1926, she was 12 years 8 months old. Her social behavior was at about the level for this age, and her teachers were coldly critical, unable or unwilling to reconcile her conduct with her physical size and intellectual maturity. She made very few friends. She was graduated from high school in June, 1929, with the reputation of being lazy. She excelled in the languages, but her work in other subjects was mediocre.

After she was graduated from high school, funds were not available for Elizabeth to attend college away from home or to pay tuition. Consequently, because she must live at home she enrolled in a State Teachers College, though she had no desire to become a teacher. She was 15 years 8 months old at this time, and her work was very uneven in excellence. When the time arrived for practice teaching, she was assigned to teach high school pupils of about her own age, and failed in this branch of the work, so that she was not graduated. She received, however, an honorable discharge from the college. During these years, 1929–1933, her situation was further complicated by the passing of a state law prohibiting students below 17 years of age from attending the State Teachers College. As Elizabeth was then still below the age specified in the new law, she was forced to withdraw and wait for time to pass, resuming her studies as soon as she fell within the law.

When Elizabeth was discharged from the Teachers College, interested friends made attempts to secure for her a subsistence and tuition scholarship at some good liberal arts college, but no such opportunities were found.   One college otherwise interested in granting a tuition scholarship now found her "too old," she being then aged 19 years.

The scholastic history of Elizabeth is too long to be told here in greater detail.   It affords an instructive and tragic example of the blindness of current educational practice in dealing with children who test in the highest ranges of intellect.   At 22 years of age Elizabeth lives at home, without suitable occupation, writing poetry and helping with the tasks of the household.   Her education as conducted has not provided her with any recognized equipment for entering into the intellectual life of her world, although she possesses one of the best intellects of her generation.

The case of J. M.   The history of J. M., a 10-year-old girl of IQ 190 (S–B), was presented by Washburne (*34*) in 1924.   This girl was a pupil in the public schools of Winnetka, Illinois, where the plan of individualized instruction is followed, with individual subject promotions.

At the age of 10 years 6 months, J. M. was 54.5 inches tall and weighed 88.5 pounds.   This is decidedly in excess of the standards for average children, as regards size.   She was doing work of good quality in the eighth grade, and could have been in high school had not the school authorities checked her progress in the seventh grade by giving her a large amount of extra work to do.   Her school record shows that she entered the public schools of Chicago in the first grade, in September, 1919.   The teacher of first grade immediately discovered that she knew too much for that grade and brought about her placement in the second grade.   There she remained until the following April, when her family moved to Winnetka.

In Winnetka, J. M. entered the second grade and was

promoted in June. Her reading, tested by the Monroe and Gray tests, was up to fifth-grade standard when she reached third grade, and had reached the sixth-grade standard by December, 1920. Her progress in other school subjects was such that in September, 1921, she entered the fifth grade. Her rapid progress was halted somewhat, as she "was carrying a double language course, finishing the fourth grade and beginning fifth-grade work simultaneously." When in May, 1922, she began the sixth-grade work, she completed it in two weeks. "June, 1922, found her, therefore, doing advanced sixth-grade reading, through with sixth-grade spelling, almost through with sixth-grade arithmetic, and promoted to the seventh grade in language. She was then nine years old." In the course of this progress, the grade standard in penmanship was last to be achieved. The perplexities which now arose in connection with this child's education are set forth as follows, by Washburne:

In spite of the fact that she was so clearly ready for seventh-grade work in the fall of 1922, we hesitated about having her come from the lower grade school to our junior high school. She was smaller and younger than any of the children in the junior high, and we felt that she was already so far advanced that still more progress was perhaps undesirable. But she had formed a warm attachment for two girls a year or so older than herself, both possessed of high IQ's, and she felt that there would be nothing for her to do in the sixth grade if we held her back. This was so obviously true that we admitted her to the junior high school with an agreement that she would remain there until she was twelve years old.

We felt that while she doubtless could do the work of the junior high school within a year, or at the most in a year and a half, since our junior high contains only the seventh and eighth grades, she ought not to go to the senior high school too young. We agreed to give her a widely enriched curriculum of electives and special courses, to keep her active and happy for three years.   But it didn't work!

When she found that no effort on her part would get her through any sooner, she stopped making effort.   The end of the first year (June, 1923) found her with seventh-grade cooking, seventh-grade art, and seventh-grade pottery, all incomplete.   She had taken up general science toward the end of the year, and of course had not finished it either.   She had, on the other hand, completed all of the seventh-grade English and arithmetic, including some advanced work; had done exceptionally well in French.   In dramatics she first had a know-it-all attitude, owing to her mother's success in amateur theatricals, but later did very good work.   In social studies she had been inclined to superficiality, trusting to her quick grasp on a single reading of the material (Rugg's *Social Science Pamphlets*) and doing little real thinking.   But she was interested, and finished the course within the year.

The general feeling of the teachers, and of J. M. herself . . . was that she had "loafed on the job" a good deal, had been over-confident, and had "let down" generally when the stimulus of rapid advancement was taken away.   This gives us some inkling as to what would have happened to her in a regular school system, where the class lockstep is the rule. This year J. M. is taking a straight eighth-grade course with one elective, and is tying up the loose ends left undone at the end of last year.

. . . The child's strong desire to move forward with the children who are now her friends, and the undesirable effect on her of our last year's experiment in holding her back regardless of her effort or ability to go forward, have resulted in our decision to let her graduate this coming June.

Her parents, however, have requested that we keep her in our junior high school for a postgraduate year, because they feel that the influence of this school is needed by J. M.   We shall, therefore, try to provide a special course for her next fall. If we find out that it does not work out successfully, we will enter her in the senior high school in February, 1925.   If, on the other hand, we find that we can give her the sort of education that will be helpful to her in our junior high school and that she responds rightly, we shall hold her here until June, letting her enter the senior high school at the age of twelve and one half years.

Interpreting and summarizing our experience with J. M.: Our system of individual instruction has permitted her to make full use of her intellectual ability. When we tried to depart from it to prevent her progress from becoming too rapid, she showed a lack of interest and in some parts of her school work she did not work up to capacity, and even became to a slight extent a discipline problem. Given, however, an incentive to first-class work and the training in social behavior which we are trying to give in our junior high school, J. M. developed successfully and well. On the whole, our system has enabled us to deal with her flexibly and as an individual. It has prevented us from prolonging our mistakes. Probably no system, or uniform plan, can be made to fit children of such exceptional mental endowments. The most we can hope for is a flexibility which will enable us to deal with such children as individuals, feeling our way as we go along.

As for family background, J. M. originates from ancestors of very superior intelligence. Her parents were both tested by means of Army Alpha and both scored far above the generality of adults. Her father was educated as an electrical engineer but subsequently went into investment banking. J. M.'s paternal grandfather was an architect, trained in Manchester School of Science. He also attended the University of Edinburgh. The paternal great-grandfather was an architect and shipbuilder, expert in laying out factories, and he was descended from a line of builders. The paternal grandmother was an English woman, educated by her aunt, "who had advanced ideas on what a girl should study." The father of this grandmother was a dealer in building materials.

On the maternal side, J. M.'s grandfather was first a teacher, then a merchant, who became very wealthy, and a mayor of a Southern town for eighteen years. The line of his descent was through Southern planters. The maternal grandmother was the daughter of a college professor, who in turn was the son of a physician and surgeon, coming from a long line of physicians. The mother of the maternal grandmother was descended from wealthy farmers. It is of some interest that for three generations at least, J. M. and her immediate progenitors were born when the parents were thirty years or older, in some cases being more than sixty years old.

The case of E. B. This child was described in 1924, by Stedman (*22*), as having "the highest IQ yet reported." Exception was taken some years ago by the present writer to this description, on the ground that the test by which E. B. registered an IQ of 214 was not the first given to the child. She had been tested previously by Stanford-Binet, at the age of 5 years 9 months, earning an IQ of 175. When tested in the Psychological Department of the Los Angeles city schools at the age of 8 years 11 months, E. B. made the record of a superior adult, earning an IQ of 214 (S–B). The record is thus ambiguous, and will be included here only because we cannot say how much allowance should be made for "test wisdom" on second test. However, subsequent history points to 175 IQ as the more probably correct status for this child, since when she was tested at the age of 21 years 1 month, by Lorge and Hollingworth (*16*), using CAVD, Levels M, N, O, P, and Q, and other tests of cultural and specifically scientific knowledge, the result placed her among individuals who in childhood had tested between 170 and 180 IQ (S–B).

E. B. was born on September 21, 1913.   When 4 years 6 months old she was placed in a convent school on account of her mother's departure for France.   She was not enrolled as a pupil but was allowed to sit with the high first grade when she wished, because her chum sat there.   In four months, at the close of the school year, it was discovered that she could read any page in the reader which had been used as a text, and any page in the public school first reader, which she had never seen before.   Accordingly, though not yet 5 years old, she was "promoted" to the second grade.

At the close of the next school year she was promoted to the fourth grade, aged 5 years 9 months.   Before E. B. was 6 years old she had read practically every book listed by the public library at Des Moines for children of the first six grades.   At the age of 9 years 4 months she was doing eighth-grade and post-eighth grade work.   Her favorite books at the age of 9 years include Barrie's *The Little Minister, Sentimental Tommy* and *Tommy and Grizel;* Hugo's *Les Misérables;* Dickens's *Oliver Twist, Our Mutual Friend,* and *David Copperfield;* Eliot's *Silas Marner* and *Mill on the Floss;* Bunyan's *Pilgrim's Progress;* Hutchinson's *If Winter Comes* and *This Freedom.* . . . Until she entered the opportunity room, E. B. never had a child companion, and was unpopular with children.   She was friendly but shy, and unable to comply with the play standards of other children.   In the opportunity room she made better social adjustments.   She is cheerful, affectionate, and considerate to the point of self-denial.   She obeys implicitly, but is forgetful in the commission of small duties, perhaps because engrossed with more interesting matters.   She thinks along economic and political lines, and can hold her own even with many adults in conversing on these subjects. . . . Health is excellent.   She has had the usual children's diseases, but has recuperated very quickly. . . . E. B. is of French, English, and Scotch descent.   The father finished high school at 13, and was an A and B student at the University, taking gold

medals for original composition. He is a writer and an editor.
. . . The paternal grandfather is a lawyer, teacher, and
author. The paternal grandmother has mathematical ability.
E. B.'s mother entered school at 8 years, and completed high
school at 15. She then entered business college, and completed
the course in less than three months. She then entered college, working her way through with consistently A records.
She was editor of a national magazine at 25, and at the time
of investigation was an editorial writer on *Screenland*. . . .
The maternal grandfather's history is unknown. It is thought
that he was average; but the maternal great-grandfather was
probably superior. At 21 he could neither read nor write, but
just at this time a public school was established near his home.
He entered, and finished the course for the entire eight grades
in sixteen months. . . . E. B.'s mother states that E. B. first
spoke words with meaning at 7 or 8 months of age, and that
she walked at 10 months. When she was 3 years old her
parents discovered that she knew the alphabet, which she seems
to have learned by asking questions about printed signs. She
has had very little formal instruction at home, for her mother
has been active in newspaper work most of the time, usually
working at night.

E. B. entered college in a large city at 12 years 0 months
of age. The girls in this college are very highly selected for
intellect, and E. B. did not do outstanding work among
them. She encountered many difficulties, but graduated at
the age of 16 years 9 months with a creditable rating. At
the age of 20 years she married, holding also at that age a
very responsible post in charge of cash for the metropolitan
branch of one of the largest manufacturing and distributing
companies in the United States. It is her aim to become a
writer.

Verda. In 1925 Terman (*26*) reported two children not elsewhere described, with IQ's above 180 (S–B), Verda and Madeline (page 63), both discovered during the census of the gifted taken in California.

The occupational level among Verda's male ancestors has been largely in the professions and in business. Her father is a successful life insurance salesman, and shows musical, mechanical, and literary ability. He is of Scotch-Irish extraction. Her mother is of French and English ancestry, a descendant in direct line from Governor Bradford, of colonial New England, and is related to many notables. Verda has no brothers or sisters.

The child's first words were articulated at 7 months, and she talked in sentences at 15 months. She hummed a tune at 17 months; could name all the primary colors at 22 months; could count to 13 at 25 months. Her first poem (said in rhyme and meter) was composed at the age of 2 years 9 months. This was recorded by her mother. She did not herself put on paper her literary compositions until the age of 5 years, when she learned to print. After this the stories she composed were no longer recorded by her mother. Soon after she was 4 years old she brought a book to her parents and read to them. Up to that time she had had no formal instruction in reading but she had been read to.

Verda did not enter school until she was 8 years 7 months old, beginning in the high fourth grade.

Her IQ was first determined at the age of 11 years 1 month by an incomplete test, made as a demonstration before a group of teachers in the limited time of fifty minutes, and was calculated at 175. When at age 11 years 7 months she was fully tested in a standard situation, she passed every test provided on Stanford-Binet, proving at an IQ ("corrected" [2]) of 186. Through four years of high school she received an "A" grade in every academic subject, with the exception of one semester of French and one of biology, in which the grade was "B." She was graduated from high school at age 16 years 9 months.

According to her own testimony, Verda's usual amount of study during her senior year was only six hours a week outside of school hours. "She is fond of parties and dances, and is very active in student life, particularly through her literary contributions. She rates herself as rather disliking study. She would rather read, play the piano, compose music, stories, or plays, or spend time with her friends." (In 1926 she won a gold medal in a piano-playing contest.) She has shown a wide margin of energy and ability over and above what is necessary for a "straight A" record in high school.

There is much more in the description of this child that is interesting, but the case cannot here be quoted in full.

Madeline. At the age of 6 years 7 months Madeline yielded an IQ of 192 (S–B). She was then in the third grade, but her scores on Stanford Achievement Tests corresponded to fifth- and sixth-grade norms. At 7 years of age, her parents' chief concern in regard to her was to prevent her from reading too much.

At 7 months of age Madeline was able to distinguish all the pictures on the walls of her home when they were named to her. She could identify the pictures of six American poets when she was a little over a year old. She knew the common flowers by name before the age of 3. Her mother reported that "reading seemed to be born in her." She could count

---

[2] Correction is attempted according to a formula for records exceeding the top of S–B, but this formula has never been actually validated.

to 100 at 3 years, played parchesi at 4 years, and "carried the powers of 2 mentally to the 20th, as a Sunday afternoon pastime before the age of 6." At 7 years of age she was writing poetry with religious thought expressed.

Entering school in the first grade at the age of 4 years 11 months, Madeline was held in the ordinary course on account of her age and in order to improve in handwork, in which she seemed deficient. She was listless and bored at school, and developed habits of procrastination and time-wasting. In high school, however, she began to take an interest in the work offered, and at the time of report she was finishing the ninth grade with "A" ratings in all except an occasional course which she regarded as uninteresting or meaningless.

> Often when she is sent out to the back yard at night to dispose of kitchen refuse, she fails to return until her mother goes in search of her. Her mother always finds her studying the heavens. Madeline has recently developed a strong interest in astronomy, has devoured several books on the subject, and is planning to become an astronomer.

The health of this child has always been good. She has had the usual children's diseases, and contracts colds, but has never been seriously ill.

Madeline's ancestry is very superior. On the paternal side, the grandfather was of English-Irish descent; the grandmother, of Scottish-French descent. Teaching and preaching have been the usual occupations. On the maternal side, the grandfather was of German-Dutch descent; the grandmother, of English descent. The child's parents are both university graduates, and they have done graduate work. She has two younger sisters, of 167 and 162 IQ (S–B), respectively. The family is in very moderate financial circumstances, having taken responsibility in the care of relatives.

Rosemarie. In 1928, Schorn (*20*) reported upon a girl aged 4 years 6 months, who tested at 8 years Mental Age in the Psychologisches Institut at Würzberg. This report gives her an IQ of 184. She was brought to attention because she could read fluently at the age of 3 years 6 months, without having been schooled.

The case of this child illustrates some of the points of misunderstanding of such children by those who have not seen several like them. Because she could not perform motor tasks in advance of her years, it was concluded that she "was not generally bright."

The case of K. In 1934 Goldberg (*11*) described the case of K, a boy who achieved an IQ of 196 (S–B) when tested at the age of 6 years 7 months.

K was born June 25, 1927, in New York City, of Jewish parents, and is an only child. The parents state from memory that K started to walk at 14 months of age, and could talk rather fluently at the age of 1 year 6 months. Dentition began at 8 months of age. His health has been very good, and he has had no serious illnesses.

When K was 20 months old, he knew his alphabet and within a short while after that he was able to recite it backwards. At about the same time he had a set of blocks, which offered him additional opportunity for developing a well-nigh astounding feat. He could by looking at one of the figures on a given block call off from memory the other five objects on the remaining sides. This he was able to do for almost the entire set. At about 2 years of age K knew his own name and address and what is more significant the addresses and telephone numbers of the entire family, numbering about a dozen.

By studying a calendar he learned to tell on what particular day a certain date would fall. For example, if he were asked on what day of the week July 16 would fall he would indicate Thursday. . . .

K began to read at about 4 years of age. He was given no formal training in the beginning mechanics of reading. The only assistance he received was a suggestion that he "pronounce words by syllables." At this time he was already reading simple words easily.

K is of Jewish origin. Mr. K at the time of K's birth was 32 years of age, and Mrs. K was 35. Neither K's mother nor his father has had the benefit of college training. They are for the most part self-educated. Mr. K is a proprietor of a small retail business.

At the age of 6 years 7 months K's height with shoes was 47.3 inches, and his weight was 52 pounds. He is well nourished, and his physical condition was found negative for all unfavorable indications. When asked for the year, in the test at year IX (S–B), K said, "It is 1934, but if you believe in the Jewish calendar, it is 5694."

The case of B. Witty and Jenkins (36) have reported the case of B, a gifted Negro girl, who was tested at the age of 9 years 4 months, earning an IQ of 200 (S–B), "corrected" score, and of 187, "uncorrected" score.[3] At the time of testing, B was in the low fifth grade at school, her mental age being 17 years 5 months at least ("uncorrected" score). She had received but one double promotion though others were offered by the school, because B's mother is afraid that the child will get too far from her age group.

B was discovered by asking a teacher to nominate the "most intelligent" and "best student" among children in her class. B was nominated as "best student," while a girl four years older, whose IQ turned out to be below 100, was nominated as "most intelligent." This circumstance is illustrative

[3] See footnote page 54.

of the lack of insight which necessarily exists in relation to such children where teachers have no special instruction in regard to them. The report continues:

> The following items were secured from B's baby book, and from the mother's reports. B, an only child, was born November 18, 1924. The mother was then 27 years of age, and the father 31. B weighed 6¾ pounds at birth, 14 pounds at 3 months, and 17½ pounds at 9 months. At 9 years and 5 months, B weighed 60 pounds and was 50 inches in height; this is normal for a child of her height and age (Baldwin-Wood norms).
>
> B walked a few steps at 8 months (under the excitement of running after a dog), but walked no more till she was 12 months old. She employed short sentences when she was about 16 months of age. Her mother reports that B expressed her thought in sentences, rather than in isolated words, almost from the beginning of language development; she excited considerable comment among friends by displaying an extensive vocabulary and by using nursery rhymes at age 2.
>
> B was taught to read by her mother at age 4, by the "picture-story" method. (She knew the alphabet long before.) A few lessons only were given her and thereafter B read and has continued to read independently.
>
> B has had no serious illnesses or accidents; her health history appears normal and her physical condition at the present time is excellent. Furthermore, she seems unusually well balanced from the standpoint of mental hygiene. B exhibits regularity in habits, sleeps soundly, seldom reports dreams, displays no unusual fears, and adapts herself quickly and successfully to the demands of her child-group.
>
> B's parents appear distinctly above the average both in intelligence and in academic training. The mother finished a two-year normal course and taught for a number of years in a metropolitan school system. The father is an electrical engineer, a graduate of Case College of Applied Science; he has pursued graduate studies at Cornell University, and has done

some college teaching. At present he is a practicing electrical engineer. . . . Her maternal great-grandfather (who is still active and robust at age 82) was private secretary to each of four executives of a large railroad system. . . . Her paternal grandfather was an inventor and manufacturer of polishes and waxes. . . .

The mother reports B to be of pure Negro stock. There is no record of any white ancestors on either the maternal or paternal side.

B has not much ability or interest in music. Her favorite subject is science, and chemistry attracts her to the extent that she wishes to become a chemist.

Child R. In 1936, Zorbaugh and Boardman (*38*) described a boy, R, of IQ 204 (S–B). They mention also three other children of IQ above 180, tested at New York University's Clinic for the Social Adjustment of the Gifted, but R is the only one described.

R was brought to the Clinic when he was 8 years old, and at that time he had on the Stanford-Binet an IQ of 204. His father, an engineer, is a well-known writer in the scientific field. His mother holds a doctor's degree in physical chemistry from a foreign university. Neither the father nor the mother has been tested, but they are both persons of very unusual mental ability. R's two younger brothers are also of very superior mentality. The family is of Jewish origin and both the father and the mother were born in a foreign country.

R, their first child, was born when the mother was thirty and the father was thirty-five. His early development was exceedingly precocious. His first tooth erupted at five months of age; he began to walk at nine months and was running at eleven months; he was talking in sentences at eleven months; he learned to read at four years of age, and was reading omnivorously before he entered school. When he entered school he had an unusual vocabulary, using such words as "casuistry" and "disproportionate." At the age of 2 he was modeling in clay, and at the age of 3 he began to design and make machines. He applied through his father to the United States Patent Office for two patents before he was 8 years old. At 8 years of age he had a large library in his home composed mostly of books of science, history, and biography, which he had catalogued himself, on the Dewey decimal system. At this age he was writing a book on electricity. Also at the age of 8 he had a small machine shop in which he was working on his machines. At the age of 6 he enjoyed discussing philosophy. At the age of 7 he would debate on the significance of religion in world development.

The day he first came to the Clinic, Claudel's experiments on developing power by raising the colder water from the lower levels of the sea had just been reported in the scientific section of the *New York Times*. R explained the theory involved much more clearly than had the scientific writer of the *Times*.

R is well developed physically, above average in height, and considerably above average in weight, likes the outdoors, especially hiking and riding horseback. At the age of 9 he showed the first symptoms of the approach of puberty. R is well adjusted to his school and his playmates, plays on their soccer and baseball teams, is well liked, and is a leader in many of their activities.

Other cases. In addition to these children who have been somewhat fully described, a few others testing above 180 IQ (S–B) have been mentioned in the literature of gifted children or their records have appeared in tabulations. In 1923 Dvorak told of a boy of IQ 183 (S–B) who was examined at the University of Minnesota. This boy was conspicuously maladjusted at school. He "hated school," and did poor work there. He was 8 years 7 months old at the time of examination, and passed the tests at a mental level of 15 years 9 months. The educational authorities were unsympathetic and resistant to advice, but finally placed the child in the fifth grade, where both work and conduct improved greatly. This observer also mentions a boy of 189 IQ (S–B) who was tested at the same University.

Cyril Burt, writing of mental tests in the schools of London, cites an English boy of 190 IQ, but does not give a description of him. The value of these mere mentions is slight because there is no elaboration and no subsequent history of the cases which would be useful for purposes of generalizations.

GENERALIZATIONS

The preceding pages (25–61) describe in some detail 19 cases rating 180 IQ or better, if those be included (3 cases) that were reported before the Stanford Revision came into use. Although the reports are lacking in uniformity and vary in emphasis, it is possible to glean from them a few generalizations concerning origin and development among the gifted.

Origin is extremely varied as regards racial stock. In describing the 14 American children, German descent is mentioned 3 times, French 3, Scottish 5, English 5, Swedish 1, Scotch-Irish 1, Dutch 1, Jewish 1, Negro 1. There is one German child.

The occupational status of the fathers all fall in Class 1 or Class 2 of Taussig's rating — professional, clerical, or business proprietors. Social-economic status wherever mentioned is said to be moderate. None is stated to be very wealthy or very poor.

Age of parents at birth of the exceptional child covers a wide range.

Development is decidedly ahead of schedule for the group in all respects. Reported age of walking (7 cases stated)

≠anges from 7 months to 14 months. Talking in sentences, in the 10 cases in which it is given, ranges from 8 months to 19 months. In 13 cases the age of reading is assigned, this being always 3.5 or 4 years.

General health is, whenever mentioned, always reported as good, and except for the twins, born prematurely, physique is superior.

In the array of 19 cases there are 12 girls and 7 boys, whereas of the 12 cases to be reported in succeeding pages of this study only 4 are girls. In the grand total there are 16 girls and 15 boys.

BIBLIOGRAPHY

1. BERKHAN, OSWALD. "Das Wunderkind Christian Heinrich Heineken." *Zeitschrift für Kinderforschung,* Vol. 15, pages 225–229 (1910).
2. —— "Otto Pöhler, Das Frühlesende Braunschweiger Kind." *Zeitschrift für Kinderforschung,* Vol. 15, pages 166–171 (1910).
3. BINET, A., et SIMON, TH. "New Methods for the Diagnosis of the Intellectual Level of Subnormals." *L'Année Psychologique, 1905,* pages 191–244.
4. —— "The Development of Intelligence in the Child." *L'Année Psychologique, 1908,* pages 1–90.
5. BUSH, A. D. "Binet-Simon Tests of a Thirty-nine-Months-Old Child." *Psychological Clinic,* 1914.
6. COX, C. M. *The Early Mental Traits of Three Hundred Geniuses.* Genetic Studies of Genius: Vol. 2. Stanford University Press, Stanford University, California; 1926.
7. DOLBEAR, K. E. "Precocious Children." *Pedagogical Seminary,* Vol. 19, pages 461–491 (1912).
8. DUFF, F., and THOMSON, GODFREY H. "The Social and Geographical Distribution of Intelligence in Northumberland." *British Journal of Psychology* (1923).

9. GALTON, FRANCIS. *Hereditary Genius.* The Macmillan Company, London; 1892. (First Ed., 1869.)

10. GESELL, ARNOLD. "Mental and Physical Correspondence in Twins." *Scientific Monthly* (1922).

11. GOLDBERG, SAMUEL. "A Clinical Study of K, 196 IQ." *Journal of Applied Psychology,* Vol. 18, pages 550–560 (1934).

12. HARTLAUB, G. F. *Der Genius im Kinde.* Hirt, Breslau; 1930.

13. HIRT, ZOE I. "A Gifted Child." *Training School Bulletin,* Vol. 19, pages 49–54 (1922).

14. I. E. R. Intelligence Scale CAVD, Levels A to Q. Printed in 5 parts. Teachers College, Columbia University, New York; 1925.

15. LANGENBECK, M. "A Study of a Five-Year-Old Child." *Pedagogical Seminary* (1915).

16. LORGE, I., and HOLLINGWORTH, L. S. "The Adult Status of Highly Intelligent Children." *Journal of Genetic Psychology,* Vol. 49, pages 215–226 (1936).

17. QUETELET, M. *Letters on Probability.* Translated by Downes. Layton & Co., London; 1849.

18. ROOT, W. T. *A Socio-Psychological Study of Fifty-three Supernormal Children.* Psychological Monographs, 1921, 29, No. 133, pages 134 ff.

19. RUSK, R. R. "A Case of Precocity." *Child Study,* 1917.

20. SCHORN, M. "Zur Psychologie des Frühbegabten Kindes." *Zeitschrift für Psychologie,* pages 105, 302–316 (1928).

21. SPEARMAN, G. "General Intelligence Objectively Determined and Measured." *American Journal of Psychology,* Vol. 15, pages 201–293 (1904).

22. STEDMAN, L. M. *Education of Gifted Children.* World Book Company, Yonkers-on-Hudson, New York; 1924.

23. TERMAN, LEWIS M. "A New Approach to the Study of Genius." *Psychological Review,* Vol. 29, pages 310–318 (1922).

24. —— *The Measurement of Intelligence.* Houghton Mifflin Company, Boston; 1916.

25. TERMAN, LEWIS M., and FENTON, J. C. "Preliminary Report on a Gifted Juvenile Author." *Journal of Applied Psychology*, Vol. 5, pages 163–178 (1921).
26. —— et al. *Mental and Physical Traits of a Thousand Gifted Children.* Genetic Studies of Genius: Vol. 1. Stanford University Press, Stanford University, California; 1925.
27. —— et al. *Ibid.*, Genetic Studies of Genius: Vol. 3. Stanford University Press, Stanford University, California; 1930.
28. THORNDIKE, E. L. *An Introduction to the Theory of Mental and Social Measurements.* Science Press, New York; 1904.
29. —— "Animal Intelligence." *Psychological Review Monograph Supplements*, Vol. 2, No. 8 (1898).
30. —— et al. *The Measurement of Intelligence.* Bureau of Publications, Teachers College, Columbia University, New York; 1926.
31. *Tehetsegproblemak* (Problems of Talent). Thirteen lectures by various authors, delivered before the Hungarian Society for Child Research and Practical Psychology, Budapest; 1930.
32. VON SCHÖNEICH, CHRISTIAN. *Taten, Reisen und Tod eines sehr klugen und sehr artigen 4-jährigen Kindes, Christian Heinrich Heineken aus Lübeck.* Zweite veränderte Auflage. Göttigen, 1779 (Erste Auflage, 1726).
33. WADDLE, C. W. "Case Studies of Gifted Children," Part I. Twenty-third *Yearbook*, pages 185–207, National Society for the Study of Education. Public School Publishing Company, Bloomington, Illinois; 1924.
34. WASHBURNE, C. W. "Case History of J. M.," Part 1. Twenty-third *Yearbook*, National Society for the Study of Education. Public School Publishing Company, Bloomington, Illinois; 1924.
35. WITTE, K. *The Education of Karl Witte.* (Translated by L. Wiener.) Bruce Publishing Company, Milwaukee, Wisconsin; 1914.

36. WITTY, P. A., and JENKINS, M. D. "The Case of 'B' — a Gifted Negro Girl." *Journal of Social Psychology,* Vol. 6, pages 117–124 (1935).
37. YERKES, R. M. (Editor). "Psychological Examining in the United States Army." *Memoirs of the National Academy of Sciences,* Vol. 15 (1921).
38. ZORBAUGH, H. W., and BOARDMAN, RHEA K. "Salvaging Our Gifted Children." *Journal of Educational Sociology,* Vol. 10, pages 100–108 (1926).

PART II

Twelve Cases New to Literature Concerning Tested Children

Chapter Four

CHILD A

CHILD A is a boy, born June 18, 1914. He was brought by his parents to Teachers College, Columbia University, in the latter weeks of 1920, for mental tests. This was on the advice of the principal of the school A attended, for the boy was a school problem. He did not adjust himself readily to the work of the classroom in the second grade where he was at that time placed, at the age of 6 years 6 months. The school had found A ready for work beyond the second grade in reading and arithmetic, but because of his age and size it had decided to place him in second grade. The record made at that time and subsequently reads as follows:

FAMILY BACKGROUND

A is descended from German Jews on both sides of his family. His parents are not related by blood so far as can be known. He is of the third generation to be born in the United States.

The paternal grandfather is living [1920] and well, a tailor by trade. He is "very handy" in making helpful devices to use in his shop. The paternal grandmother is living [1920] and well, a competent housewife, who has evinced no noticeable intellectual interests.

No dependent or incompetent relatives of the father are known.   It is usual for the progenitors in the paternal branch to die between the ages of 80 and 100 years.   The paternal great-grandfathers of A died aged 86 and 89 years, respectively.   The paternal great-grandmothers both died at 40 years.   The paternal great-great-grandmothers died at 101 and 102 years, respectively.   There have been no constitutional diseases in the ancestry.

A's father has but one sibling, A's paternal uncle, who is a successful dentist.   He married a teacher, and has two young daughters, A's cousins.   One of these, about 6 months older than A, has twice been tested by Stanford-Binet, her IQ's being 170 and, a year later, 161.   At the age of 8 years, this girl had reached the fifth grade in public school. She now [1920] attends a special class organized for children of her age who test over 150 IQ.   The other of these cousins was tested by Stanford-Binet on November 9, 1923, yielding an IQ of 129.   These two girls are the only first cousins A has.

A's maternal grandfather is living [1920] and well.   He is a cloth salesman, but he has always seemed dissatisfied with this vocation.   He had to go to work at an early age. The maternal grandmother is living [1920] and well, a competent housewife, not especially interested in intellectual pursuits.

No dependent or mentally incompetent relatives of the mother are known.   All are self-sustaining.   There are no constitutional diseases in the maternal ancestry.   It is usual for the progenitors on the maternal side to die between the ages of 60 and 70 years, but one of A's maternal great-grandmothers lived to the age of 90 years. A's mother has but one sibling, A's maternal uncle, a salesman, who is unmarried.

Father. A's father is a large, strong man, now following the profession of organization engineer. He is a high school graduate and a graduate of Webb Academy, holding a diploma from the latter as marine engineer and marine architect. He has invented and patented a complete combustion furnace, and has designed a set of torpedoes which were used in the Japanese-Russian war. During the war of 1914–1918, he participated in the development of a fleet destroyer, and designed a boat superior to previous models for transporting nitrocellulose. He made the original layout for one of the largest steel plants in the United States. His rating on Army Alpha is 180 points. His grip is 70 kg. in the right hand and 64 kg. in the left hand (Smedley's dynamometer). He was 29 years old when A was born.

Mother. A's mother was graduated from high school at the age of 18 years. Before marriage she was in business, as an executive in charge of advertising for one of the largest drug concerns in this country. She has handled business affairs involving large sums for a tobacco company. She also did some newspaper work. Formerly she had excellent health, but she has not been entirely well since the birth of her children. She was 27 years old when A was born.

Noteworthy relatives. In the paternal branch these include cousins who founded the Banking House of Tuch, in London. The father's maternal grandfather (A's great-grandfather), a tailor, devised and patented a union suit, said to have been the first union suit. He also invented an improved buckle for adjusting men's vests in the back. It was said of him, "He was always trying to invent things."

Noteworthy relatives of the mother include the founder of the Lemaire Optical Goods firm. This firm has an international reputation for fine lenses. A cousin of the mother is a judge. Another relative was a leader of Jewish reform movements.

Immediate family. A is the first-born child. He has one brother, three years younger than himself. This brother is large, strong, and handsome. His IQ on repeated tests, at intervals of a year, has stood at 145, 152, 145, 161. He too displays the special interest in mathematics which characterizes A. For instance, at the age of 5 years he set himself the project of counting all his footsteps until he had counted a million consecutive steps. This project he carried out, his parents submitting to the numerous inconveniences incident to it. The growth of this brother affords an interesting comparison with that of A, since we have here two children, both of extremely superior intelligence, of the same ancestry, and living under the same school and home conditions, one of whom is nevertheless as superior to the other — in terms of IQ — as that other is superior to the average child.

PRESCHOOL HISTORY

The preschool history of A has been elicited from the parents and from the "baby book" kept by them. A was born at full term, and the birth was normal in all respects. He weighed 7 pounds 9 ounces, and was breast fed for the first several months of life. He began to articulate words at 10 months, and at 14 months could pick out letters on the typewriter at command. At 12 months he could say the alphabet forward, and at 16 months he could say it backward as well. His parents had no idea that he could reverse the alphabet until one day he announced that he was "tired of saying the letters forward" and guessed he would "say them backward." The concepts of "forward" and "backward" had thus been developed by the age of 16 months. At 12 months he began spontaneously to classify his blocks according to the shape of the letters on them, putting V A M W N together, Q P O G D together, and so forth. This love of classifying has remained one of his outstanding characteristics. As an infant, he would for hours thus amuse himself with his alphabet blocks.

When 18 months old he was able to carry out simple errands involving not more than three or four items. By the time A was 30 months old he could copy all the colored designs possible with his kindergarten blocks. Before the age of 3 years he enjoyed rhymes, and would amuse himself rhyming words together. From the time he was old enough to be taken out to walk, he would point out letters on billboards and signs with keen interest and delight, crying, "Oh, see D! There's J, Mother! There's K and O!" Also before the age of 3 years A objected to stories containing gross absurdities. For instance, he rejected the story of the gingham dog and the calico cat who "ate each other up." A pointed out that this could not be, "because one of their mouths would have to get eaten up before the other mouth, and no mouth would be left to eat *that* mouth up." He was irritated by this obvious lapse from logic and requested that the story be read to him no more.

A learned to read for himself during the third year of life, and read fluently before he entered school.

The photograph in Figure 1 shows one of A's amusements at the age of 10 months — balancing and rolling simultaneously a large ball between his hands and another between his feet as he lay on his back in his crib. This activity illus-

FIG. 1. CHILD A AT THE AGE OF 10 MONTHS.

trates his power of motor coördination in infancy, and it is especially interesting in connection with the errors of judgment made by A's teachers to the effect that "A is below average in control of his body."

SCHOOL HISTORY

First year. A has always attended private schools. He started school at the age of 5 years, in Philadelphia. Here he was placed in the kindergarten, though the question was raised by teachers as to the greater advisability of placement in the first grade. After a few months in this school the family moved to New York, where A entered an excellent private school at the age of not quite 6 years. By this time he had developed many numerical processes by himself. On one occasion the mother went to speak to the teacher regarding the advisability of teaching such advanced processes to so young a child at school, and the teacher replied in great surprise that she had been on the point of asking the parents not to teach so young a child these matters.

Second year. In the autumn of 1920, A entered a private school which he attended for several years. It was here that he was considered to be a school problem. It was recognized that he was ready scholastically for a grade much beyond his age and size. As a compromise he was placed in the second grade. Soon the teacher of the second grade advised that he be considered for the third grade, as he did not "fit" into second-grade work. Thereupon he was brought to Teachers College for educational guidance. The report stated that A stood far ahead of the other second-grade children in reading and arithmetic but that he was "poor in carrying out projects," and did not seem interested in the activities of the second grade.

After mental examination of A, revealing an intelligence level of 12 years 2 months, it was explained that there had never been worked out an established appropriate procedure for variants of such rare occurrence. The advice given was to place A in the third grade; for although his Mental Age was then more than 12 years (his physical age at this time was 6 years 6 months), many of the 8-year-olds in this school would approximate A's mental capacity, since the median IQ of the pupils there was about 120. A was accordingly placed in the third grade, where he had the good fortune to meet a teacher of extraordinary knowledge and ability. At the end of that year he was promoted to the fourth grade.

Third year. In the autumn of 1921 A was in the fourth grade, with the same teacher he had had in the third grade.

Outside of school hours he took special work in sports and games with a group of young boys. At the end of that year he was promoted to the fifth grade, and placed in a special fifth-grade group which had been formed of the brightest children of this status in the school. During this time a special effort was made to develop A in social activities and to interest him in group projects, with the result that "he became much more a member of the group." Nevertheless, he still liked to "lie down on his back and look up at the ceiling," instead of joining in common projects. "His mind often seems to be miles away."

Fourth year. In the autumn of 1922 A was in the fifth grade, composed of the special group referred to above, with classmates about two years older than himself, whose IQ's ranged above 140. At the end of that year he was promoted to the sixth grade, at age 9 years. He seemed happy and contented during his fourth year in school but displayed many characteristics which might well try the patience of any but a very wise teacher. The tendency to become absorbed in his own line of thought continued, giving an impression at times of indifference, absent-mindedness, and non-coöperation. Also, he was "slow to take advice." He decided, for instance, not to learn French, as he was "not interested in it." He persisted in this attitude until it was clearly explained to him that people who go to college must know French, whereupon he applied himself and learned the language. The relative difficulty in handwriting, shopwork, and other manual tasks which such a child experiences in comparison with older classmates is also a problem for the teacher.

Fifth year. In the autumn of 1923 A entered the sixth grade. He was at this time 9 years old.

JUDGMENTS OF TEACHERS

Teachers' judgments of A show the usual disagreements and errors. His superior intelligence has been recognized to some extent by nearly all. One teacher, however, has felt his superiority to be merely for reading and arithmetic. Several teachers have judged A to be inferior in respect to manual dexterity and motor coördination, forgetting that their comparison was based always on older children, A's classmates. Only one teacher bore this fallacy of judgment in mind in reporting her estimates. For instance, one of the supervisors who had observed A, reported that he was below the average child of his age in penmanship. A was then 6 years old. This supervisor seemed not to recall that the average child of that age has no penmanship whatever. Direct quotation from teachers' estimates will best show how A has been appraised.

He was quite a desirable pupil, and we should have been glad to keep him. *From the headmaster of the school A first entered.*

Though ahead of the class in arithmetic and reading, he reasons like a child of 6. He has undeveloped judgment. *From a teacher, in 1920.*

He seems to like the third grade, and the children like him. Intellectually he is able to carry the work of the grade, and while he is not yet very responsive in manual work, I think he can gain the muscular control he needs here as well as in a lower grade. He has made a splendid effort in the matter of penmanship. He is still very imperfectly adjusted to the school situation, but in time will find himself able to meet the requirements, I am sure. *From report of a classroom teacher, for February 1 to March 18, 1921.*

Although A still has lapses of inattention during class lessons, in general he complies with class requirements and he has learned to use his free time without direction. His gain in penmanship has been marked. *From report of a classroom teacher, for March 21 to May 27, 1921.*

He is doing well, but needs handwork. *From report of a special teacher, 1921.*

He is slow to take advice but has shown big improvement over last term. He seemed to go ahead suddenly. *From report of a special teacher, 1921.*

He has got little from the playground. Doesn't "get into the game," and is a trial to his mates. *From report of a teacher in charge of playground, 1921.*

Manifests considerable musical ability. Lovely voice, and true to pitch. *From report of a music teacher, 1921.*

A is making excellent progress both socially and in his work. Mr. W reports that his shopwork is good, considering his age, and that it is improving. Miss C says there is continued improvement in art. I find that his writing of figures is improving more than written English. He does not like to write, and is apt to neglect written homework. *From report of a classroom teacher, for November 17, 1921, to January 31, 1922.*

A is the youngest child in his group (he is 7 and in the fourth grade, in which the average age is about 9). It is difficult to classify him in general terms as the first in scholastic standing, as he is with a group which numbers nine or ten superior children with IQ's running from 140 to 175; but in scholastic standing, with the exception of written work, he is among the best. If one compares his age with that of the others, his ability is of course most marked. Even in this group he is conspicuous for his accuracy and lucidity of statement and for the clear thinking this indicates.

One noticeable indication of his intelligence is his ability to criticize his own concepts; unless he understands every detail of a subject, he does not consider that he understands it.

His ability in academic work seems well distributed, though strongest in mathematics. For this grade he is markedly low in art and industrial work; but he would be average in second grade, where his age would under ordinary circumstances place him. His artistic feeling is all for music and literature. He is moderately interested in drawing, but doesn't like modeling and does not want to draw unless it is for some special purpose, or because everybody else is doing so and it is the social thing to do. For example, he has made posters and designs for holiday cards, which, while very crude, had an idea to express and were suitable for their purpose. He enjoys shopwork and here does better technically than in other types of handwork. I think he is rather clumsy with his hands, even for his age, though not much below the average child. With his mental ability he can learn to do anything in which his interest is aroused.

This ability to attack any sort of problem is shown in his physical work. He makes an excellent effort and comprehends what is to be done, but in bodily coördination, in muscular strength, and in rhythmic response he would rank in the lower half of a second grade. *From a specially requested report of a classroom teacher, June 20, 1922.*

In short, I am fully convinced that A requires most of all training which will develop a proper harmony and rhythm between mind and body. *From the report of the instructor in the special boys' group, to which A belonged, outside of school, April 19, 1922.*

A's teachers seem to hold the universal opinion that he is not doing well in his work unless prodded or specially urged. It was to be expected that the handwork, such as art and shopwork, would be hard for him, but he seems to do poor work and at the same time to be entirely satisfied with it, his teachers say. Miss B finds he is not an observer of nature, but rather inclined to tell what he has read in books.

However, on the academic side, in French and the regular classroom studies, he seems to require the same prodding. His sleepiness and inattention are quite marked at times. When aroused, I find him capable of good thinking, and excellent memory work. I have been afraid to overstimulate him, but in order to accomplish the work of the fifth grade creditably we must develop in him more of a feeling of responsibility on his own account.   His immaturity shows rather clearly in some of these respects.   Of course his work is more than passing, because of the fine coöperation at home and his own vigorous response when sufficiently urged.   *From report of a classroom teacher, for September 18, 1922, to January 31, 1923.*

It is still a problem to get A to make contributions to the work of the class.   His mind works along lines of special interest at the time.   Although urged by the parents to push A a little harder, I have hesitated to do much urging.   One fears to stimulate unduly.   And yet I find that A is learning in many ways all the time.   There are still, of course, some definite needs.

Mr. P reports no marked improvement on the physical side. However, on the side of participation in the sports of the group, I find a great improvement in A.   He appears to be enjoying himself during a ball game, and even catches a ball occasionally.

Miss B says she hopes that A will have some real country and nature during the summer.   He needs a chance to roam and think and observe for himself rather than to learn facts from books or other people.

In the French class his interest and attitude have improved. *From report of a classroom teacher, for February 1 to June 15, 1923, on the occasion of A's promotion to the sixth grade.*

These remarks from teachers bring clearly to notice some of the difficulties in adjustment to school procedure when a child has a 12-year-old capacity for thinking and the body of a 7- or an 8-year-old, combined with the life of a 6-year-old. Motor control is, of course, far behind abstract thinking; writing is slow and feeble, while reading is rapid and fluent; shopwork is poor but arithmetic is excellent; he can surpass 8- and 9-year-olds — even those of superior intelligence — in the classroom, but in playing with them he cannot catch a ball and is always the last to be selected when sides "choose up," because he is a handicap in any playground competitions.

From these remarks and estimates it is also easy to see how such a child may provoke adverse comments from teachers, may be found unsuited to school organization, and eventually even be reputed stupid or "foolish." Fortunately for A, most of his teachers have had unusual training and have been rigidly selected, besides, for insight and personality. If you have read Edison's biography, you will recall that under teachers less highly selected young Thomas "did not get on in school," was regarded as "foolish," and eventually was removed from school by his mother, who educated him at home, she herself being a teacher.

These difficulties of discrepancy between mental development and physical development are seen to be greatest in the earliest years of childhood. The judgments show that as A grew from his sixth birthday to his ninth birthday, he became less and less conspicuous in his poor penmanship and in his inaptitude at games.

MENTAL MEASUREMENTS

General intelligence tests of A have been made as follows:

DATE	BIRTHDAY AGE OF A	STANFORD-BINET				ARMY ALPHA POINTS	
		MA		IQ			
		A	Norm	A	Norm	A	Norm
December 30, 1920 .	6–6	12–2	6–6	187	100	(Not given)	
January 2, 1922 . .	7–6	14–4	7–6	191	100	76 0 (Form 5)	
April 22, 1922[1] . .	7–10	14–8	7–10	187	100	(Not given)	
February 22, 1923 .	8–8	(Not given)				95 0 (Form 7)[2]	

[1] Demonstration test before a class of teachers.

[2] The score of 95 points on Army Alpha, Form 7, on February 22, 1923, corresponds to a mental level of 16 years 0 months by Stanford-Binet. This (if translatable into IQ) would result in an IQ of 184.

Mechanical skill. On January 2, 1922 (aged 7 years 6 months), A was given the *Stenquist Assembling Tests of General Mechanical Ability* and he made a score of 4 points only. He could tell what mechanisms were to be constructed from the materials in five out of the ten instances, but he was not "handy" enough to put them together. (The test depends very much upon size and strength of hands and upon the degree to which motor coördination is developed. Young children, therefore, of whatever degree of intelligence, are unable to succeed in it.)

Musical sensitivity. On February 22, 1923, Seashore's *Tests of Musical Sensitivity* yielded results as follows, using the figures for eighth-grade children for comparison, because of A's Mental Age:

TEST	PERCENTILE (EIGHTH GRADE) A	PERCENTILE (ADULTS) A'S FATHER
Consonance	Below 27th	36th
Pitch	91st	81st
Intensity	41st	26th
Time	Below 17th	78th
Tonal memory	70th	9th

Design. On January 2, 1922, the examiner made the following note in reference to A's performance with Milton Bradley color cubes (with which he always asks to play when he comes to the laboratory):

> The child can construct the most complicated designs with Milton Bradley's color cubes in less than three minutes each, from memory — the design being exposed to vision and studied for one minute. Three colors are involved — red, blue, yellow, and white.

TRAITS OF CHARACTER

A has not been rated by any scale for traits of character as, for instance, were the children reported by Terman. There are at hand only statements by persons who know A. The parents both say that A has no troublesome traits of character except "a tendency to fail to take his own part in a fight." If a child strikes him, he often does not strike back but simply does nothing. His parents feel that this indicates a lack of "give and take" that is essential to getting along in the world. The parents describe him as "especially honest, truthful, reliable, affectionate, kind, generous, and modest, with strong control of his emotions."

Traits of A which are faulty from the point of view of teachers are absentmindedness, lack of interest in group activities, untidiness, and obstinacy. One teacher estimated him as "a little bit selfish." The desirable traits most often mentioned by teachers are kindliness, amiability, affection, good humor, reticence, and precision in treating the data of thought. The following are quotations from teachers:

> I am so sorry about A's coat. I laid it on his desk, as he was cooking when it came. . . . Evidently he didn't notice it on his desk when he came in later. Knowing A's absent-minded habits, I ought to have called his attention to the coat.

> A is not neat nor orderly.

> A still has lapses of inattention during class lessons.

> He is slow to take advice.

> He is affectionate and kindly, while not over-demonstrative.

> The class in which he has been for a year and three months was slow in accepting him, but now they appreciate his intellect and his good humor, and treat him with the kindly tolerance of older brothers and sisters. A responds to this attitude well and loves to fool and frolic with the others, somewhat kitten

fashion. In the goal ball games he wants to play though he is simply a figurehead, and he knows enough to obey the rules and not get in anyone's way.

In working with a group, A is inclined either to be dictatorial or to insist upon doing everything himself. This may be because of youth or because he sees so clearly what is to be done, but I think he is a little selfish and obstinate. A is a very lovable child with a tender heart and a good deal of emotional capacity, generally kept hidden, so he is not difficult to manage. It is difficult, however, to make him assume responsibilities about material or work which is irksome, such as writing, and he is very untidy.

It has been a pleasure to have A in my class. He has been friendly and pleasant in his relations with his teachers as well as with his classmates.

The physician who attended A when his ankle was twisted in an accident (mentioned later in this account) rated him very high for courage.

The character traits which have stood out repeatedly and most noticeably in the course of visits to the laboratory for mental tests appear to the present writer to be amiability, reticence, emotional control in the face of mishaps (such as falling off a chair in a strange place and bumping his head severely), and obstinacy in pursuit of his plans and activities. He does not seek advice, and does not take it readily. He is easily bored by unnecessary repetitions of matter once presented. For instance, in certain mental tests, where the standard procedure demands that the same question be asked several times (Stanford-Binet fables, "What lesson does that teach us?"), A grew more and more restive at each repetition, and finally said, "We don't need that every time, do we?"

The nickname is an important datum in estimating a child.

A's nickname among the children at school is "Sleeping Beauty." This name was given, the teacher thinks, because of A's abstraction and because he was never ready in games.

PHYSICAL MEASUREMENTS AND HEALTH

Physique measurements. The following measurements were made by the present writer, using the standard scales and stadiometer of the Teachers College Laboratory. The measurement of cranial circumference was made with a reinforced fabric tape.

Date	Wt. (lbs.) A Norm	Ht. (stand., in.) A Norm	Ht. (sit., in.) A	Ht.-Wt. Coeff. A Norm	Cranial Cir. (in.) A
January 1, 1921 .	56.0 44.8	48.0 46.6	25.5	1.01 .96	
September 17, 1921[3]	58.0	128 cm.			
January 2, 1922 .	66.5 51.7	50.3 48.3	26.5	1.26 1.07	
February 22, 1923 .	68.7 55.9	52.7 50.1	28.1	1.24 1.12	21.3

In the case of the measurements made in clothing, subtracting .5 inch, the height of heels, from standing height, and 4 pounds for clothing from weight, we see that in all measurements of physique taken, A decidedly exceeds Baldwin's norms for the selected children in good private schools.

Grip measurements. Grip in the hand has been repeatedly measured with Smedley's dynamometer, with the following results:

Date	Grip (Kg.)			
	Right Hand A Norm		Left Hand A Norm	
January 1, 1921	13.0	10.0	10.0	9.0
February 22, 1923	16.0	13.0	14.0	12.0

[3] Measurements made without clothing, by Dr. Herman Schwartz.

The superior size of A is, therefore, accompanied by superior strength of hand.

Growth curves of A and his brother compared. In the case of A and his young brother, we have two boys of the same ancestry, living in the same school and home environment, both falling into the highest one per cent of the population as respects intelligence, yet very widely separated in terms of IQ. The repeated measurements show that the children do not become either more alike or more different as time passes, but that each remains a constant, maintaining a static relationship to the other in mind and body. The pressure of the similar environment does not bring them closer together in ability.

Nervous stability. The supervisor who judged A's penmanship to be inferior to that of the average child of 6 years, also interpreted this difficulty in writing to be a symptom of nervousness, especially when considered in connection with his abstraction and general maladjustment to work of the second grade. For this reason the parents obtained statements from two physicians who knew A well, as to the child's nervous stability. The physician who removed A's tonsils wrote as follows:

I am glad to state that he is as free from any nervous stigmata as is possible for any child of his age. Because of his brightness, he was treated as an older child before his tonsil operation, and what was about to be done was explained to him, and he underwent the anesthesia in a perfectly natural manner. His convalescence was unusually rapid, and at no time did he show the slightest indication of any neurosis. From careful observation I can truthfully say that A would pass the severest tests, and show no abnormality.

The other physician wrote:

> At the time I examined A in 1917 I found no neuropathic stigmata. In fact, he impressed me as a boy who was rather well developed physically. By physically I mean inclusive of his nervous system.

A's parents rate him as "well balanced." The present writer would rate him as far above the average child of his years in nervous stability.

Organic condition. Physical examinations reveal no defect except a serious degree of "progressive myopia." To correct this, glasses are worn and the use of the eyes is limited.

Medical history. A has always been healthy. He has never been subject to a chronic disorder. He sleeps well and has a keen appetite for food. As an infant there was never any trouble in feeding him. He cried very little, and was easy "to care for." When he was 3 years 6 months old he was almost run over by an automobile, but escaped with a twisted ankle. After that, for about a year, he had a series of boils. At the age of 5 years A was threatened with a mastoid infection and the drum of his right ear was pierced, liberating a large quantity of pus. Hearing was not, however, impaired. Adenoids and tonsils were removed at the age of 6 years. These had never been especially troublesome, but the parents decided on the operation because A breathed through the mouth. He has not had "children's diseases," and except for the incidents narrated, his medical history is negative.

MISCELLANEOUS CHARACTERISTICS

Diversions. At the age of 5 to 6 years A had much difficulty in playing with children of his own age because he could not be satisfied with play involving merely sensory stimulation and diffuse motor activity. He always tried to divert the play to some planned end, to *organize* it, in ways not appreciated by others of his age. When he was 6 years old, boys of 12 to 14 years of age were preferred by A as playmates, and he would join them whenever they would accept his company. However, he had and continued to have chums of approximately his own age.

At the age of 6 years 6 months A's favorite diversions were reading, playing games of intellectual skill (like geographical Lotto), and playing in sand (building). At the age of 8 years 8 months his favorite diversions were reading, chess, and pinochle.

Imaginary land. At the age of 3 to 6 years A had an imaginary land which he called "Center Land." This fantasy appears to have started when his brother was born. When this event occurred A asked just how it happened. His mother thereupon gave him the real physiological facts. To these he made no immediate comment. Several days later he said he had no doubt his brother did come into the world in just that way, but that he, A, did not. He, A, originated in Center Land, where he chose his father and mother. Thereafter, the imaginary land developed rapidly. In this land children stayed up all night. They could play with fire whenever they wished. He lived there in a hundred-story house, with an elevator he could run by himself. Two playmates, "Katharine" and another child, lived there also. By the age of 6, this imaginary country had almost ceased to engage him, and at the age of 9 he no longer thinks of it.

Religious experiences. Between the ages of 6 and 8 years (Mental Ages 12 to 15 years) A became very religious.

Prayer was regarded as extremely sacred, and God was much reverenced. Now, at the age of 9 years (Mental Age beyond the limits of ordinary maturity), he is no longer seen to devote himself to these observations.

Career ideas. At the age of 6 years 6 months A wanted to become "an eye doctor." "I like to tend to mother's eye. I like to tend to people's eyes." At the age of 8 years 8 months, in answer to the question, "What will you be when you grow up?" A replied, "I will do something with arithmetic in it; whatever has the most mathematics in it."

Reading interests. To the question, "What do you like to read?" A gave the following responses:

(Age 6 years 6 months) "True books, like *The Fall of Jerusalem* — that's the best one, and Burgess *Animal Books,* Burgess *Bird Books, Our First Flag, The Arabian Nights.*"

(Age 8 years 8 months) "Books about people who *really* lived."

A has always preferred books of fact to books of fancy — "true books," as he called them; but he now enjoys fairy tales more than he did when he was younger. This may be because the fact behind the fancy now makes a stronger appeal. The following list represents six months' reading, from the age of 7 years 0 months to 7 years 6 months, some of the books being read to A, to reduce eyestrain.[4]

On Plymouth Rock	S. A. Drake
Four Great Americans	J. Baldwin
Stories of New York	A. T. Lovering
The Children's City	E. Singleton
The Burgess Bird Book	Thornton Burgess
The Burgess Animal Book	
The Empire State	J. W. Redway

[4] The Burgess books had been read often before.

Around the World with the Children	F. G. Carpenter
East o' the Sun and West o' the Moon	G. W. Dasent
Miles Standish	H. W. Longfellow
The Wreck of the Hesperus	H. W. Longfellow
Fables	Bulfinch
Aesop's Fables	
Tales and Teachings from the Pentateuch	M. M. Joseph
The Little Gray Grandmother	Carolyn S. Bailey
Stories of the Bible	Louise M. Pleasanton
The Pied Piper of Hamelin	R. Browning
Tanglewood Tales	N. Hawthorne
First Jungle Book	R. Kipling
Second Jungle Book	R. Kipling
Poems	J. W. Riley
Poems	Eugene Field
Poems	R. L. Stevenson
The Wonder Book of Knowledge	
The Blue Bird	M. Maeterlinck
Historic Boyhoods	R. S. Holland
The Friendly Stars	M. E. Martin

This list gives an idea of the reading preferences of A, at the age of 7 years. Within the year following, the preference for biography and autobiography developed.

Interest in astronomy. Because other very young children of more than 180 IQ known to the present writer had been especially interested in astronomy — particularly Child E — it was desired to observe what would be the reaction of A if knowledge of astronomy were made accessible to him. Books which had interested Child E at the age of 6 to 7 years were therefore made accessible to A. He at once became interested in the heavenly bodies and their movements.

Tendency to classify and diagram. A's love of classifying — first noted at the age of about 12 months — is a conspicuous characteristic. He classifies events, objects, names, numbers, and other data of experience. He can think in terms of diagrams and sometimes draws a diagram to clarify or condense his meaning.

Lightning calculation. A's keenest intellectual interest is probably in numbers, and he has responded very readily to his father's instruction in short-cut methods of calculation. By March, 1922, he could very quickly square any number up to 100; multiply any two numbers of a sum not to exceed 200; square any number up to 1000 ending in 5 such as 865, 935, etc.); square any number up to 10,000, ending in 55 or in 555; solve problems in proportion, such as $9 : 21 :: 21 : x$, $8 \div 42 :: x \div 21$, $8 : 9 :: 10 : x$; subtract the square of one number ending in 5 from the square of another number ending in 5, where the difference between the two numbers is 10, or 20, or 30 (e.g., 2255^2 or 2245^2 or 3345^2 or 3325^2). Also at that age he could calculate series of operations, thus: "Take 2, square it, square that, divide by 4, cube it, add 17, take the square root, add 7, square it, square it, give the result," his calculations taking about five seconds each.

Editor's Supplement

The author's original write-up of Child A ends with the above, written early in 1923. From records in the author's files the following further data concerning later development may be added:

December 26, 1923
AGE: 9 years 6 months
SCHOOL GRADE: Sixth
TEST RECORD: Given Stanford-Binet by L. S. H. with Mental Age of 16–11. This would give IQ 178, but the comment is made, "Can no longer be measured by Stanford-Binet."

On this day also given Army Alpha, with a score of 128 points, this being the score assigned to chronological age 17 years 8 months.

PHYSICAL MEASUREMENTS:

Standing height	54.2 inches
Sitting height	27.9 inches
Weight	74.3 pounds
Head circumference	21.5 inches
Right grip	14, 17, 18
Left grip	14, 12, 14

TEACHERS' REPORTS. (Private school, September 22–December 19, 1924) "A's reports show that he has attained high credit in mathematics and history; low credit in French, shop-work, art, music, and physical training; average credit in other subjects. His written work shows improvement.

"He presents the usual problem of the unadjusted. There is now more alertness in his manner, but still a lack of the will to do work because it is a group demand. Something more of maturity has come to him with his greater freedom. He has started the manual-training problem with some sense of self-discipline.

"If he will now attack his work with the mental grip of which he must be capable, and give to the group the benefit of his ability, it will be a joy to have him among us."

December 22, 1924

AGE: 10 years 6 months

SCHOOL GRADE: Seventh

TEST RECORD: On Stanford-Binet, passed 4 of the 6 Superior Adult Tests, failing on Tests 1 and 4. Alpha score, 166 points.

PHYSICAL MEASUREMENTS:

Standing height	56.2 inches
Sitting height	29.4 inches
Weight	80.5 pounds
Head circumference	21.5 inches
Right grip	18, 18, 16
Left grip	19, 17, 15

December 22, 1925
AGE: 11 years 6 months
SCHOOL GRADE: Eighth
Test record: Passed all tests on Superior Adult level, Stanford-Binet. Took two forms of Army Alpha. Form 7, 162 points, and on Form 5, 168 points.

PHYSICAL MEASUREMENTS:		*Norm*
Standing height	58.1 inches	56.7 inches
Sitting height	29.4 inches	
Weight	88.8 pounds	75.5 pounds
Head circumference	21.7 inches	

November 18, 1926
AGE: 12 years 5 months
TEST RECORD: Score on Army Alpha, 175 points

PHYSICAL MEASUREMENTS:		*Norm*
Standing height	60.0 inches	57.8 inches
	(in shoes)	
Sitting height	30.0 inches	
Weight (without coat)	93.0 pounds	84.6 pounds

January 12, 1929
AGE: 14 years 7 months
SCHOOL GRADE: Third Year High School
TEST RECORD: Score on Army Alpha, 194 points

PHYSICAL MEASUREMENTS:		*Norm*
Standing height	64.2 inches	62.2 inches
Sitting height	32.5 inches	
Weight (clothed)	118 pounds	98.9 pounds
(stripped)	114 pounds	

October, 1929, to February, 1930
SCHOOL GRADES:

English Literature	C +
English Composition	C
German	B —
Geometry	B +
Trigonometry	B +
Science	B +

January and June, 1931
AGE: 16 years 6 months to 17 years
SCHOOL GRADE: Now a freshman in college
TEST RECORD: Was given CAVD test, Levels M, N, O, P, Q,
at two different sittings — one in January, the other in June.
Score 422 points. (According to available information 400
points is twelfth-grade college entrance score in high-type colleges, while 421 points is the upper quartile score of candidates
for advanced degrees in Teachers College, Columbia University, the median being 415.)

January 20, 1932
At the age of 17 years 7 months, in the third year of college,
he scored 204 points on Army Alpha, Form 8, a score made
only by the top one per cent of college juniors, seniors, and
graduate students.

November 23, 1939
Notice was received of A's marriage.

Chapter Five

CHILD B

CHILD B is a girl, born November 25, 1912. She was discovered in a private school in the course of a systematic survey made by Dr. E. H. Malherbe, who was at the time a graduate student at Teachers College, Columbia University. To Dr. Malherbe the present writer is indebted for introduction to this child, and also for data on first tests as well as for other information.

FAMILY BACKGROUND

Child B is descended from colonial settlers in this country. Her ancestors came chiefly from the British Isles, as set forth in her family history. Her parents are not related by blood so far as can be known.

The paternal grandfather was of English descent; the paternal grandmother of Irish descent. No dependent or incompetent relatives of the father are known. All are self-sustaining.

The maternal grandfather was of Irish-Spanish blood. The maternal grandmother was of Irish descent. No incompetent or dependent relatives are known.

Father. Child B's father was born in Vermont and was

42 years old when B was born.　He is a high school graduate and a graduate of the United States Military Academy at West Point.　He passed the entrance examinations for the latter institution at the age of 16 years and was at that time the youngest student ever admitted to the Academy.　He has held posts of extraordinary trust in the pursuit of his profession, and is at the time of this writing an officer of high rank in the United States Army.

Mother.　Child B's mother is a graduate of a Catholic parochial high school and of the College of Mount St. Vincent.　She was married at an early age and her career has been that of housewife and mother, no profession having been followed previous to marriage.　Although she is the mother of seven children and mistress of a large household, B's mother found time to attend courses in law and economics at Columbia University while the family lived in New York.　She was 39 years old when B was born.

Noteworthy relatives.　Relatives of note in the paternal branch include B's great-grandfather, who was a physician, founder of the Vermont Academy of Medicine in the early years of the nineteenth century, and a professor of surgery there.　There are also among relatives an admiral of the United States Navy,[1] a physician of wide reputation, a commander of the United States Navy,[2] and a practical tin- and coppersmith who was an inventor.　This family branch as a whole finds its average level of achievement in the professions.

The maternal branch includes a woman of extraordinary business ability, a priest who was a scholar and organizer of

---

[1] Rear Admiral John W. Phillip.　(Callahan, E. W.　*List of Officers of the United States Navy and of the Marine Corps.*　Hamersley & Co., New York;　1901.)

[2] Commander E. T. Woodward.

marked ability, and a mining engineer of unusual achievement. The performance level of the family lies, on the
average, in business and the professions.

Immediate family. B is the sixth born of seven siblings.
Of these children, two — the brother born two years before
B and the brother born five years after B — have had mental
tests. The older brother was measured in the course of the
mental survey made by Dr. Malherbe. His IQ (S–B) at
the age of 10 years 6 months was 167. This is not a full
measure of this brother, as he passed many tests at the highest
levels of performance provided by the scale. A still older
brother passed the entrance examinations for Columbia College, from which may be inferred intelligence above the
average. The younger brother's IQ (S–B) at the age of
6 years 10 months was 138.

PRESCHOOL HISTORY

The preschool history of B has been elicited from the
parents. She cut her first tooth at 7 months. She began to
talk at 9 months of age and to walk at 15 months. As soon
as she was able to walk out with her nurse or her mother, at
about the age of 24 months, B began to notice the letters on
billboards and to spell out words. By the time she was in
the third year of life she could read fluently in simple books.
(The brother whose IQ is referred to above as 167 did not
read until he was about 4 years 6 months of age.)

SCHOOL HISTORY

B has always attended private schools. She began her
school life in kindergarten, at the age of 3 years, and attended
the same school until the age of nearly 9 years. At the age
of 8 years 4 months she had reached only the fourth grade,

whereas in the battery of educational tests given as a part of the school survey she surpassed at that age the seventh-grade standards for public schools.

In appraising the great discrepancy between school progress and ability in this case, it is necessary to bear in mind that children in some private schools are highly selected as regards intellect. The median IQ in this particular school was shown by the survey to be much above 100; so that B was not so hopelessly misplaced in the fourth grade there as would have been the case had she attended public school. The fact of competition with selected children reduces the discrepancy, though it is still very great.

At the age of 8 years 9 months, B entered a private school in Washington, D. C. Here she was placed in the sixth grade, "skipping" the fifth grade. Her school reports have always been very excellent, "almost always E in every subject."

In the autumn of 1922 B entered the seventh grade, aged 9 years 9 months. She was the youngest pupil in a class of about 20 children, and held first rank. "She leads in every regular subject except catechism, geography, and history." B "likes all subjects except catechism, giving first place, at the age of 9 years, to arithmetic. Her school marks for 1922–1923 are as follows, the marks indicating as is usual: 100, perfect; 90, very good; 80, good; 70, fair; 60, deficient."

At the age of 11 years B entered high school and is doing good work there, but without much stimulus of competition, as there are but a few pupils in her grade.

Unlike several of the children who have an IQ of more than 180, B has never been a school problem. She has always been a "good mixer" with children of her school

B's Marks, Grade VII. Age 9 Years 10 Months

SUBJECT	1922 October 31	1922 December 15	1923 January 31	1923 March 27
Catechism	95	90	80	94
Grammar	92	94	85	90
Composition	87	88		85
Spelling	93	95	100	98
Letter writing	85	85		80
American history	85	80	88	90
Geography	94	87	90	94
Arithmetic	90	90	100	90
Oral French	95	95	96	95
Penmanship	D	C		75
Reading	90	91		85
Choral singing	80	80		95
Drawing	90	90		90
Plain sewing	80	85		85
Rules of observance	90	100	97	94
Bible history	94	90	86	93

grade, and has taken part in their activities. Being a very large, strong child, she has not been so much "out of it" in motor skill as to be conspicuous among older schoolmates. As evidences of unusual manual dexterity the following may be mentioned: at the age of 5 years B knitted on steel needles a pair of socks which were worn by her little brother; at 6 years she made edible rice puddings; at 7 years of age she made cookies.

TRAITS OF CHARACTER

No one among parents and teachers has mentioned any character trait considered faulty. The virtues most frequently mentioned and emphasized are modesty, reliability, self-direction, poise, good humor, amiability, and "being a good sport."

JUDGMENTS OF TEACHERS

It is remarkable that no adverse comments have been offered by any of B's teachers. All teachers have rated B high in character and intellect. The chief error in judgment lies in not ranking her as high as she really stands. This error arises partly from the fact that teachers in the private schools B attended deal with selected children whom they may come to think of as representing the average of child ability. The judgments of B's teachers may be quoted as follows:

Remembered in our kindergarten chiefly for her vivid imagination. *From the head mistress of the school.*

One of the most popular children in the school. *From a teacher.*

It is some time since I had B as a pupil, but I am glad to tell you my impressions of the child as I remember her.

She was a very quiet, unassuming member of the class. She had remarkable powers of concentration, always finished her work well in advance of the others and then found work for herself until the class was ready to go on with a new subject.

With the children in both work and play she made no effort to lead them, and although they recognized the fact that her work was superior to theirs, they showed no resentment toward B because she never made them feel her superiority.

B showed a mental poise that I have rarely, if ever, found in a child. It was not so much a matter of a sudden keen grasp of a subject, which might or might not be permanent. She seemed to have the power, which is usually met only in mature minds, of weighing, reasoning, and then placing for permanent use the matter with which she was dealing.[3]

Always B appealed to me as a normal child, with unusual mental poise. She was not at all uncanny or tiresomely intelligent. *From a former classroom teacher.*

[3] At this time B's intelligence was about that of the average adult, according to mental tests, though the teacher made this comment without having that knowledge.

MENTAL MEASUREMENTS

Measurements of general intelligence of B have been made as follows:

DATE	BIRTHDAY AGE OF B	STANFORD-BINET MA	IQ	ARMY ALPHA POINTS B	Norm
March 3, 1921	8–3	15–8	189		
April 8, 1922	9–4	17–6	188	84 (Form 5)	0
December 29, 1924 . . .	12–1			142 (Form 5)	

PHYSICAL MEASUREMENTS

B was measured at the age of 9 years 4 months and again at the age of 12 years 1 month, in light indoor clothing, with the following results:

Height and weight.

DATE	WT. (LBS.) B	NORM[4]	HEIGHT (IN.) B	NORM[5]	HT.-WT. COEFF. B	NORM	CRANIAL CIR. (IN.) B
April 8, 1922 . . .	106.0	61.5	56.0	52.0	1.88	1.18	22.4
December 29, 1924 .	123.0	82.8	61.6	57.7	1.99	1.44	22.5

B greatly surpasses Baldwin's norms (making the usual allowance for heels and clothing).

Grip measurements. Measured with Smedley's dynamometer, B's hand grip scores as follows:

[4] Baldwin's norms for children 9 years 6 months old.
[5] Without shoes.

DATE	GRIP (KG.)	
	Right Hand	Left Hand
April 8, 1922	13.0	11.0
December 29, 1924	20.0	18.0

Superior size is therefore accompanied by superior strength.

MISCELLANEOUS CHARACTERISTICS

Diversions. At the age of 9 years B listed her favorite diversions thus: "All sorts of outdoor games; then reading; then drawing; then playing with dolls, sometimes."

Imaginary land. "When I was 8 years old my imaginary countries were generally of grownupness, where I figured as chief actress and queen."

Career ideas. At the age of 9 years B was asked, "What will you be when you grow up?" B responded promptly, "A doctor." Then she added, "I will learn to sing, too. Perhaps I'll sing to the patients. There are so many things to do. I'll try to combine several things." Now, at the age of 12 [1925], she is ambitious to become "a celebrated authoress, actress, artist, and musician."

Reading interests. When asked how many books she had read (April 8, 1922), B replied, "Oh, hundreds and hundreds. We have plenty of books." It is characteristic of her that she reads over and over again a book that especially pleases her. Thus she had read nearly all of Louisa Alcott's books twice each, and had read *Lady Luck* — at that date her favorite book — several times. She had read a great many books written for boys, and remarked, in trying to describe her preferences, "I like boys' books best. They have more in them than girls' books."

Tendency to organize other children. B is the only one of the children here reported who shows any success or interest in leading or organizing fellow children. She organizes "clubs" and games. When shown the Civil War code, in the course of mental tests, she remarked, "I must remember that, for it will be fine for my Clip-Clap-Club."

Chapter Six

CHILD C

CHILD C is a boy, born June 15, 1913. He was brought to the writer's attention by the principal of Public School 157, Manhattan, who wrote as follows, requesting an examination in the laboratory at Teachers College, Columbia University:

> I have in the 5A grade of this school a boy . . . who seems to be somewhat of an infant prodigy. His verbal memory, especially, is phenomenal, but he is underdeveloped on the physical side, takes no interest in Manual Work, and does not like to play with other children.

FAMILY BACKGROUND

Child C is descended, in both lines, from German Jews. His parents are not related by blood.

The paternal grandfather was a successful businessman. The paternal grandmother was a competent housewife. A paternal uncle is a judge in New York City. No incompetent relative in this branch is known; on the other hand, there is no one of great eminence.

On the maternal side, one of C's mother's brothers is a physician, a cousin is a writer, and another cousin is a judge. No incompetent relatives are known in this branch.

Father. C's father is an accountant. He did not graduate from elementary school but went to work at an early age. He was 40 years old when C was born.

Mother. C's mother is a high school graduate. She was 35 years old when C was born. She is a housewife, and had no paid occupation before marriage. C is an only child, never having had any siblings.

PRESCHOOL HISTORY

The following information was gathered from C's mother. The child cut his first tooth at the age of 9 months. He began to walk at the age of 1 year 3 months, and to talk fluently at the age of 1 year 4 months. He learned to read almost as soon as he talked, and at the age of 3 years could read simple matter.

When he was 4 years old, C went one day into a store with his father. While the latter was making his purchases the child took a book from the shelf and began to scan it. The shopkeeper noticed the child looking attentively at the book and said, for a joke, "Boy, if you will read me that book, I'll give it to you." Instantly C began to read fluently and carried the book away from the astonished merchant.

On another occasion, when he was about 5 years old, a woman noticed C searching about the house and said to him, "Are you hungry?" His reply was, "Yes, I'm hungry for a book."

Apparently C has never had an imaginary land. His favorite recreation has always been reading.

SCHOOL HISTORY

C's school life began at the age of 6 years. He did not attend kindergarten. His teachers recognized him as "out of the ordinary" — but not in any appreciative way. They thought him "queer" and "odd." In spite of perfect work, he was advanced at only a little more than the usual rate, being placed in Grade 5B at the age of 9 years 5 months. His obvious misplacement and unhappiness here caused the principal of the school to seek advice regarding C's education.

After mental tests had revealed the mental level of a superior adult, C was invited to enter the Special Opportunity Class then just organized at Public School 165, Manhattan. Here he was associated with twenty-five classmates of his own age whose IQ's ranged from 150 to 175, the median of the group being about 164 IQ.

In this class C gradually became adjusted to the work in such a way that at the end of the school year (1923), when asked whether he would prefer to stay in the Special Opportunity Class or go on to high school, he unhesitatingly chose to stay with the special class. "It will be more interesting," he said. He therefore finished elementary school at the age of 12 years, although at 10 he was judged by his teachers to be fully prepared in knowledge to enter senior high school. There is no doubt that he could have been made ready to enter college at the age of 12 years.

When asked at the age of 9 what he would be when he grew up, the following conversation took place:

Q. What do you think is the most interesting vocation? What would you like to be when you grow up?

A. Well, the answer to those two questions is not the same one.

Q. Then tell us first what you think is the most interesting vocation.

A. Science, especially astronomy.

Q. And what vocation would you like to follow when you grow up?

A. To be a medical doctor.

Q. But why not be what is most interesting?

A. Because a person cannot make much money being an as-tronomer. I never heard of anyone at the Lick Observatory earning fifty thousand dollars a year.

Q. But do medical doctors earn fifty thousand dollars a year?

A. It is possible for one to do it. Some of them do.

Q. Do you think being a medical doctor is the most lucrative occupation?

A. No. It would be more lucrative to get into Standard Oil.

Q. Then why not go into Standard Oil?

A. Because it isn't so interesting as being a medical doctor.

Q. Which is the more useful occupation — medical doctor or astronomer?

A. Medical doctor. Because a man does not care much for a blazing star a million miles away if his wife is sick. Anyone cares more for a *person* two feet away than for a *thing* a trillion miles away.

The ambition to become a medical doctor has persisted for three years and gives an impression of permanency.[1]

Scores of anecdotes could be cited to illustrate the interests and the fine intelligence of this boy. In walking through the halls of the college with him, on one occasion when he had come for a mental test, the present writer saw what seemed to be an exhibition of Chinese costumes in a glass case, and called C's attention to it, saying, "Look at this exhibition of Chinese work." C looked closely at the exhibit for several moments without comment, and then said, "Well, I believe it is Japanese work, isn't it?" He then proceeded to point out certain minute differences which are found be-tween the work of Japanese and Chinese and which were later verified by an authority on the subject.

When he went with his class to visit a new high school

[1] C is now, 17 years after the recording of this comment, engaged in the profession of medicine. Editor.

building in the city, he was missed as the others began to move from one corridor to another. After search, he was found in the chemical laboratory copying in a notebook the names of all the chemicals in the bottles as they appeared on the labels.

In the Opportunity Class C was appreciated by these children of more than 150 IQ as he had never been by the unselected children in the regular classes. They recognized his encyclopedic knowledge and respected it. They eventually elected him to two posts of responsibility among them. These were totally new experiences for C.

Another new experience for the boy was that of being equaled by another child in an intellectual performance. Although C led the special class in marks, as would be expected, he was nevertheless occasionally equaled or surpassed in one or two subjects in the month's record. He learned for the first time how to adjust himself to successful competitors in his own particular field.

TRAITS OF CHARACTER

A few faulty character traits in C have been noted by teachers. One teacher said, "He is somewhat of a prig." This impression appears to have been based partly on his lack of desire to play with children of his own age and partly on his use of "long words." Soon after C entered the Special Opportunity Class for gifted children, another boy equaled him in an assignment and put out his hand to C, saying cordially, "Let's shake." C had never had the experience of being equaled by a fellow pupil and he turned away, refusing to shake hands. However, he has now learned to react most cordially to those who equal him, though he bitterly dislikes to be equaled or passed in mental work.

Never in any sense a leader or guide among the unselected children of the school from which he came, C was soon elected to the position of monitor by the children of median IQ 164. They were heard to say: "C is just; C can make us behave." One child (IQ 164) exclaimed in admiration, "C knows *everything*."

On the other hand, C arouses some feelings of jealousy and antagonism as well as admiration because he does not hesitate to contradict erroneous statements or to rectify imperfections in what others say or do. He is not very tactful in human relationships.

The virtues most frequently ascribed to C by those who know him well are reliability, honesty, bravery, and loyalty. He is a stickler for the exact; no statement is right unless it is exactly right. It is easy to see how this trait might antagonize average children of C's age, and even teachers and others in authority.

MENTAL MEASUREMENTS

Measurements of general intelligence of C have been made as follows:

DATE	BIRTHDAY AGE OF C	STANFORD-BINET MA	IQ	ARMY ALPHA
September 26, 1922 . .	9–3	17–7	190	On October 30, 1922,
April 18, 1923	9–10	18–6	188	he scored 146 points (Form 9)

PHYSICAL MEASUREMENTS

Measurements of C's physique have been made as follows:

Date	Wt. (lbs.)	Ht. (stand., in.)	Cranial Cir. (in.)
September 26, 1923 . . .	60.5	53.9	. . .
January 8, 1924	. . .	. . .	20.7

C is one of the few of the bright children studied who does not exceed Baldwin's norms in physique. However, at the age of 11 years 7 months he was 57 inches tall and weighed 69.9 pounds. His appetite for food has never been very satisfactory, but in spite of this his general health has been good.

Editor's Supplement

The author's original write-up of Child C terminated at this point, in 1923. But during the following 16 years she remained in constant contact with C, interviewing him and testing him periodically, and in many ways sponsoring his secondary, collegiate, and professional education. Many pages of these records are in her files, accompanied by collections of C's work, newspaper notices, correspondence, photographs, and data from further interviews with the parents. It seems best to summarize these records chronologically, and with some brevity, since it would not be at all feasible to reproduce the material in full.

October 15, 1923

C filled out an "Interest Blank" at P.S. 165, Manhattan, where he was then in the eighth grade, at the age of 10 years 4 months. He was at this time, or had been, class monitor and editor of the class paper. "Likes and dislikes" were expressed, strongest "preference" of subjects, and judgment of "what is easiest."

Liked very much were literature, reading, spelling, mathematics, French, games and sports, and geography.

Most disliked were painting, water colors, etc.; penmanship; composition.

"Easiest" and also *"best liked"* was English literature.

Preferred kind of reading was encyclopedias, biography, current events, and history.

Things most like to do were studying, general reading, sedentary games, playing alone.

Most disliked things to do were using tools or working with apparatus and machinery, drawing, dancing, practicing music.

[This dislike for manual activities remained with C. In later years, although his drawings in science courses were admirable, he made an unsatisfactory laboratory assistant when set to using the typewriter or mimeograph, or to drawing graphs and charts not for his own use.]

Fig. 2. A Sketch by C.

February, 1924

At this time the Special Opportunity Class teacher (P.S. 165, Manhattan) rated C, on a school information blank, for a long array of "physical, mental, social, and moral traits," using a 7-step rating scale (1 being the highest scale).

Ratings of 1 were given for —

Truthfulness	Common sense
Desire to know	General intelligence
Originality	

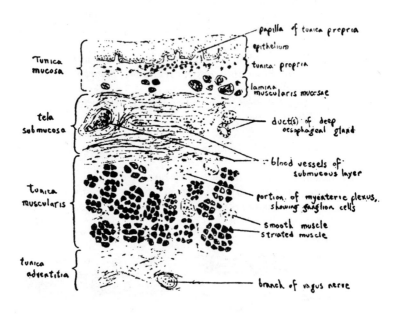

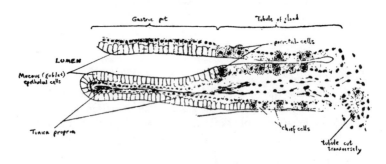

Fig. 3. A Page from One of C's Notebooks.

Ratings of 2 or 3 were given for —

Prudence and forethought   Conscientiousness
Self-confidence   Permanency of moods
Will power and persever-   Desire to excel
   ance   Cheerfulness and optimism
Freedom from vanity and   Leadership
   egotism   Sensitiveness to approval or
Sympathy and tenderness   disapproval

Ratings below 3 (average or below) were given for —

Health   Fondness for large groups
Physical energy   Popularity with other children
Musical appreciation   Generosity and unselfishness
Appreciation of beauty   Mechanical ingenuity
Sense of humor

September 15, 1924

At this time the author (L. S. H.), who had known C for two years, independently rated him on this same array of traits by the same rating scale technique.

Ratings of 1 were given for —

Prudence and forethought   Sympathy and tenderness
Self-confidence   Conscientiousness
Will power and persever-   Truthfulness
   ance   Desire to know
Appreciation of beauty   Originality
Sense of humor   Common sense
Desire to excel   General intelligence

Ratings of 2 or 3 were given for —

Cheerfulness and optimism   Sensitiveness to approval or
Permanency of moods   disapproval
Leadership   Freedom from vanity or ego-
Popularity with other chil-   tism
   dren   Mechanical ingenuity

Ratings below 3 (average or less) were given for —

Health   Generosity and unselfishness
Physical energy   Fondness for large groups
Musical appreciation

The only striking differences between the two sets of ratings are in sense of humor and appreciation of beauty, in which C was rated low by the teacher and high by the author. It appears to the Editor, who also has a more or less intimate acquaintance with C, that a composite of these ratings, made when the child was 11 years old, gave an adequate portrayal of him as an adult of 27.

April 18, 1925

At the age of 11 years 10 months, C was again given the Stanford-Binet examination by L. S. H. His score was 18 years 6 months, and he was recorded as being "no longer measured" by this test.

January 16, 1926

At this time C was in a private high school, being then 12 years 7 months old.

On these data his score in Army Alpha (Form 5) was 195 points.

He was given an early form of the IER Test for Superior Adults, CAVD, and the score is given as 43.5 (perhaps this should be 435). The comment of the scorer in the Institute of Educational Research was: "This puts the boy well into the college graduate class. He excels about 75 per cent of the Yale Law freshmen."

January 26, 1927

C was now age 13 years 7 months, and he was in the second year of high school.

He was given the IER Scale CAVD for Superior Adults in two installments, beginning January 30 and finishing February 13. The score was 435 points, and the comment is, "As good as best Yale Law School freshmen and as high as top 4 per cent to 5 per cent of Teachers College candidates for M. A. degree."

Also in January, 1927, in the psychological laboratory of Barnard College, C was given by the present Editor an array of tests for which norms were available for Barnard freshmen, from the work of F. E. Carothers (*Psychological Examination of College Students*). The scores made are in the following tabulation expressed in terms of the PE of the distribution of 100 Barnard freshmen.

SCORES MADE BY C AT AGE OF 13 YEARS 7 MONTHS IN TERMS OF PE OF DISTRIBUTION OF 100 BARNARD FRESHMEN

Unless otherwise indicated, the score is "plus."

TEST	C's SCORE
Word Building (AEIRLP)	3.22 PE
Completion (Trabue A)	3.09
Directions (Woodworth-Wells)	2.78
Word Recall (Mulhall)	2.72
Analogies (Woodworth-Wells)	1.66
Logical Recall (Proverbs)	0.49
Naming Opposites (Woodworth-Wells)	0.16
Substitution (Digit-Form)	0.07
Color Naming (Woodworth-Wells)	− 0.06
Cancellation (Digits)	− 0.15
Word Recognition (Mulhall)	− 0.27
Logical Recognition (Proverbs)	− 0.64
Number Checking	− 0.81
Verb-Object Associations	− 0.86

On those of the above subtests most nearly like the content of present general intelligence examinations, C is clearly above the standard for the freshmen group, being in fact at the very top of the list, about 3 PE above average.

Most of the things on which C scored (slightly) below average are simple and more or less mechanical. This result may perhaps be confirmed by his score in Stenquist Assembling Test, Series I, given on the same day. His T-score was 58, placing him only a little above average (67th centile) among 13-year-old children. It will be recalled that C was uniformly rated low in "mechanical ability" and also expressed a lack of interest in "working with machinery."

On this day C was also given the Rosanoff High Standard Frequency Test (Word Association) based on Class A words

only.   The available standards (Rosanoff) and also C's score
are given in the following:

```
Fifth grade, total value . . . . . . . . . .  15
First year high school . . . . . . . . . . . 100
First year college . . . . . . . . . . . . . 375
Master's degree  . . . . . . . . . . . . . . 600
Starred men of science  . . . . . . . . . . 800
C's score. . . . . . . . . . . . . . . . . . 823
```

August 23, 1931

At the age of 18 years 2 months, C was in his third year of
college (Columbia).   On this date he was again given IER
Intelligence Scale CAVD, Levels M, N, O, P, Q, and his
score was 446 points, which is as high as any score recorded
on this scale.

December 26, 1932

At the age of 19 years 6 months, in the fourth year of college,
C scored 210 points on Army Alpha, Form 8, a score
equaled only by the top 1 per cent of college seniors.

LATER SCHOOL HISTORY

Subsequent to the Special Opportunity Class, in 1923, in
P. S. 165, Manhattan, C completed his high school work,
first in a private school and later in a public high school
(George Washington) in New York City.   During these
years he received various academic honors and prizes, or
medals, for proficiency.

In the high school from which he was graduated in 1929,
he was vice-president of the French Club.   He won a city-
wide contest in French composition, for which he received a
medal.   He was elected to Arista, the high school honor
society, and ranked third in his class upon graduation, with an
average grade of 94 (the two better were 96 and 94.5).   In
connection with his high school work he was awarded a state
scholarship of $150.

Upon graduating from high school, C applied for and competed for a Pulitzer scholarship, and he was awarded a scholarship as the highest-ranking boy among the competitors. This enabled him to enter Columbia College, to which he was admitted in 1929.

He was graduated from Columbia, taking the premedical course, in 1933, being elected to Phi Beta Kappa. During the previous year he also won a current events contest conducted by a metropolitan newspaper, with a prize of $150.

C was admitted to the New York University Medical College, from which he was graduated with the degree of M.D. He is now (1940) serving his interneship in hospitals in New York City.

$\mathcal{C}hapter$ $\mathcal{S}even$

CHILD D

CHILD D is a boy, born March 9, 1910.[1] He was first described by Terman, who tested him in 1917. D, like E, was brought to the attention of the writer by the principal of the Horace Mann Kindergarten (Teachers College, Columbia University) as being a child of remarkable endowment. He was at that time 7 years 4 months old and had a Mental Age of 13 years 7 months, with an IQ of 184 (S–B).

FAMILY BACKGROUND

D is descended from Russian Jews in the paternal branch and from English Jews in the maternal branch.

Father. D's father immigrated to America at an early age. He is a high school graduate and was a student of engineering but abandoned these studies in the third year to do newspaper work, and later entered the advertising business in a large city. His leisure is spent in writing, and he has published a number of books, including three novels and

[1] This child was described in some detail in Chapter IX of *Gifted Children,* 1926, and the earlier part of the present account is taken from that chapter. In the later part additional items are given, taken from the author's 1924 manuscript, and there are a few editorial additions.

a philosophical drama dealing with religion. His first book, a novel, was published when he was 21 years old. He was 28 when D was born.

Mother. D's mother went to school for only a few weeks and has been largely self-taught. Before marriage she was statistician and registrar in a large philanthropic organization. She has published stories, reviews, and poems, and a book on education. She has always taken part personally in the education of D. She was 26 years old when D was born. D is an only child.

Noteworthy relatives. Noteworthy relatives beyond the first degree of kinship include the following: a chief rabbi of Moscow, who was exiled for aiding the Nihilists; a distinguished lawyer; a man who by his own efforts became a millionaire; a concert pianist; a composer and virtuoso; a writer; and "a relative decorated for science in Poland."

The maternal great-grandfather was a famous rabbi who compiled and published a Jewish calendar covering a period of 414 years. This calendar contains, in regular order, the exact period of every new moon's appearance, the sabbaths, festivals with scriptural portions for each, and the equinoxes of the solar year according to the prescribed and authorized Jewish laws and corresponding to dates in the common era. The tabulations have been carefully compiled from various works of ancient rabbinical astronomers, with annotations in Hebrew and English.

This rabbi was also the great-grandfather of the four first cousins of D, whose intelligence quotients have been taken, and who rated 156, 150, 130, and 122, respectively. A second cousin in the maternal line yielded at the age of 6 years an IQ of 157.

PRESCHOOL HISTORY

D cut his first tooth at 4 months of age. He could say words at 8 months and talked in sentences at 11 months. In November, 1910 (8 months), he said "little boy" when his shadow appeared on the wall. D could stand, holding to chairs, at 9 months of age, and he walked alone at 11 to 12 months. At the age of 18 months, while sitting on his mother's lap as she sat before a typewriter, he learned to read by looking at the letters. The records kept by the mother indicate that he "learned to read and count in 1911." One such record reads, "October 11, counts all day long."

At 8 months of age D strung in succession 5 yellow and 5 red balls and then began on blue, when the activity was interrupted. In March, 1912, he was using words to express relationship, such as "will" and "shall" (correctly), "but," "and," "my," "mine." At 2 years 6 months his vocabulary (incomplete) was 1690 words.

D's earliest memory goes back to 2 years of age, when he saw a rat and thought it was "a little brownie." An example of the quality of the questions asked by D in the first 36 months of life is one he asked in October, 1911 (19 months): "Has every door two knobs?" "Why?" His mother reports: "He was always asking unexpected questions."

This child was not placed in school at the usual age because he did not fit into the school organization. At the time he should have entered kindergarten D could read fluently and could perform complicated arithmetical processes. His intellectual interests were far beyond those of even the highly selected children of a private kindergarten. Therefore, his parents kept him out of school and obtained the companionship of other children for him by sending him to a playground.

D was first seen by the present writer [L. S. H.] while he was attending this playground, in the year 1916–1917. It is very interesting to note how D made social contacts with the other children while pursuing his own interests. For instance, he published a playground newspaper called "The Weekly Post." [2] He composed, edited, and typed this paper, issued at intervals, and it had a regular playground circulation.

TRAITS OF CHARACTER

No faulty traits of character have been ascribed to D by parents or teachers interviewed. He was rated for character by Terman's method under Terman's direction, with a result of 1.93 from parents' estimates and 1.90 from teachers' estimates (the median score, for comparison with average children, being 3.00). D is thus rated by parents and teachers alike as well above the average in character. The desirable traits most often mentioned are refusal to lie, loyalty to standards once adopted, readiness to admit just criticisms, unselfishness, and amiability.

MENTAL MEASUREMENTS

General intelligence tests of D show the following results:

DATE	BIRTH-DAY AGE OF D	STANFORD-BINET		ARMY ALPHA POINTS		THORNDIKE TEST FOR FRESHMEN (POINTS)	
		MA	IQ	D	NORM	D	NORM
August, 1917 .	7–4	13–7	184				
January 29, 1921	10–11	Passed all for Super. Adult.		185 (Form 5)	—		
June, 1922 . .	12–3					106	70–80

[2] A facsimile of a page from this paper is reproduced on page 244 of the author's book, *Gifted Children* (The Macmillan Company, New York; 1926).

It is thus seen how greatly D surpasses the average child in mental tests. In the five years which have elapsed since D's first test there has been no tendency to become mediocre. At the age of 7 years he showed an IQ of 184; at the age of 11 years he exceeded by a wide margin on Army Alpha the median score for postgraduate students in first-rate universities; at 12 years he far exceeded the median score of college freshmen on Thorndike's test for that group. The validity of these scores is consistently borne out by the school history.

PHYSICAL MEASUREMENTS AND HEALTH

The following measurements, as of May, 1922, were made in the gymnasium of the high school attended by D: [3]

| Weight (lbs.) | | Height (in.) | | Ht.-Wt. Coeff. | |
D	Norm	D	Norm	D	Norm
76.0	82.8	64.0	57.7	1.19	1.44

D's health has always been excellent and no physical defects are known to his parents. He is rated as very stable nervously. His slenderness has been rated as a defect by one examiner; although he greatly exceeds the norm in height, he falls below in weight. He is therefore very tall and slender in appearance, which is characteristic of his father and uncles.

MISCELLANEOUS CHARACTERISTICS

Diversions. At the age of 7 years D's favorite amusements were skating, "Mechano," reading, playing ball, writ-

[3] A note shows that on March 16, 1926, at just 16 years of age, D's height was 71.5 inches and his weight 115 pounds, stripped. EDITOR.

ing, tabulating, solitaire, chess, and numerical calculation in all its forms. As development has proceeded, he has continued most of these recreations, turning more and more, however, to games of intellectual skill. He likes other children and likes to be with them; he has established relations with them by editing newspapers for them, teaching them about nature, and the like. Play in the sense of mere purposeless sensorimotor activity has not been enjoyed by him.

Imaginary land. From the age of about 4 years to about the age of 7, D was greatly interested in an imaginary land which he called "Borningtown." He spent many hours peopling Borningtown, laying out roads, drawing maps of its terrain, composing and recording its language (Bornish), and writing its history and literature. He composed a lengthy dictionary — scores of pages — of the Bornish language. The origin of the words "Borningtown" and "Bornish" is not known. It seems possible that D's imaginary land may have arisen out of the mystery of being born.

Gift for music. D has had piano lessons for several years, and he has displayed remarkable ability to deal with the mathematical aspects of music. A sample is shown of his musical composition, illustrating his understanding of musical symbols and his ability to interpret through this medium. He composed music before he had any instruction in playing musical instruments. He read certain booklets which came with Ampico and decided to compose. He can compose music which he cannot himself play.

Gifts for form and color in drawing. D's talent for color, for drawing and design, has been marked from the time he could wield a pencil. His drawings, paintings, and designs would fill a book by themselves. A sample of his original work at the age of 10 years is reproduced.

FIG. 4. PART OF A COMPOSITION BY D AT AGE 8 YEARS 7 MONTHS.

Fig. 5. Drawn by D at Age 9 Years 9 Months.

This conventionalized bird is a fragment from his decoration for the chest in which he kept his "scientific work" at that time. This oblong chest he painted Chinese red, with three figures on the front. These were the conventionalized bird here shown, a conventionalized nest with eggs, and a conventionalized butterfly — all painted in striking combinations of yellow, blue, green, and red.

D loves color, and one of his favorite playthings has been a sample folder of silk buttonhole twists of three hundred shades. Between the ages of 8 and 9 years he would go over and over these, classifying the colors in various ways, scoring them for beauty, and renaming them to satisfy his appreciation of them. Some of these names will give an idea of his appreciation:

spotted pale	dark darking green
darkling green	regular green
shame blue	paper white

spoiled pink	apron blue
soft light pink	beau yellow
meadow beauty pink	visitor's green
cat black	alien white
royalest red	feeling blue

One of his favorite games (aged 8 to 9 years) was to assign a numerical value to each of the 300 shades and then to list them for "highest honors." "Royalest red" nearly always won in these contests.

Origination of new concepts and new words. From earliest childhood D has felt a need for concepts and for words to express them that are not to be found in dictionaries. His occupation in this field he calls "wordical work." Some examples are recorded by his mother in the following note dated December, 1916.

> Was having his dinner and being nearly finished said he didn't care to eat any more, as he had a pain in his actum pelopthis. He explained that his actum pelopthis, actum quotatus, serbalopsis, and boobalicta are parts of the body where you sometimes have queer feelings; they don't serve any purpose. He said he also had a place called the boobalunksis, or source of headaches; that the hair usually springs out from around the herkadone; that the perpalensis is the place where socks end, and the bogalegus is the place where legs and tummy come together. He also named one other part, the cobaliscus or smerbalooble, whose function is not explained. The definitions are exactly as he gave them in each instance.

On February 23, 1917, his mother wrote:

> He has not referred to these places since. I do not know where he got the idea for such names, unless possibly from *The Water Babies*. He would probably refer them to some Bornish source.

The invention and classification of the Bornish language already referred to is another example of D's "wordical work." He has also invented hundreds of words which have not been included as Bornish. An example of his handwriting, illustrative of words he has invented, classified, and recorded for pleasure, is here shown.

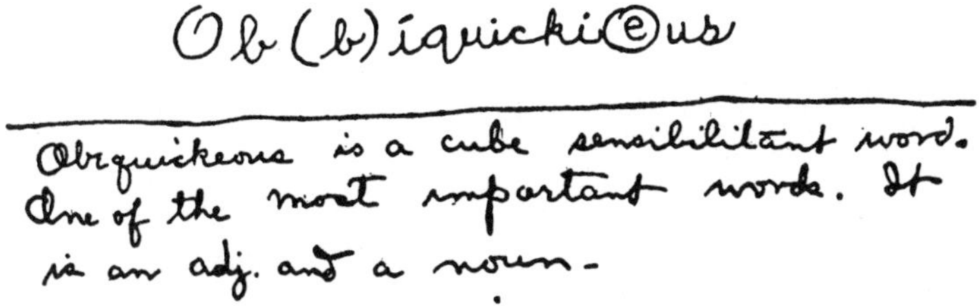
Ob(b)iquicki(e)us

Obiquickeous is a cube sensibilitant word. One of the most important words. It is an adj. and a noun.

FIG. 6. ONE OF D'S VERBAL INVENTIONS.

Invention of games. D has invented many games. To illustrate this aspect of his mental capacity, there are his designs for three-handed and four-handed checkers.[4] D held that these would be better games than two-handed checkers because they are more complicated. A description of the games invented by D, together with his mathematical calculations concerning the chances and probabilities in each, would fill many pages.

Calculation and mathematical ingenuity. It is difficult to say that D is more gifted in one mental function or group of functions than in others, for his ability is so extraordinary in all performances that without means of measurement one cannot tell in which he deviates farthest from the average.

However, it is to be observed that the quantitative aspects of experience have always played a very striking role in all his performances. Even in his dealing with color he turned

[4] See *Gifted Children*, pages 246–247.

to mathematics and made his values quantitative. Throughout childhood he spent hours playing with numerical relationships. These calculations cover hundreds of pages. There is reproduced here a sample of such work, chosen at random from scores of like material. There is no doubt in the mind of the present writer [L. S. H.] that D could, by practice with short-cut methods, easily become a lightning calculator. By the age of 12 years D had finished college entrance requirements in arithmetic, algebra, geometry, and trigonometry, all with high marks.

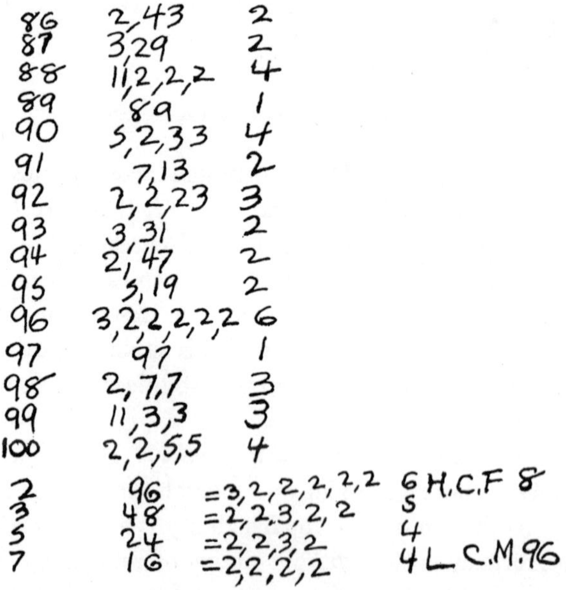

Fig. 7. Playing with numbers, Child D, age 7, to find what number under 100 has the greatest number of factors, counts up factors in each and awards "highest honors" to 96.

Tendency to classify and diagram. To classify the data of experience has always been one of D's chief interests.

One such tabulation was of parts of speech in various stories and poems.[5] Figure 8 is a sample taken from many pages of reclassification of birds. The caption, "Proper Scientific Name," represents the name considered by D to be better than those now recognized by ornithologists. His classifications of words, numbers, colors, musical notes, objects, and so forth would fill a large volume. He often constructs diagrams to clarify or condense meaning.

```
Classification of birds seen in summer 1918. Classified in Feb.,
1919. "Proper Scientific Name" is the improved name given by D--.

Found  Name         Genus      Scientific      Proper Scien-
Here  (Popular)    or,etc.     N  a  m  e      tific Name.     Equal
*... Towhee......Species...Erythopthalmus.......Pipilo Eryth.......**?..
X...Wh.-eyed Towhee..Sub-Species..E.Alleni..P. Leucopthalmus...***..
X...Green-tailed  " ..Genus... Oreospiza...........Pipilo...........**?..
X...Blue Grosbeak...Species...Caerulea......... ..Cyanea...........***..
*...Indigo Bunting.. "   ...Cyanea.............Caerulea........ ..***..
X...Painted      "   ...  "   .....Ciris.. .........Pictus.........**?
X...Lark Bunting.... "   ..Calamospiza Melanocorys..Melanospiza Leucoptera
                                                                  ***...

*...Barn Swallow..  " ...Erythrogastra.........Leucurus..........***..
*...Tree      ...Genus....Iridoprocne...........Hirundo..........***..
*...Red-eyed Vireo..Species...Olivacea...........Erythropthalmus...Yes..
....Wood Warblers..Family...Mniotiltidae...... Dendroicidae......**?..
*...Black & White Warbler..Species..Varia........Striata...........**?..
*...Yellow Warbler..Species...Astiva...........Xantho or Auro......Yes..
*..,Sh.-Billed Marsh Wren..Genus..Cistothorus...Telmatotytes. ......?..
*...Red-br. Nuthatch..Species..Canadensis......Borealis.............Yes..
                                    ....Erythrogastra........**?..
*********************************************************************
```

FIG. 8. A SAMPLE OF D's CLASSIFICATIONS.

Interest in science. By the age of 10 years D's chief interest had come to center in science and it continued to center there. His classifications of moths, birds, and the like and his observations of their life cycles are "monumental." There are volumes of these recorded observations as in Figure 9.

Figures 10 and 11 illustrate his interest in physical science. They have been taken from his notebooks and state problems

[5] *Ibid.*, page 245.

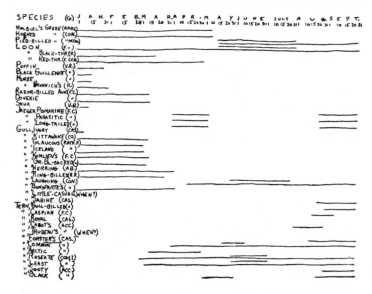

FIG. 9. ONE OF D'S RECORDS OF OBSERVATIONS. LIFE CYCLES OF BIRDS.

which occurred spontaneously to him and for which he tried experimentally to find solutions. During a series of experiments "to determine the path of a tack," it is reported that "the house was full of tacks" which had been used in attempting solutions.

SCHOOL HISTORY

In the September following his ninth birthday D entered upon formal instruction in the junior high school. In the autumn following his tenth birthday he entered senior high school, from which he was graduated at the age of 12 years, with a scholastic record which won for him two scholarships.

He was admitted to a large Eastern college at the age of 12 years 6 months (1922–1923), and made a superior record

of the problem: "Determine the appearance of a finger, F, to two eyes, E_R and E_L , focussed on a pole R at point P_S along lines $E_R R$ and $E_L R$."

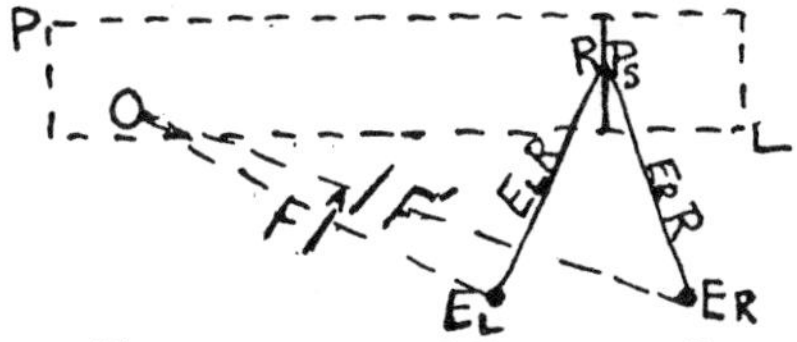

Thru R pass plane PL // to the plane of the eyes. Draw a line from E_L (which is nearer to F than E_R) to F, cutting PL in O. Draw $E_R O$; thru F pass a plane // to PL and crossing $E_R O$ in A. Thru A pass F' // F.

F' and F are the positions of F to E_R and E_L.

D.

So it can be shown that 2 other eyes would see F in positions F and F''.

∴ 4 eyes focused on R see F as F, F, F', and F''.

D.

Fig. 10. Copy of Work Done by D "For Fun," March 28, 1921, Aged 11 Years 1 Month.

throughout the course. It was very interesting to see that D continued to discover means of obtaining social contacts in spite of the great difficulties due to his extreme youth and his intellectual deviation. Thus it is not easy to plan how a 12-year-old boy might successfully participate in college athletics when the median age of college freshmen is over 18 years, but this problem was not too difficult for D. He presented himself to compete for the post of coxswain on the freshman crew where, other things being equal, light weight is an advantage.

He was graduated from college, with Phi Beta Kappa honors, in 1926, at the age of 16 years 2 months. At that time he was ambitious for a career in science.

Discussion

of the determination of the course of a freed tack, T, connected with other tacks by rubber bands.

A.Fig.1.

When connected to a tack T' by band B.
Draw T T, or L.
T freed will travel along L, answer.

B.Fig.2.

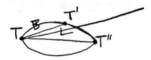

When connected to 2 tacks T' and T'' by 2 bands B and B'.
Answer: Along L, the bisector of
T' and TTT''.

C.Fig.3.

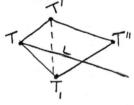

The same as B, but only 1 band B.
Answer same as to B.

D. Fig.4.

When connected to 3 tacks by any number of bands.
Draw T' T, , and treat as in B and C.

D.

FIG. 11. THE PATH OF A TACK. WORK DONE BY D AT AGE 11 YEARS.

Editor's Supplement

D undertook graduate work, with distinction, in the field of chemistry. He became an industrial chemist with an important position in the research phases of the motion-picture industry. Word has been received of his death in September, 1938.

Chapter Eight

CHILD E

CHILD E when first seen was a boy 8 years 4 months of age. He was born June 17, 1908, and the first psychological measurements were made November 4, 1916. The circumstances that led to acquaintance with him were as follows:

A child of exceptional intelligence was desired for demonstration before a class at Teachers College, Columbia University, engaged in the study of the psychology and treatment of exceptional children.[1] E was suggested because of his remarkable school record. The consent of the parents was secured and the psychological examination was made before a class of about thirty students.

This was not, of course, the ideal circumstance under which to perform a mental test for scientific record. The presumption would be that the audience would tend to reduce the child's performance, so that whatever error there might be from this source would be in the direction of making the child appear less exceptional than he really was. Of course no one knew beforehand that such a phenomenal record was about to be made; for had such an unusual result been expected this child would have been kept for examination under more favorable laboratory conditions.[2] For an account of this testing, see under "Mental measurements," page 140.

[1] See Preface, pages xi-xii.

[2] EDITOR'S NOTE. This child was observed by Leta S. Hollingworth over a period of nearly a quarter century. She published three accounts of his

134

FAMILY BACKGROUND

Little or nothing is known of E's paternal relatives. His father was separated from them before the age of recollection.

Of E's maternal ancestry fairly complete genealogical records are available.[3] Five persons bearing the surname of the mother settled in New England before 1650. These were probably all related to each other. The individual who was E's direct ancestor first appeared in New England in 1639 and settled at Cambridge, Massachusetts. This family attained great distinction in the six generations recorded in the New England genealogy. A son of the first ancestor in America was a royal councilor and the greatest merchant of his day in New England. A grandson was royal governor of Massachusetts, and later of New Jersey; he was also a patron of learning. A great-grandson was chief justice and lieutenant governor of Nova Scotia. A great-great-grandson was a royal councilor of Nova Scotia; some of his children settled again in England, of whom a son was a distinguished naval officer, attaining the rank of

development, and the present chapter is in the main a composite of these three reports, to which are added such supplementary items as are available. The articles referred to are as follows:

Garrison, Burke, and Hollingworth. "The Psychology of a Prodigious Child." *Journal of Applied Psychology* (June, 1917).

Hollingworth, Garrison, and Burke. "Subsequent History of E—— Five Years after the Initial Report." *Journal of Applied Psychology* (June, 1922).

Hollingworth, Leta S. "Subsequent History of E—— Ten Years after the Initial Report." *Journal of Applied Psychology* (October, 1927).

[3] Bartlett, J. G. "The Belcher Families in New England." *New England History and General Register,* Vol. 60, pages 125–136, 243–256, 358–364.

Belcher, Jonathan. "The Belcher Papers." *Collection of the Massachusetts Historical Society,* Vols. 6 and 7.

Appleton's *Cyclopedia of American Biography,* Vol. 1 (1887). (Jonathan Belcher.)

rear admiral in the British navy. These genealogical records, and other records of New England families which intermarried with this family, have not been brought up to date.

The maternal surname appears first about 1176 in the records of England, and was apparently Norman-French in origin. The remote male ancestor [4] from whom the mother of E derives the middle part of her maiden name was born in Providence, Rhode Island, March 11, 1753, a descendant of early colonial settlers in America. He was graduated from Rhode Island College (now Brown University) in 1773 and later took a medical degree at the University of Pennsylvania. In 1783 he was appointed Professor of Materia Medica and Botany at Brown. In 1819 he was elected a delegate from the Rhode Island Medical Society, of which he was vice president, to the convention which formulated the National Pharmacopoeia. He took an active part in the organization and proceedings of the Rhode Island Society for the Encouragement of Domestic Industry. In 1824, with his son, William, he published *The Farmer's Guide*, "a comprehensive work on husbandry and gardening." He participated in the Proceedings of the American Academy of Arts and Sciences, and delivered many lectures on botany. He died at the age of 81 years, leaving among descendants a large proportion of persons in the learned professions.

Father. E's father, while still a college undergraduate, produced a Latin play which was performed in a Boston theater. Since graduation from college he has maintained a

---

[4] Drowne, Henry R. "Family Record of Solomon Drowne." *New York Genealogical and Biographical Record*, Vol. 5, No. 35, pages 171–172. New York; 1904.

Drowne, Henry T. *Genealogy of the Family of Solomon Drowne, M. D., of Providence, Rhode Island, with Notice of His Ancestors, 1646–1879.* Providence Press Company, Providence, Rhode Island; 1879.

keen interest in educational matters. He organized a special library of insurance in Boston which is now used as a reference library all over the world. He is at present [1939] engaged in business; has written several books; is a university lecturer on insurance; has served on many important city commissions. Unusual mental endowment is clearly indicated by the fact that he rose entirely by his own direction and effort to a post of honor in an intricate field of knowledge. He was 45 years old when E was born.

Mother. E's mother was a qualified physician and a specialist in bacteriology. For some years she held a position as bacteriologist in one of the municipal departments of New York City. After the birth of her son she devoted a great deal of attention to his education and welfare, keeping records of his development, supervising his health, and acting as his teacher. She often accompanied him to school, sometimes registered for courses along with him, or herself took courses calculated to make her more useful in his training. She gave an exceptional amount of attention to his formal educational program and cultivated with him numerous extracurricular intellectual activities. During E's college career the two were often seen together on the campus.

EARLY HISTORY [5]

E was his parents' fourth child, three girls having been born before him, all having died. Birth was difficult. He was bottle fed. His parents were both in middle life at the time of his birth. He cut his first tooth at 8 months — a lateral incisor. He walked at thirteen months.

[5] Developmental history and history of personal health were elicited from the mother, who, being a physician, is especially competent to speak on these points. The family history and the facts concerning his extra-school linguistic achievements were also given by the mother.

Up to the age of 2 years E did not say a word. He then began to talk, and before he was 3 years old was able to read such books as *Peter Rabbit*. Conversation with him was carried on in German, French, Italian, and English equally. When he did begin to talk he could say in these four languages all the words he knew.

Health. E's health has been exceptionally good from infancy. He has had no disorders or diseases except measles, and an occasional attack of indigestion. He is exceptionally free from colds.

Physical measurements. The figures given below as *averages* are for a boy of 8 years 4 months who is the same height as E. The average height for a boy of this age is 49.7 inches. The measurements here given for E were transcribed from the gymnasium records of the school he was then attending.

MEASUREMENTS	CHILD E OCTOBER 30, 1916	AVERAGE FOR AGE 8 YEARS 4 MONTHS AT HEIGHT 54.3 INCHES
Weight	89.3 pounds	70.5 pounds
Height	54.3 inches	54.3 inches
Girth of chest	31.8 inches	25.6 inches
Girth of chest, expanded	32.4 inches	26.8 inches
Lung capacity	100.0 cubic inches	112.0 cubic inches
Strength, right forearm	30.9 pounds	39.7 pounds
Strength, left forearm	22.0 pounds	37.5 pounds

It will thus be seen that E is considerably larger than the average boy of his age, though of less lung capacity and forearm strength.

Other characteristics. E has clear, well-molded features. He does not like physical exercise of any kind but has had special attention along this line, such as lessons in swimming, dancing, and horseback riding. He sleeps eleven hours and goes to sleep immediately upon going to bed.

SCHOOL ACHIEVEMENT

E went to kindergarten from the age of 3 years to the age of 5 years. From 5 to 6 he was out of school on account of school organization (he could not be accepted in the first grade). From 6 to 7 years he attended an open-air, ungraded school and did the work of the second to the fourth grades. From 7 to 8 years he was in the fourth grade in regular school classes, and at the time of first observation by the writer, when he was 8 years old, he was in the sixth grade.

He was thus three full years accelerated in school grading, according to age-grade norms, but was still three years retarded in school according to his Mental Age. (Terman makes special note of the fact that superior children are almost invariably retarded in school grading according to Mental Age.) His mother stated that under private tutors E had at this time covered the work of the seventh and nearly all the work of the eighth grade. His school standing, on his last report preceding this initial account, was as follows (the highest attainable rating is 1, the lowest, 4):

Courtesy	1	Composition	2	Penmanship	3
Promptness	1	Grammar or		Industrial Arts	1[7]
System	1	Language	2	Fine Arts	4[8]
Spelling	2	Mathematics	3[6]	Music	2
Reading or		Geography	1	Physical Educa-	
Literature	1	History	1	tion	4
				Science	1

[6] Private tutors grade E as 1 in mathematics.

[7] In industrial arts credit is given for *knowing* industrial processes, as well as for ability to carry out the processes.

[8] In fine arts credit is given for manual dexterity only.

In addition to his regular school work E, by the time he was 8 years old, had covered the following special work in language and mathematics, either with a tutor or with his mother:

Mathematics: Algebra as far as equations; geometry.

Latin: Partial knowledge of the four declensions (he has been taught by the direct, informal method, and reads easy Latin).

Greek: Worked out the alphabet for himself from an astronomical chart, between the ages of 5 and 6 years.

French: Equal to about two years in the ordinary school.

German: Ordinary conversation.

Spanish: Attended class with his mother — reads and understands.

Italian: Reading knowledge and simple conversation.

Portuguese: Asked his mother to take this course at the Columbia Summer School because he could not be registered himself.

Hebrew: A beginning.

Anglo-Saxon: A beginning.

Astronomy: He has worked out all the constellations from Mac-Cready, and displays a very great interest in this subject.

One evening this winter he noticed a new planet near the Twins. He said it was Saturn but his mother thought it was Mars. E went home, worked the position out from the chart and found it to be Saturn.

Miscellaneous: He has a great interest in nature, wherever found, and is already able to use Apgar intelligently.

His writing is not equal to his other accomplishments. He is very slow at it and for this reason dictates most of his "home work" to a stenographer.

History is his chief and absorbing interest among school subjects.

MENTAL MEASUREMENTS

At the time E was first tested, at Teachers College, Columbia University, in November, 1916, the Stanford revision of the Binet-Simon measuring scale was used for the determination of the child's mental level.

General intelligence. The examiner [L. S. H.] began with the "ball-in-the-field" test. E responded at once with the superior solution, thus giving a preliminary cue to the quality of his mind, and the examiner proceeded immediately with the other tests at the 12-year level of intellect. E passed all the 12-year tests with facility and ease, giving responses of excellent quality. From the 12-year level the examiner then worked forward in all the higher levels through Superior Adult. This is, of course, a long examination, and in view of the actual age of the child it was deemed best to give the tests at two separate sittings, when it was seen that he would cover the whole upper range of the scale. The examination was therefore accomplished in two sittings of about fifty minutes each. The final record of E shows that he measures on the scale as follows:

	YEARS	MONTHS
Levels 1 year to 7 years............	....	....
8	....	....
9	....	....
10	....	....
12	12	....
14	....	16
Adult	....	15
Superior Adult......	....	12
Total	15	7

Since his actual age is 8 years 4 months and his Mental Age is 15 years 7 months, his IQ is 187. On the curve of the distribution of intellect he stands eleven times the probable error (11 PE) removed from the norm, a position occupied by but one child in more than a million. He stands as far removed from the average in the direction of superiority as an idiot stands removed from the average in the direction of inferiority.

An analysis of his performance shows that E has extraordinary appreciation of the exact use of words and of the shades of difference between words. He gave correct meanings for 64 words out of the 100 in the vocabulary test. His vocabulary thus includes 11,520 words. The score of the Average Adult is 65 words. Thus he just missed scoring on this Average Adult test. Samples of his definitions are as follows:

scorch — is what happens to a thing when exposed to great heat.
quake — is a kind of movement, unintended.
ramble — is a walk taken for pleasure.
nerve — is a thing you feel by — for instance, cold.
majesty — is a word used to address a king — your majesty.
Mars — is a planet.
peculiarity — is something you do that nobody else does.
mosaic — is a picture made of many small pieces of marble.
bewail — is to be extremely sorrowful.
tolerate — is to allow others to do what you don't like yourself.
lotus — is a kind of flower.
harpy — is a kind of half-bird, half-woman, referred to in Virgil.
fen — is a kind of marsh.
laity — is *not* clergy.
ambergris — it comes from a whale.
straw — the stalk of a cereal plant.
lecture — someone giving a very long talk about something to an audience.

E also has a prodigious ability for comprehending and formulating abstract ideas, and for working with symbols. He gave the differences between the abstract concepts under Average Adult as follows:

a — laziness and idleness. Laziness is that you don't *want* to work; idleness is that you *can't*, for a while.

b — evolution and revolution. Evolution is making things from the beginning; revolution is changing them.

c — poverty and misery. Poverty is when you don't have anything; misery is how you feel when someone insults you.

d — character and reputation. Character is what he *really* is; reputation is what they *think* he is.

E succeeded in reversing the clock hands three times without any error in less than a minute for each trial. He was able to reproduce the thought from the selection beginning "Many opinions have been given about the value of life" as well as a Superior Adult. He solved the three mental arithmetic problems under XIV, 5, in less than a minute each, absolutely without error. These performances serve to illustrate his precocious power over symbols and over abstractions.

His attention, concentration, and capacity for sustained effort are illustrated by the fact that he was able to repeat five digits backward twice out of three trials absolutely without error, before a class of thirty adults. His memory span for digits repeated forward is at least 8. (He was not tried with more than 8 digits.)

During the examination he showed neither embarrassment nor any tendency to "show off." He was alert, interested, and gave his attention strictly to the business in hand. He always knew when he had failed on a test, and gave up with great reluctance. For example, he was unable to solve the problems under XVIII, 6, in the time allotted; but he carried these data away in his head, and held to them tenaciously till he had solved the problems. In several instances after he had given his reply he recast it in better form. In short, he exemplified in remarkable degree all the characteristics which Binet finally chose as symptomatic of intellectual power; i.e., (1) the ability to make and maintain a given direction; (2) the capacity to make adaptations for the purpose of obtaining a desired end; and (3) the power of autocriticism.

Special tests. Following the procedure described by Seashore, and using the set of forks recommended by him, E was tested for pitch discrimination, being given seven trials with the whole series of forks. His record was as follows, # meaning a correct answer and — meaning a false one.

SERIES	VIBRATION DIFFERENCES									
	30	23	17	12	8	5	3	2	1	.5
1	#	#	#	#	#	#	#	#	#	#
2	#	#	—	#	#	#	#	#	—	—
3	#	#	#	#	#	—	#	—	—	#
4	#	#	#	#	#	—	#	—	#	—
5	#	#	#	#	#	#	#	#	—	—
6	#	#	#	#	#	—	#	#	#	—
7	#	#	#	#	#	—	#	—	#	#

His threshold for pitch discrimination would thus seem to be not greater than five vibrations, and would probably be found to be as low as three if a more complete test were possible. This is a very good record, according to Seashore's standards.

E gave free associations to the first 50 words of the Kent-Rosanoff list of words, both stimulus and response words being oral. The stimulus words and responses follow:

STIMULUS	RESPONSE	STIMULUS	RESPONSE	STIMULUS	RESPONSE
table	dinner	smooth	surface	needle	slim
dark	night	command	army	red	color
music	soft	chair	cushion	sleep	fast
sickness	fatal	sweet	sugar	anger	sick
man	tall	whistle	blew	carpet	bagger
deep	ocean	woman	lady	girl	pretty
soft	couch	cold	coal	high	mountain
eating	dinner	slow	train	working	people
mountain	snowcapped	wish	I	sour	lemon
house	brick	river	Hudson	earth	big
black	dog	white	color	trouble	great
mutton	beef	beautiful	dress	soldier	brave
comfort	your	window	glass	cabbage	green
hand	dirty	rough	surface	hard	surface
short	man	citizen	U. S.	eagle	swift
fruit	orange	foot	bare	stomach	ache
butterfly	moth	spider	black		

At once after giving some of these responses E explained why he had given them. Thus he explained that "carpet bagger" had to do "with Civil War history." After giving "beef" in response to "mutton" he smiled and said, "That's a joke, isn't it?" When asked why he thought it a joke he replied that he thought very few people would give that answer. After the test he was told that 97 people in a thousand gave "beef" in response to "mutton," and he at once said, "Ten per cent, that's not so very many."

It was impossible, for lack of time, to give E the complete list of 100 words usually given in this test. Using the 50 as a basis for calculation, 78 per cent of the responses are "common responses" in the Kent-Rosanoff sense of the word, a number of common responses which children do not usually show until after the age of 10 years. His "median of community" (a measure not yet standardized for age levels) is 1.4 per cent.

E was given the Pintner form of the Knox Cube Test, and achieved 11 of the 12 lines arranged by Pintner. The average record for the 16-year-old is only 8 lines, and this is the highest level for which this test is yet standardized.

The usual "tapping" test was given, tapping continuously with the right hand, with the stylus, for one minute. The record was 239 taps only, which is lower than the average 8-year-old record.

Given three minutes in which to make up words out of the letters A-E-I-R-L-P, E made the following: a, rip, pie, lie, ale.

He was given thirty minutes in which to put together the pieces in the Stenquist Construction Box II, and was not able to put any of the pieces together. He began at one end of the box, examined each set of materials in turn, tried to put them together in an indiscriminate way, put them back, and went on to the next set of materials. He remarked, "I don't seem to be able to put any of them together. It seems that all I can do is to find out what each of the things is for." He recognized that various sets of pieces were "a mousetrap," "a lock," "a bell," etc., but made a zero score from the point of view of construction. At the end of twenty minutes he gave up and turned away from the materials.

It is interesting to compare the child's record in construction tests and his comments regarding these tests, with his school record in industrial arts and fine arts. E receives the best possible rating in industrial arts because he has keen insight into processes and can explain how to construct a mechanism or perform an operation clearly and minutely, though he is unable to carry out his own instructions. For instance, he can tell exactly how to make a boat, but he cannot make the boat himself. There is thus an interesting distinction here between "constructive ability" and "manual dexterity." Similarly, in fine arts E has many ideas for decorative schemes, but he is unable to execute these ideas with his hands.

SOCIAL HABITS, TASTES, ETC.

E does not care to play, and would never do so unless forced. He is very impersonal and agreeable in his attitude toward other children. His chief diversion is reading and his favorite book at the age of 8 is *Ivanhoe*. He has no hobbies at this age. In the spring of 1916, after careful and thoughtful preparation, he was confirmed in the Episcopal church. His desire is to be a clergyman and to become a missionary. When asked what he would consider the most fun in life, he replied, "To have statistics of my imaginary country." This country is on Venus. It is inhabited by people and has a navy like ours. E does not volunteer much information about his interests. All these items had to be elicited by questioning.

LATER MENTAL MEASUREMENTS

In the spring of 1920 E took the Thorndike Mental Tests for Freshmen, for entrance to Columbia College. An official letter from the Director of Admissions at Columbia College states that, "In the Freshmen Tests he was number two, out of 483 entering Columbia College." He was at this time 12 years 0 months old; the median age of his competitors was about 18 years.

On September 29, 1921, E was examined by means of the Army Alpha (Forms 5 and 6, examiner L. S. H.) for the purpose of recording his mental development. On Alpha, Form 5, he made a score of 194 points, finishing several of the tests, without error, before the time limit. On Form 6, which was taken subsequently, on the same afternoon, his score was 201 points; and with these, too, some of the tests were finished in about two thirds of the time allowed, without error. As the method of scoring Alpha does not provide for a time bonus, this cannot be taken into account in the formal score.

In April, 1927, at the request of the writer [L. S. H.] E took the tests of the IER Intelligence Scale CAVD, Levels M–Q. This series of tests is described in a recent publication.[9] Briefly it may be said here that this instrument was chosen for the purpose in hand because it is the most thorough method available for approximating in quantitative terms the intelligence of the best among college graduates.

E's score on this test, at Levels M–Q, was 441 points. The score of the average adult is not yet known, but the median score of college graduates in professional schools of first-rate standards is 415 points, with an upper quartile at 421 points. The best scores yet made by college graduates hover about 440 points.[10]

Thus E rates plus 4 PE in relation to college graduates in first-rate professional schools, ranking with the best minds revealed in any group so far tested. These groups may each be expected to include some of the best intellects existing. The comparative groups are, of course, older than E. Some of them are composed of persons over 30 years of age on the average, while all are past 20 years. E was 18 years 9 months of age on the date when he took the test, in comparison with these groups. The number of years lived in an

[9] Thorndike, E. L. *The Measurement of Intelligence.* Bureau of Publications, Teachers College, Columbia University, New York; 1927.

[10] I am indebted to Dr. Ella Woodyard and to Professor Ralph B. Spence of Teachers College, Columbia University, for this information.

intellectual environment, other things being equal, probably affects results to some extent in favor of those who have lived longer.

A score of 441 points on the IER Scale corresponds to a score of about 116 points on the more widely known Thorndike Tests for College Freshmen. The top one per cent of college graduates make a score of 108 or better on the latter test. E, therefore, surely rates at least in the top one quarter of one per cent of college graduates. [E, it will be noted, was at this time at the average age of college freshmen.]

At the age of 8 years E rated plus 11 PE in general intelligence (by Stanford-Binet) as compared with the generality of 8-year-olds. It seems likely that in these later measurements he rated at about the same status, in relation to the generality of 18-year-olds, since his status is plus 4.3 PE in relation to highly selected groups of college graduates.

E, at the age of 18, was probably mature — or nearly mature — intellectually. However, in view of recent findings in regard to the growth of intelligence among pupils in high schools, we cannot be sure that at this age he has quite reached the maximum of possible accretions of power from inner growth.[11]

LATER PHYSICAL MEASUREMENTS

On September 29, 1921, E's physical measurements were as follows:

Standing height .... 64.2 inches
Sitting height .... 31.7 inches
Weight (summer clothing) .... 166 pounds

[11] Thorndike, E. L. "On the Improvement in Intelligence Scores from Fourteen to Eighteen." *Journal of Educational Psychology* (1923).

At this time his health continued to be excellent; in fact, he has never had a serious illness of any kind.

E was measured again in October, 1926. By this time he had probably achieved his maximum stature. His age was then 18 years 4 months. He was still in excellent health, the only illness in the intervening five years being a "light case" of scarlet fever. At this time the measurements were:

Standing height ....6 feet 1 inch
Weight (stripped) ....194.75 pounds

LATER SCHOLASTIC RECORDS

In the spring of 1917 E finished the sixth, seventh, eighth, and ninth grade work at the Horace Mann School, New York City. He was then just 9 years old. Thereafter he attended the Friends Seminary, New York City, and was graduated from the high school there in the spring of 1920, with an excellent record and excess credits, at the age of 11 years 10 months.

By this time E had also passed the comprehensive examinations of the College Entrance Board for Harvard College. The official communication from Harvard authorities, making statement to this effect, has been seen by the writer. E's maternal ancestors had attended Harvard (one of them having graduated from there at the age of 18 years, according to records), but E expressed a desire to attend Columbia and received permission to take the mental tests with the applicants of 1920. He was admitted to Columbia College with the freshmen of 1920, with 14 points of advance credit toward a B.A. degree.

There is at hand an official statement of E's academic status on June 1, 1921, at the age of not quite 13 years. He had then 46 points of academic credit toward a B.A. degree in Columbia College. During his freshman year he made 32 points, maintaining consistently a grade of B, except in two subjects. In physical education his rating was C, and in contemporary civilization he made A the first semester.[12]

E attended the summer session of 1921 at Columbia, making five credit points, all A grade, and in September, 1921, was a sophomore with many points of credit in advance of minimum sophomore status. In addition to having passed the comprehensive examinations for college entrance, he had passed the examinations in trigonometry, solid geometry, chemistry, and physics, and was at this time 13 years 3 months of age.

EXTRACURRICULAR ACTIVITIES

E was of course a conspicuous freshman because of his extreme youth, and he was hazed by the sophomores for refusing to wear a prescribed necktie. One of the New York newspapers commented on his conduct under hazing as follows:

> He has demonstrated that he is nevertheless a regular fellow. He did it first by bringing about a conflict in which he himself was the much buffeted prize of battle, and then by glorying in his bruises instead of making them the basis of a grievance. He is a good sport as well as a good scholar, and being both he ought to go far.

[12] It is worth saying that in contemporary civilization the final examination had been objectively standardized by Dr. B. D. Wood, expert in educational measurement, and did not depend on the estimate of instructors. "E's score on the objective examinations of both terms was in the highest tenth of the highest percentile" (B. D. W.). The instructor's estimate, as well as the result of the objective examination, enters into the term grade and, indicated above, in this course; so that the final grade in the second semester is but B.

E also participated in the class play, given in 1921, humorously consenting to impersonate himself.

Manual work had no more charm for him at this date than it had when he was 8 years old.   That he *can* work with his hands and with materials when motivated is suggested by an incident connected with the Liberty Bond drive.   His teacher relates that E wanted to pay for his own bond; so he made jelly, working at it until very good jelly was made, and sold it for the purpose specified.

In recent years E has developed a keen interest in detective stories.

TEACHERS' COMMENTS

Comments from E's teachers during the last five years up to this date [1921] are indicative of their estimates:

The regular course of study has been so easy that he has, in several subjects, notably English and history, accomplished a great amount of voluntary work outside the course.

An excellent mixer with other students.

His weekly visits have been a pleasure and anticipation, and his ability to understand without English the spoken Latin and the authors as I have read them aloud to him has been extraordinary.

Has done very remarkable work in science, particularly in theory.

I predict for him a great scholastic record in college.

I consider it a privilege to have had something to do with teaching him.

Possesses a *power* in Latin that few persons ten years his senior can boast.

Has shown devotion to the best interests of the school.

SUMMARY UP TO 1921

In the five years which have elapsed since E was first tested mentally he has shown no tendency to become mediocre. His gifts have not grown less; he maintains his superior status in mental tests. As for achievement, he has passed during this interval from the sixth grade of the elementary school, half through the second year of college. Average children, the country over, born when this child was born, and measuring 100 IQ when he measured 187 IQ, are now in the seventh grade of the elementary schools.

E still wishes to be a clergyman and to go abroad as a missionary. To this end he interests himself especially in history, the languages, and anthropology.

It is an interesting theoretical question as to how far human intelligence may vary from the norm in the direction of superiority. The case of this child has been placed on record largely because it seems probable that such cases represent very nearly the extreme possible limit of variation in the human species as it now exists.

At 8 years of age his IQ stood at plus 11 PE (1 PE being, according to Terman, equal to 8 IQ [13]). The probabilities are usually regarded as slight that cases beyond 5 PE will occur. Perhaps the range in human intellect is much greater than probabilities would lead us to guess.

Since the initial report of this child's qualities, readers have occasionally asked with what meaning the word "prodigious" was used in reference to him. It was used in the dictionary sense of "wonderful," "extraordinary."

In these reports there is no intention to approve or to disapprove the educational regimen pursued. Who knows what should be the educational treatment of a child standing at

[13] See note, foot of page xii.

11 PE in intellect? The sole intention is to record the identification and development of a deviation so extreme that the chances are theoretically almost nil that it would occur at all.

EVENTUAL SCHOLASTIC RECORDS

In June, 1923, E was graduated from Columbia College, with the degree of B.A. He took general honors, Phi Beta Kappa honors, and the English Seminary Prize, awarded by the Society for Promoting Religion and Learning "for the best essay in sermon form on an assigned topic." He was within eleven days of his fifteenth birthday when he was graduated. He was elected to Phi Beta Kappa at the age of 14 years, probably the youngest person ever elected to that organization.

E was graduated with excess credit (8 points) toward the M.A. degree. This degree was awarded him in June, 1924, when he was not quite 16 years of age, more than enough work for it having been accomplished. He was matriculated for the Ph.D. degree before he was 16 years old, and by the age of 18 years 9 months had practically finished all the requirements for that degree except completing the dissertation. The dissertation topic had been then approved, in the field of history, and E was at work on the material.

In October, 1926 (aged 18 years 4 months), E entered upon his professional studies for the ministry in the theological seminary of his choice. Since the age of 15 he had done special work at the seminary. He had read prayers in one of the city churches as a lay reader since the age of 16 and was at this time a candidate for ordination as deacon, but this ordination could not take place before the twenty-first birthday.

In the initial report of E it will be found that he had decided before he was 5 years old to be a clergyman.   It now
appeared that his professional course toward that end would
be completed in 1929.

Professional course will be finished in 1929

The subject of the thesis, on which I am now working, is definitely approved and published (decided June, 1925); the other requirements are practically finished.

Appolonius, Diocetes of Egypt (3rd century B.C. Egyptian history, 1923)
Worked on order of Pliny's letters (1924-25)
At present reading Greek papyri.
Making my turn in Modern European History, worked on Irish constitutional history (1924-1925)

Fig. 12. A Memorandum from E.

RESEARCHES OF E

When E was 10 years old he made an original contribution in connection with the Pentateuch, and was made a
member of The Oriental Society of Research in Jerusalem.

At 13 years of age E was first admitted to the Bodleian
Library, at Oxford, for purposes of research.

In 1923 E presented his M.A. essay — "Appolonius,
Diocetes of Egypt" — which pertains to Egyptian history of
the third century B.C. and is on file in the Library of Columbia University.

E has also done research (1924–1925) on the order of
Pliny's letters; on Irish constitutional history (1924–1925);
and was in 1926 and 1927 reading Greek papyri.

The subject of his dissertation to be submitted in partial

fulfillment of the requirements for the Ph.D. was reported as "Feudal Estates in Byzantine Egypt." [14]

SUMMARY OF DEVELOPMENT

A summary of E's development over the period from 1916 to 1927, given in the table on the opposite page, shows clearly that the superior magnitudes, both of mental caliber and of physical size, so markedly present at the age of 8 years, are maintained as growth terminates.

EDITOR'S SUPPLEMENT

Although no follow-up inquiry has been made since the year 1927, a few items gleaned from clippings found in the author's files are relevant. These are newspaper accounts, chiefly in connection with E's being ordained as deacon, and later elevated to the Protestant Episcopal priesthood. These articles recite that E —

Received his B.A. at the age of 15 years.

Received his M.A. degree the following year.

Was ordained deacon on December 21, 1929, at the age of 21.

Received his Ph.D. the following year at the age of 22.

Also received the degree Bachelor of Sacred Theology, in June, 1929.

[14] EDITOR'S NOTE. This dissertation was published in 1931 by the Columbia University Press under the title *Large Estates of Byzantine Egypt*.

Among later publications, of which there is record in the files, are:

"National Elements in the Career of St. Athanasius," *Church History*, pages 3–11 (December, 1933).

"Dura — An Ancient City of the East," *Natural History* (The Journal of the American Museum of Natural History), Vol. XXXIV, No. 8, pages 685–701 (December, 1934).

Militant in Earth. Pages 255. Oxford University Press, New York; 1940. A book which "shows how Christianity has presented a spiritual and social front against opposing phases of civilization, whatever they may have been during 2000 years."

	Child E	Norms for Private Schools [15]
Born June 17, 1908, as shown by birth certificate and hospital records		
November 4, 1916		
Height	54.3 inches	49.5 inches
Weight	89.3 pounds	54.2 pounds
Intellect	IQ 187 (S–B)	IQ 100 (S–B)
Scholastic status	6th grade, elementary	3d grade, elementary
September 29, 1921		
Height	64.2 inches	58.2 inches
Weight	166.0 pounds	89.5 pounds
Intellect	194 points, Army Alpha, Form 5	47 points, Army Alpha
Scholastic status	4th semester, college	8th grade, elementary school
October 26, 1926		
Height	73 inches	67 inches
Weight	194.7 pounds	150 pounds
April 1, 1927		
Intellect	441 points, IER Tests	Not yet known
Scholastic status	B.A. 1923 M.A. 1924 Ph.D. candidate Also finishing first year in Theological Seminary	Has left school to go to work

Was elevated to the priesthood in the Protestant Episcopal Church at the age of 24 (June 19, 1932) at a special ordination service at the Cathedral of St. John the Divine, New York City.

[15] Norms for height, weight, and scholastic status are taken from B. T. Baldwin, as established at Horace Mann School, Francis Parker School, and the elementary and high schools of the University of Chicago.

As a graduate student too young for the priesthood, he had held a fellowship in the General Theological Seminary, teaching Greek and history.

There is also an announcement of his marriage in September, 1939.

See also Editor's Note on publications, foot of page 156.

Chapter Nine

CHILD F

CHILD F was a boy whose ability was identified as the result of a mental survey made with group tests in P.S. 14, Manhattan.[1] His score in these tests was unbelievable, and he was summoned for testing with the idea that he must have been coached. An individual Stanford-Binet test, however, showed a phenomenal record similar to all other tests given him, including an Army Alpha. He was referred to a Special Opportunity Class at that time being organized in P.S. 165, Manhattan.

FAMILY BACKGROUND

Although detailed study of F's ancestry is available, a brief summary of the facts appears to be all that is here needed, for the ancestry throws little light on the boy's extraordinary mental ability.

F's paternal grandfather was of Scottish parentage, born in Canada. He was a reasonably successful worker in the printing trade, appears to have been well balanced and socially adjusted, and showed no exceptional traits. He had little education and no special interests. He died of apoplexy at 51 years of age.

[1] This chapter was written by H. L. H.

F's paternal grandmother, born in Albany, New York, had a public school education (probably). She is still living [1924], clerking in a store after her husband's death. She appears to have no special interests outside her home life; is said to be quick and nervous, easily excited, and prone to worry.

F's maternal grandfather was born in New York State, of German parentage. He is still alive [1924], at the age of 70, and is very active. His education was limited, but he is an excellent reader and is well informed. He is fond of music, is an active churchman and a choir leader. He is said to be quick-tempered, impulsive, and affectionate. He mixes well with people, and has some leadership qualities. He has always worked as a paper hanger and painter, his business being on a small scale.

F's maternal grandmother was born in New York State; the nationality of her parents is not recorded. She had a public school education. Her interests are limited to home and Red Cross activities. She is friendly and sociable, impulsive, affectionate in disposition, and has a keen sense of humor.

F has several uncles and aunts, none of whom presents any qualities of striking interest. All appear to be normally effective and well adjusted, competent on a small-town scale, enjoying their homes, and taking part in local activities and organizations.

F has one brother, younger than himself, born April 2, 1920. He was given a Stanford-Binet examination, May 13, 1924, by Leta S. Hollingworth, being then 4 years 1 month of age. His Mental Age was 6-0, yielding an IQ of 147. This brother has strong musical inclinations, was a choir boy, and subsequently took instruction in singing.

Father.   The father of Child F was born in Albany, New York.   He had a high school education and business college training.   He has always done clerical and office work, especially bookkeeping.   He is fond of athletics, reads only newspapers and magazines, is quick, alert, and active, has an even temperament, is seldom worried.   He has no interest in clubs or organized activities.   Seems to take an interest in his children.   (In later years the father lost the balance and evenness of temperament here reported and became unemployed much of the time.   He died in March, 1935, at the age of 41, "apparently accidentally drowned.")

Mother.   The mother of F went to high school for two years and earned a teacher's certificate.   She taught two years in rural schools but disliked this work and had no patience with children.   She liked music, however, and studied piano and voice for a short time, but now pays little attention to it. She has always regretted going to high school, believing that if she had devoted that time to music, she might have had some success in it.   Her interests are limited to home affairs. She says she has few friends and does not mix well with people.   She appears calm and does not worry, is sensible in her dealings with her children, takes no part in organized activities, but always sends the children to Sunday School. She is a very good home manager, and runs things effectively on small resources.

PRESCHOOL HISTORY

F was born in upper New York State, November 14, 1914. The period of gestation was of normal length; at birth he weighed according to the father 9 pounds, according to the mother 11.5 pounds.   No records of early infancy were kept, so that many such details are given from memory, either by the father or by the mother. The child was the mother's first-born. She reports that much of the infant's weight at birth was due to his enormous head, which necessitated instrument birth. Birth was difficult, the mother was severely injured, and the child's head "was so distorted from the instruments that it was weeks before it could be molded into normal shape."

F was bottle fed from birth to one year. His first teeth appeared at about 10 months. He talked (short sentences) at about 12 months, learned to walk alone (several steps) at 14 months, learned to read at between 4 and 5 years of age. His childhood illnesses were measles, whooping cough, chicken pox, and scarlet fever, all between 6 and 8 years of age. Cried little as a baby. His mother says "he was a lovely baby to take care of." No sensory defects or signs of physical weakness. Adenoids were present, to be removed shortly after the initial interview in 1924 (age 10 years). He sleeps soundly.

EARLY SCHOOL HISTORY

F started school at the age of 5 years 10 months, in a two-room rural school in upstate New York in the town where he was born. He could already read well at that time; it was first noticed that he could read when he was "around 5 years of age." Riding in streetcars, he would take words apart and put them together again. He had learned the letters before his third year.

At school he was received in the first grade. It was soon found that he was memorizing his reader and the teacher gave him a more advanced book. This school was a practically ungraded one; the first four grades were together in one room, and grades five to eight were in the other room.

The teacher did not know what to do with F; so he was allowed to go into the second room and listen, in an orderly manner, to the fifth to eighth grades.

When he entered New York City schools at the age of 7 years 10 months, the rural teacher gave F a transfer for the fifth grade. The mother presented the letter of transfer to the Manhattan principal, who pooh-poohed the idea that the boy could belong in the fifth grade at that age. He refused to accept the recommendation from the ungraded school and placed F in the third or fourth grade. After the first week the boy's teacher reported that he did not belong in that grade. When the principal insisted that F could not go into the fifth grade, the boy himself spoke up and said if they would give him an examination they would see that he could do it. The principal ordered him to keep still and not to talk so much. He was, however, eventually placed in the fifth grade in the year in which his eighth birthday occurred. At the end of that year he was promoted to Grade 6A, then into 6B, and he was shortly after received into the Special Opportunity Class at P.S. 165.

He had always been fond of school up to this time, although he later developed a distaste for it and became a chronic truant. He spent much of his time helping the teachers, carrying books, and running errands, in order to keep occupied. When his mother requested his transfer to the Special Opportunity Class, the principal of the school he was attending, at first refused, saying that he liked to have bright pupils in his classes too. After futilely arguing for half an hour, the mother finally threatened to move to another part of town, thus forcing a transfer, whereupon the principal relented and gave the transfer. F said he liked the new school because he was allowed there to say what he thought.

In his early school years he once won a prize, which was to be a book. Several books, supposedly of interest to boys, were offered him from which to choose. He looked them over and then said if it made no difference to the teacher, he would rather have a dictionary instead. This volume was given him, and it was used constantly thereafter.

EARLY TEST SCORES

In March, 1924, at the age of 9 years 4 months, F was given a mental test, using Army Alpha, by L. M. Potter. He was then in Grade 6B, P.S. 14, Manhattan. His score was recorded as 124 points. But there is also a copy of an Army Alpha Test, Form 7, given F in the fall of 1924 upon his entrance to P.S. 165, on which the score is 163 points.

On April 14, 1924, at the age of 9 years 5 months, F was given a Stanford-Binet test by M. V. Cobb, in P.S. 165, Manhattan. His Mental Age shown at that time was 15–2, and an IQ of 162 was reported. Strength of grip measures were also recorded as of May 15, 1924. These were made by Leta S. Hollingworth, three trials for each hand. The records were (median of three), right, 10.5; left, 9.

On April 22, 1925, at the age of 10 years 5 months, F was given a Stanford-Binet examination by Leta S. Hollingworth as a demonstration before a class of 60 adults. His Mental Age was 19–0, and the IQ is recorded as "over 182, unmeasured by the scale."

On May 8, 1926, at the age of 11 years 6 months, F was again tested with the Stanford-Binet [by L. S. H.]. He passed at this time all the Superior Adult tests and was thus unmeasured. He was at this time in his first year of senior high school.

January 7, 1933, at the age of 18–2, while a college freshman, his score on Army Alpha, Form 8, was 198 points.

Music tests. F showed no active musical interests but became very fond of listening to good music, being particularly fond of string quartets. As was the case in every field to which his interests turned, he quickly acquired a fund of information about it which he took pleasure in exhibiting.

F was given the Seashore Music Tests four times [by L. S. H.] over a period of 11 years. Perhaps the record of these successive examinations will have some intrinsic interest, and such a tabulation is here provided.

SEASHORE TESTS OF MUSICAL TALENT SCORE (Per Cent Correct)

	MAY 7, 1924 9 YEARS 6 MONTHS	DECEMBER 23, 1924 10 YEARS 1 MONTH	JUNE 18, 1925 10 YEARS 7 MONTHS	JUNE 14, 1935 20 YEARS 7 MONTHS
Pitch	79	82	78	81
Intensity . . .	76	—	94	94
Time	71	62	—	70
Tonal memory .	80	—	88	98
Consonance . .	64	—	74	76
Rhythm	72	—	88	86

Character rating. After six months' acquaintance, on September 15, 1924, when F was about 10 years old, he was rated by Leta S. Hollingworth for various estimated traits on a 7-point rating scale as follows:

Extraordinarily good (Grade 1)

Prudence and foresight, will power and perseverance, appreciation of beauty, sense of humor, sensitiveness to approval or disapproval, desire to excel, freedom from vanity and egotism, conscientiousness, desire to know, originality, common sense, general intelligence.

Decidedly superior (Grade 2)
  Self-confidence, musical appreciation, leadership, popularity with other children, sympathy and tenderness, truthfulness.
Rather superior (Grade 3)
  Cheerfulness and optimism, permanency of moods, generosity and unselfishness, mechanical ingenuity.
Average (Grade 4)
  Health, amount of physical energy.
Rather weak (Grade 5)
  Fondness for large groups.

Although there is no formal record of the fact, it is known that fifteen years later this rater would have made different judgments on most of these traits not relating to strictly cognitive characteristics. Other judges acquainted with F rather unanimously disagreed with the high ratings here accorded such traits as prudence and foresight, will power and perseverance, sensitiveness to approval or disapproval, freedom from vanity or egotism, common sense, leadership, popularity, sympathy and tenderness, truthfulness, generosity and unselfishness, and these ratings are as a matter of fact inconsistent with F's subsequent history.

HOME RATING

On May 6, 1924, the home of F was visited by a social worker trained in the use of the Whittier Scale for Home Rating. The rating was reported as 21, with a possible score of 25. Neighborhood was average, in a fair section of New York City. Details were as follows:

Necessities. Father bookkeeper with steady, small salary, adequate only for necessities. Food and clothing of good quality, conditions neat and clean but plain. Heat, light, sleeping facilities fair. Grade 4.

Neatness. Sanitary conditions good; rooms well kept and clean; apartment rear, second floor, little view. Considering the equipment, household run in an efficient manner. Grade 4.

Size. Four small rooms and bath for two adults and two children. Conditions crowded. Grade 4.

Parental condition. Parents socially adaptable; there appears to be harmony in home; parents have too few outside interests. Mother practically always at home; father at home evenings. Grade 5.

Parental supervision. Parents keenly interested in development of children. Their own education limited, which is a handicap in directing and educating the children. Little need of discipline in home, though mother is lax about carrying out threats. Parental example good. Grade 4.

MISCELLANEOUS CHARACTERISTICS

Play interests. F preferred playmates of his own age and sex. He would spend hours at a time "using marbles for soldiers and working out military formations." Being with older children in school, he was somewhat backward in joining in their outdoor games.

Reading interests. From 6 to 10 years of age F read a great variety of books, "particularly geography and history" and "averaging probably 20 hours weekly." He was especially interested in dictionaries and encyclopedias; would always look up new words in detail. Most of his leisure time was preferably spent in reading.

LATER EDUCATIONAL CAREER

As already recorded, F was transferred in 1924, at the age of 10 years, to the Special Opportunity Class in P.S. 165, Manhattan, then being organized for experimental purposes connected with the education of children of rare intelligence. He graduated from this class into senior high school. He and another boy (Child C, Chapter 6) led this highly selected group of children in achievement tests.   As he was at this time, Leta S. Hollingworth wrote of him:

> I have never met with a more interesting child than he was, and the same creativeness and inexorable logic which characterized him then have always continued.

He entered, after a brief experience in a progressive private school, a public high school in New York City, in 1925. His high school career was a checkered one, typical in some respects of his later educational history.   For one thing, he was a constant truant, and he refused to do the required work in physical education.   He had always been averse to physical activity and loathed manual work to the end of his career.   He said that the gymnasium work always left him feeling "worse," gave him colds, and was of no use to him. Perhaps his subsequent medical history throws some light on the reasons for these observations.

His truant hours were spent partly in the public library, where he read continuously in technical volumes in a great variety of fields and accumulated an amazing fund of general information and esoteric lore.   Law, theology, history, science, and literature were some of his favorite fields.

When not in the library, he would usually be at a chess club to which he had been granted access and where he had learned the game.   He rapidly developed into an expert chess and bridge player, and in Eastern chess tournaments is said to have achieved the ranking of seventh in the national list.   He always managed to appear at high school to take the necessary examinations, and passed all his subjects with good standing and even with phenomenal records.   But his inexplicable truancy and his refusal to do the required work in physical education baffled the educational authorities. They finally refused to graduate him with his class — although his record was among the best — until he had redeemed himself by doing the gymnasium work in a fifth year. In 1930 he did this, and also carried some additional courses and thus was allowed to finish high school, requiring longer than the conventional period for this because of his refusal to accommodate his own interests and ideas to the regular routine.

In spite of irregular attendance, F took some part in high school activities. His main activities, of the extracurricular sort, were chess club, chess team, poetry club, debating society, mathematics club, board of publications, program committee. He was executive member of the debating society and of the law society, vice president of the poster club, and two or three times section president. His record, of course, shows no athletic history and no physical activities engaged in.

For the four years following 1930 F continued to frequent the public library, the chess club, and the bridge games. At one time a patron friend made it financially possible for him to enter college at the College of the City of New York. He quit before the end of the first term, again because he hated the required gymnasium work and said he always got a cold and felt bad after such exercise. Although he was again and again urged by people who knew his ability not to waste it at chess and bridge, he showed no apparent interest in going on with college. He replied that he could always make a living some way or other. Uncongenial home circumstances and the general unemployment situation prevailing at the time perhaps heightened this indisposition and lack of ambition. While other boys who had been in the same grade school and high school classes with him were finding part-time employment and working their way through college, F was contented with his chess games, with an occasional bit of money won at cards, and with his hours in the public library.

In 1934 he was asked to take the CAVD tests by the Institute of Educational Research at Teachers College, Columbia University, to help determine the highest scores to be expected on this scale. He and another boy, both selected because of their known phenomenal range of information and intellectual alertness, "went through the ceiling" on this scale, thus again confirming the earlier records of his mental level so far as intelligence was concerned. On the same occasion he was given the Coöperative General Culture Test, by Dr. Lorge. In this his score exceeded that of superior college graduates.

In September, 1934, F was again persuaded, through financial assistance practically forced upon him, and after much urging and long discussion, to try college. He enrolled in Columbia College, once more a freshman. He carried a heavy program, tried to do certain outside jobs as assistant provided for him, and probably overworked. He had declined one patron's offer to give him a stipulated sum of money for the year if he would abstain from chess for that period. In fact, only vigorous prodding led him to go to college at all at this time, even with the way opened for him.

The outcome appeared to be another fiasco. In January, as the examination period drew near, he became ill, developed pneumonia, and for the second time withdrew from college before completing a term of work. In this instance his illness appeared to justify the act.

In the autumn of 1935, having been nursed back to reasonable health through patrons interested in his case, he was urged by them to make a fresh start and to try the University of Chicago plan, under which students could progress as rapidly as they were able to satisfy the requirements through comprehensive examinations. He entered the University of Chicago that fall, for the third time a college freshman, agreeing to do this without any great enthusiasm of his own but as part of what was called an "educational experiment."

Of his record on entrance the following comment was made by the chief examiner:

> The examiners have called my attention to a freak case in our records for the incoming students. . . . His performance seems almost unbelievable. On the freshman classification tests his performance was as follows: first in the vocabulary test; first in the reading test; second in the Intelligence Test of the American Council; third in the English placement test; third in the physical science placement test . . . in the freshman class of about 750 students.
>
> In addition, he also took four Comprehensives with the following grades: Biological Science, A; Humanities, B; Social Sciences, A; Physical Sciences, D.

The year at Chicago was not without episode. F was held up by two gunmen, engineered the capture of one of these, and was advised to disappear for a time during the excitement. Impetuously, and without resources except the provisions made by his sponsor for his own subsistence, he married a young Jewish girl. But the "Chicago Plan" kept its word, and by the end of the year F had passed all the Comprehensives required to give him his B.A. degree. In doing this he acquired a good deal of newspaper and popular magazine notoriety, and his photograph, and that of his young wife, were often reproduced in the public prints.

Although he fancied he would like to be a lawyer, F finally decided to go in for graduate work. Some uncertainties prevailed in connection with his acceptance by some of the graduate schools because, although he had been three times a college freshman (a point never brought out in the newspaper accounts of his educational progress), he had completed but one year of college residence.

Eventually he was awarded a graduate fellowship in Teachers College, Columbia University, for study toward the Ph.D. degree in Education, and he completed a year of work there, accomplishing, in addition to the class work, a minor experimental study, a report of which was subsequently published. For the following year he was appointed Assistant in Psychology at Barnard College. At the last moment, just before the beginning of the new term, he decided to shift to law, which was one of his boyish ambitions. He was enabled to return to Chicago for this purpose.

Chess, bridge, and racing continued to intrude themselves into his activities, although he was pledged to abstain from them. His marital affairs did not run smoothly; contrary to his promises he incurred additional indebtedness; but he continued to carry on his law studies with passable records. Then he suddenly became seriously ill and was discovered to have an inoperable abdominal cancer. Again his educational career was interrupted and he returned to New York for care and treatment. Before another year was over, in December, 1938, he died of this affliction, at the age of 24 years.

In spite of a brilliant mental endowment, early discovery, much educational encouragement, and material assistance, a Bachelor's degree and a few chess prizes and bridge victories represent F's final achievement. The chief causes of this relative failure to make the most of his potentialities appeared externally in the form of character traits. His parents said of him that it was never necessary to stimulate his desire to learn; they also reported him to be "willful and headstrong." These unpropitious traits were as a matter of fact apparent in his early school days. They became magnified as he was given freer opportunity for self-expression and activity. We know so little about the identification and genesis of character traits that the case makes little or no contribution to our understanding in this direction. It is not known how early the physical disability that finally terminated the picture had been operating; it may even have been at the bottom of what appeared socially as a personality defect.

Chapter Ten

CHILD G

CHILD G is a boy, born in Brooklyn, New York, May 26, 1923. Records of his test scores that are available date from 1930, at which time he was 6 years 6 months old. A record of his development has been kept by his parents, who take an unusual interest in educational problems. They have freely and intelligently coöperated in the frequent objective examination of G, and have consulted with teachers concerning problems of adjustment and educational development.

FAMILY BACKGROUND

G is of Hebrew parentage, and all four of his grandparents attended Hebrew school. His paternal grandfather was a tailor, his maternal grandfather an installment dealer. G's father is a lawyer; in an Army Alpha test he made a score of 178 points. His mother, before her marriage, was a typist and stenographer. There are among the relatives a doctor, a lawyer, a rabbi, a college professor. A cousin stood highest in a city-wide achievement test given to public school pupils in New York City. His only brother, younger than he and the only sibling, has an IQ of 150–155 (see record, page 184).

EDUCATIONAL HISTORY

In January, 1934, Edna W. McElwee published a preliminary account of G's school achievement up to that time.[1] A few months later G's father published an account of the boy's reading interests.[2] Data recorded in these two reports have been made use of in the present chapter.[3]

G learned to read before going to school, but at this time his parents did not realize that he was exceptional. After a term in kindergarten he was promoted to Grade 1A, after a few weeks to 1B, and then to 2A. At the end of the term he was placed in 3A. Then he was doubly promoted each term for a time, entering the 6A grade at the age of 8 years 6 months. The principal reported:

> He absorbed information easily and quickly and, regardless of the grade in which he was placed or the length of time he had been in the grade, his work and his ratings were always much beyond those of his classmates.

During these early years G preferred being alone with his books to playing with other children. His parents intelligently sought advice on the correction of this and encouraged him, successfully, to play with other children, first with those younger than he, and then with children of his own age. He made a ready adaptation, and in time had a group of boys with whom he played and who were sometimes invited by his father to accompany them on Saturday afternoon excursions. He developed an interest in all sorts of ball games and became a good swimmer.

[1] McElwee, Edna Willis. "Seymour, a Boy with 192 IQ." *Journal of Juvenile Research*, Vol. XVIII (January, 1934), pages 28–35.

[2] "The Reading of a Gifted Child." By his Father. *Journal of Juvenile Research*, Vol. XVIII, No. 2 (April, 1934), pages 107–111.

[3] This chapter was written by H. L. H.

G read widely, and his parents from the beginning exercised some supervision over the character of the books provided for him, and they read to him at bedtime, about an hour daily.   There were included in his reading not only a large selection of children's books and stories but also books of history, mythology, biography, poetry, science, and art.

The Saturday excursions to places of interest were a regular institution, and these interests were readily tied to G's reading.   Among the places thus visited were the zoo, botanical gardens, aquarium, navy yard, fleet, airport, museums, art galleries, Hall of Fame, numerous factories and industrial plants, fire department, public utilities, observatories. Plays and concerts were attended, and good taste in music was encouraged.   Educational use was made of radio programs.   G learned to play the violin and joined the school orchestra.   At his own request he was given private instruction in Hebrew and made good progress.

At an early age — 7 or 8 years — G became interested in chemistry, and was provided with a chemical outfit for his own use.   With this he busied himself a great deal, and he kept his classmates provided with ink of his own manufacture.   He has collected both stamps and coins and also *Popular Science* magazines.

There is in the files a large collection of his remarks in childhood, recorded by his parents.   They show early thoughtfulness, curiosity, and judicious discrimination.

Of G's later educational experience Miss McElwee wrote as follows: "At eight and a half years of age he was transferred to P.S. 208, Brooklyn, where he entered the 6A group of the Individual Progress class, which had been organized for superior children.   The method of instruction had been modified and the course of study enriched to meet the needs of the pupils. . . . Tests of educational achievement given in October, 1931, soon after he entered the class, showed that his grade placement was 7.4 and his achievement quotient 86. Similar tests given in May, 1932, indicated that his grade placement was then 10.3 and his achievement quotient 97. In those seven months he had completed three years of work. . . . By January, 1933, he had gained another year and a half, and was maintaining his achievement quotient. In other words, at 9 years of age he was doing as well as a junior in high school."

His father wrote to the school at this time:

> We are happy to tell you that G is full of his school work and is very contented with the present curriculum. Inasmuch as he has always complained until this term of lack of work at school and always considered his school work a necessary evil, we feel very grateful to you for his increased interest and happiness.

EARLY MENTAL TESTS

The first recorded measurement of G's mental ability is found in a report from the Educational Clinic of the College of the City of New York, where he had been taken by his father for a private examination. The report is made by Elise S. Mustor, Assistant Director, as of January, 1930. G was then 6 years 7 months old. His Mental Age was found to be 10–9, and his IQ is reported as 163. This report also gives numerous other details which may be summarized in the following tabulation.

Report of G, January, 1930

Chronological Age 6–7
Mental Age 10–9
Intelligence Quotient 163

Height (with shoes)......... 48.5 inches
   (About 3 inches above the
   median for his age)
Weight .... 59 pounds
   (About 5 pounds above the
   median for his height)
Reading comprehension ...... Median of 5th Grade
Arithmetic reasoning .... Median of 4B Grade
Arithmetic fundamentals ..... Median of 3A Grade
Perception of form and physi-
   cal relationships .... Ranges from 7th- to 12th-year
                                level
Auditory rote memory .... 10-year level
Vocabulary .... 10-year level

Physical condition: Well nourished.   Tonsils and adenoids removed.   Breathing unobstructed.   Teeth good.   No defects
of heart, lungs, acuity of vision or hearing.
At the clinic his social responses were good.   He was well poised
and unassuming; showed very fine effort and application.

LATER TEST RECORDS

1931.   G was given a Stanford-Binet examination by **Leta
S. Hollingworth** in May, 1931, within a few days of his
eighth birthday.   He achieved an IQ of 192.   The following comment is included in the record:

> The increase over the IQ obtained at the age of 6 is not
> unusual for a very young, very bright child, although it would
> be very unusual for an average child.   I shall be glad to test
> G again when he·is about 12 years old, and when he is 16 years
> old.   Also his little brother.

1933.   On April 5, 1933, at the age of 9 years 10 months,
G was again tested by Leta S. Hollingworth, perhaps as a
class demonstration.   He was then in Grade 7B and his IQ
is recorded as 176 plus.   The following comment is made:

Children of G's present age can no longer be reliably measured in terms of IQ by any existing test if they have previously scored above 185 IQ. . . . The IQ of 176 plus merely informs us that the test has begun to "run down" in his case. . . . Next time we test him we shall have to use a test scoring in *points* only, which will place him on the centile scale for adults. . . . His physical measurements correspond closely to the norms for boys of about 11 years.

1934. There is in the files a Stanford-Binet record of G taken by Leta S. Hollingworth, March 19, 1934. His age was then 10 years 10 months and he was in Grade 8B in P.S. 208, Brooklyn. He passed without error all the tests in the scale (Average Adult and Superior Adult).

Miscellaneous records. In the McElwee report already cited the following scores are recorded, on a variety of scales, covering a two-year period (1931–1933).

DATE	TEST	AGE	SCORE
May 5, 1931 . .	Stanford-Binet	8–0	192
October 7, 1931 .	Porteus Maze	8–5	12 years
	Healy Picture Completion		13 years
	Porteus Form and Assemblying		8 years
	Thorndike-McCall Reading: Form B		6B Grade
	Stanford Achievement Test: Form A, Arithmetic Computation		8A Grade
	Trabue Language Completion, Alpha		15–10 years
May 18, 1932 . .	Elementary Reading, Los Angeles, Form 3	9–0	12A Grade
	Arithmetic Fundamentals, Los Angeles, Form 4		9A Grade
	Woody-McCall Spelling, List 5		9B Grade
	Trabue Language Completion, Beta		16–4 years
January 6, 1933 .	New Stanford Achievement Test: Form V	9–8	18 years

DATE	TEST	AGE	SCORE
April 12, 1933 . .	Powers General Science Test: Form A (25 per cent of first-year high school pupils exceed this score at end of one year instruction in general science.)	9–11	62 points
April 26, 1933 . .	Kent-Rosanoff Association Test Woody-Cady Questionnaire indicates supersensitiveness — thinks people look at him, make remarks about him, find too much fault with him, etc.	9–11	9 Individual Reactions

The New Stanford Achievement Test score of 18 years of Educational Age, achieved at the Chronological Age of 9 years 8 months, broken down into detailed sections, was as follows:

EDUCATIONAL AGE

Paragraph Meaning 17–8
Word Meaning 18–8
Dictation 16–0
Language Usage 17–2
Literature 16–8
History and Civics 19–2
Geography 20–4
Physiology and Hygiene 18–5
Arithmetic Reasoning 19–2
Arithmetic Computation 17–8

Average .... 17 years 11 months

The examiner remarks: "Using the IQ of 192, his Mental Age would now be 18 years 5 months. This would give him an Achievement Quotient of 97.3 per cent."

TRAITS OF CHARACTER

At the age of 10 years G was described by his school supervisor and parents as prudent and self-reliant, with will power, desire for knowledge, wish to excel, and originality. He was conscientious, truthful, cheerful, sympathetic, and had a sense of humor. He was modest about himself and his achievements, did not like bragging, and reproved his younger brother for such conduct. At this time he wore glasses for an error of refraction, had "a slight speech impediment and a nervous mannerism." He always wanted to do things as well as possible. He set out to improve his poor penmanship by learning manuscript writing. He was full of questions about scientific aspects of the things and processes he saw about him. He had a reliable and alert memory, even for incidental observations.

PHYSICAL MEASUREMENTS

The physical measurements referred to in the 1933 mental test (page 178) are as follows:

	G	NORMS
Standing height (in stocking feet)	53.8 inches	53.6
Sitting height.	27.7 inches	
Weight (ordinary indoor clothing except coat) . .	78 pounds	66.9
Right grip	14, 11, 10 kg.	
Left grip	9, 9, 9 kg.	

On August 2, 1937, there is a record of height and weight at the age of 14 years 2 months, as follows:

	G	NORMS
Height (stocking feet)	63.7 inches	61.0
Sitting height.	33 inches	
Weight (no coat or shoes)	121.5 pounds	94.9

HIGH SCHOOL RECORD

By February, 1937, G was finishing his sixth term in Erasmus Hall High School, Brooklyn. In the first five terms his work had averaged 90–95. Regents' marks to that date were:

French, two years	95
Plane Geometry	100
Intermediate Algebra	98
European History	91

In June of 1935 he had won first prize in "an algebra contest for the entire grade of his school." During the first four terms he had ranked fifth in scholarship and in the fifth term he tied for second place. A letter from his father records that:

In June, 1934, he scored 174 on the Terman Group Intelligence Test which was given to 27,573 boys and girls, graduates of the elementary schools, public and parochial, who applied for admission to the high schools in New York City, this score being the highest reached, and was referred to, though of course not by name, in John L. Tildsley's "The Mounting Waste of the American Secondary School," at page 3 thereof.

A letter from G dated July 5, 1938, records his graduation from high school at the age of 15 years. He there says:

At present my interest lies along abstract lines; mathematics, chemistry, and physics are my favorite subjects. The occupation I would like most to enter when my schooling shall be finished would be mathematics. However, I see no chance for a job in this field for research work as there is in, say, chemistry. Hence I feel uncertain as to whether I shall make mathematics my life work or whether I should specialize in one field or another of chemistry, my second love.

There is a copy of the principal's statement "In Re Qualifications of G, Candidate for Scholarship," at the close of his high school career. It is worth quoting here as a record of the judged characteristics of this 15-year-old boy whose thoughtful letter, just quoted from, shows his serious concern over the theoretical and practical possibilities of the various fields of his interest.

PRINCIPAL'S STATEMENT IN RE QUALIFICATIONS OF G, CANDIDATE FOR SCHOLARSHIP

Native ability. Intelligence Quotient 174 on Terman Test given at Erasmus Hall, the highest ever reached here; ranks fourth in a grade of 712 in scholarship.

Personality. Pleasant and helpful; well liked and respected by students and faculty; always agreeable, willing, eager to help others.

Loyalty. Loyalty is unquestioned; fine home background contributes to high ideals; his good example has inspired loyalty in others.

Coöperation. Has given much time to clubs, to tutoring students, and to giving clerical assistance in offices.

Integrity. Commended highly by teachers for uprightness.

Leadership. An active leader in many school activities; has strong initiative and unusual resourcefulness.

Thoroughness. Class and extracurricular work characterized by unusual care and thoroughness; carried through many long-term assignments with a minimum of supervision.

Originality. Outstanding characteristic; while working in his grade adviser's office he devised a new and superior arrangement for finding the official classes of any one of 800 students in the grade.

Partial list of activities and honors. Program Committee, five terms; Office Service, seven terms; Little Symphony, two terms; Orchestra, five terms; Arista, four terms; Junior Arista, three terms; String Ensemble, two terms; "Dutchman" Staff; "XYZ" Mathematics Tutoring Club, three terms; prize, Geometry Contest; prize, Safety Essay contest; medal, Algebra contest.

Comments by teachers. "Very efficient and reliable." "Very good assistant." "Fine work on Arista Membership Committee." "Fine boy, earnest, and willing worker." "Brilliant mind." "Diligent worker."

In June, 1938, upon graduation from high school, G was awarded a scholarship in Harvard University, which he entered in the ensuing academic year.

G'S BROTHER'S RECORD

A brother younger than G and his only sibling was tested at the age of 5 years 6 months at the Educational Clinic, College of the City of New York. His IQ (S–B) was 151. Other scores were:

<pre>
        Goodenough Drawing .... 6.0 years
        Porteus Maze 5–6
        Pintner-Patterson Performance 6–6
        Stenquist Mechanical Assembly 6–0
        Gates Primary Reading Scale .... 1B Grade
        Stanford Achievement: Arithmetic ...... 1B Grade
</pre>

This child was also measured by Leta S. Hollingworth in February, 1933, when he was at age 6–10, and the Stanford-Binet IQ was 152. Other measures made at that time were:

<pre>
        Standing height .... 50.75 inches
        Sitting height .... 27.75 inches
        Weight .... 78.25 pounds
        Found "left-handed"
</pre>

A letter from the father dated June 24, 1938, reports that G's brother "graduated from public school this week (age 11 years 6 months). He was awarded one of two history medals given in a class of 134. In the Terman Group Test given to about 1000 applicants he scored 153, which is the fourth in the group. The first one in the group was 156."

Chapter Eleven

CHILD H

CHILD H, at the time this account is written,[1] is a girl of 17 years, but the data on record terminate with her tenth year. She was born March 25, 1924, in New York City. Her parents have kept a diary of her development, and an aunt with special educational interests has made various observations and records of her and has also familiarized herself with the parents' records.

FAMILY BACKGROUND

Her grandparents on both sides were Austrian Hebrews. The maternal grandfather was a rabbi and did some writing. The maternal grandmother is said to have shown unusual mental alertness, a surprising and almost untutored aptness in numerical calculation. At 65 years of age she learned to play bridge very well, and in her old age continued to show lively interests.

Parents. H's father is a newspaper reporter. He attended college for three years. He was 29 when H was born. Her mother is a high school graduate and before marriage was a stenographer. She was 28 when H was born.

---

[1] By H. L. H.

PRESCHOOL HISTORY

H is reported as a healthy child, of average stability. She is a first-born child. She began to walk at 14 months and to talk at 16 months, according to the parents. She cut her first tooth at 9.5 months. H did not learn to read until after she was 4 years old. At this age she was fond of play and her playmates were children ranging in age from 3 to 9 years. Her favorite recreations were sedentary — drawing, painting, mosaic blocks, and the like.

At 2 years of age she was given a box of wooden beads for stringing. "She very quickly learned the art of holding the string in the right hand and the bead in the left, and became very much absorbed in her work. Suddenly she looked up and said, 'Beads, onions.'" The record continues: "Alternatives seem a preferred mode of expression at present, so that she wants 'soup, *not* peas'; her hands are 'clean, *not* dirty.'"

At 2 years 10 months, upon seeing a picture of a little girl mailing a letter, she told herself the following story:

> Once upon a time there was a little girl and she wanted to mail a letter. She went out and looked for a letter box and found one near the drug store. She mailed the letter and it came to Wawarsing and Sheve received it." (Sheve was an aunt living at Wawarsing.)

Storytelling and writing plays and verses became a favorite pastime in later childhood.

At this time H had imaginary companions. "For several days Mr. Parkey (an invented character) was her very close friend. She played with him, conversed with him, loved him, killed him, and brought him to life again." She also invented new names for her dolls — Flossie became "Woozie" and Alice became "Katch."

At 2 years 11 months she asked the meaning of the words "excitement," "guarantee," and "neatness." She constantly asked about the meaning of words. She sang songs to herself, such as "Go into the next room, where there's no steam heat." At this age she asked how babies are made. "Where do they come from? How do they come out? Why? Will a baby grow in my belly when I'm a big lady?"

At 3 years she wanted to know if people "wear out" like brushes and combs. She purchased for an imaginary house "an extrola," "a gate-legged table," "a gate-legged bookcase," and "gate-legged chairs."

At 3 years 0 months, waiting for her cereal to cool, a lump of butter put into it is slowly melting. H remarks, her eyes on the butter, "Now it's a baby — baby died — no more baby."

And noting the snow, she said, "My muffler is as white as the snow." She looks again at snow and muffler. "No, it's a *different* white."

There is on record a vocabulary compiled by the mother when H was 3 years old (May 23, 1927). It was based on a count of "all the words *used* by H regardless of whether she could tell exactly what they mean. Tenses of verbs are given but no plurals of nouns." The list includes about 1400 words, approximately classifiable as follows:

Nouns	745	Pronouns	17
Verbs	401	Prepositions	15
Adjectives	161	Conjunctions	5
Adverbs	63	Interjections	9

MENTAL MEASUREMENTS

March 24, 1927. Age 3 years. Stanford-Binet examination given by Dr. Ella Woodyard, with the following results: Mental Age, 5–6; IQ, 183.

March 8, 1930. Age 5 years 11 months. Stanford-Binet examination given by Leta S. Hollingworth, with the following results: Mental Age, 8–9; IQ, 148. At this time H was in Grade 1A.

April 21, 1933. Age 9 years 1 month. Stanford-Binet examination given by Alice M. Holmes, with the following results: Mental Age, 17–2; IQ, 189.

At this age she was in Grades 5A and 6B, P.S. 206, Manhattan, and is described as "a quiet and unassuming person, but most responsive. She would like to be with children her own mental age, for then she would get a mental stimulus and a social life that seems to be denied her now."

In this same month (April, 1933) the New Stanford Achievement Test: Advanced Battery: Form V, given by Alice M. Holmes, showed scores as follows:

Paragraph Meaning...	109	Geography	105
Word Meaning	103	Physiology and Hygiene	90
Dictation	87	Arithmetic Reasoning.	94
Language Usage	91	Arithmetic Computation	110
Literature	91	Average score	97.8
History and Civics	98		

September 11, 1934. Age 10 years 6 months. H was given Army Alpha, Form 8, by Leta S. Hollingworth. Her score was 135 points, which is median for college sophomores. H was then in Grade 7B. It is noted that "This result is just what would have been predicted from tests made by us when H was 3 years old."

November 9–17, 1934. Age 10 years 7 months. During this week H was given a number of tests by Leta S. Hollingworth, with the following results:

Stanford-Binet: Mental Age: 18–6; IQ, over 174, "unmeasured by the test."

Intelligence Scale CAVD
    Levels I–M   Score 394 points
    Levels M–Q   Score 392 points

Coöperative General Science Test for College Students: Score, 17; Percentile, 11.

PHYSICAL MEASUREMENTS

March 8, 1930

	H	NORM
Standing height	47 inches	45.2
Sitting height.	24 inches	
Weight	48.25 pounds	41.7

April 21, 1933

	H	NORM
Standing height	54.5 inches	51.1
Weight	66.5 pounds	57.5

INTELLECTUAL ABILITY

There is a collection of many records showing H's reactions and opinions from infancy up to the age of 9 or 10. These contain apt comments, sage remarks, and discriminating judgments. They reveal a lively intellectual curiosity and a socialized attitude.

H's parents have preserved copies of poems and short plays that H has written. A collection of the "best ones," selections written between 5.5 and 8.5 years of age, covers

seventeen typewritten pages. Among them are the
following.

> If I had Aladdin's lamp, you see,
> I'd give one wish to you and me.
> And then we'd wish for every toy,
> That every child should have some joy.
> *Age 5 years 6 months*

> On the clover fields he roams,
>   In the mountains,
>   At the homes,
> Makes the trees and flowers grow,
> And manufactures pure, white snow.
>   — God —
> *Age 8 years 6 months*

> There was an old soldier
>   He was all dressed in brown
> This soldier had an honor —
>   He was known all over town.

> This old soldier had a misfortune,
>   That was known too.
> His beard it covered his medal,
>   And people couldn't see through.
>   *Age 8 years 6 months*

There are in the collection brief stories, continued tales,
short verses, longer poems, dialogues, and plays divided into
scenes, with appropriate stage instructions.

From after the tenth year there is an undated poem, submitted to the examiner September 19, 1939, by the aunt of
H. This poem, entitled "The Gospel of Intolerance," won
a prize in a poetry contest. Of it the aunt writes:

It was fished out from the wastebasket by my sister.   To the question why she had thrown away the "Gospel of Intolerance," H answered that she did not think it was worth keeping, that she had no particular idea in mind when writing it, and that she was just practicing on the typewriter and thought of the phrase "They said no," and then the rest just came by itself.   Incidentally, H has never read the Bible.

"The Gospel of Intolerance" occupies a full single-spaced typewritten page.   It begins as follows:

The Gospel of Intolerance

They said no
And who shall but hear the whisper of command shall without question don his uniform and go out upon the field of death in obedience
And who shall lie asleep in the sun must be roused
And who shall sit in lavender chairs eating of the earth shall drop his spoon
And who shall lie with the woman shall turn from his passion
And all this shall be done without words as the answer to the whisper of that which is calling and that which is in command
And he who shall stuff his ears with cotton must needs be twice called

.   .   .   .

Chapter Twelve

CHILD I

THIS child, a girl, was born in Palo Alto, California, June 17, 1929. She is the daughter of one of the male children studied by Terman and reported in *Genetic Studies in Genius*. She was first observed when, in September, 1937, she entered a special class for "rapid learners" established by Leta S. Hollingworth at Speyer School, P.S. 500, Manhattan.[1] This experimental group was made up of fifty children chosen from the public schools of the city on the basis of intelligence, and their range in IQ was from 130 to 200. Of these fifty selected children, Child I was one of three whose IQ's exceeded 180.

FAMILY BACKGROUND

Child I's paternal grandfather was still living in 1939, aged 69. He had a Normal School education (South Dakota) and was teacher, farmer, and small-town merchant. His education was superior to that usually achieved by farm boys. His special interests were church, travel, and repair work on his own properties. He is described by his son as stubborn, thrifty, and industrious, with uncompromising attitudes toward worldliness.

[1] This chapter was written by H. L. H.

I's paternal grandmother died when I's father was 9 years old. She had been a teacher of music and kindergarten, and a housewife. She was educated in a Normal School and a Conservatory of Music. She was an active leader in her community, established her own kindergarten, and was socially and musically active in local ways. Her home was in South Dakota and her father was first Land Commissioner of Dakota Territory. He had led a group of homesteaders into that region about 1860. He was politically and educationally active — Commissioner of Immigration, Commissioner of Education, in the Territory.

No mentally defective or otherwise generally incompetent relatives on the father's side are known. The great-grandmother of I, on her father's side, is said to have been a relative of Phillips Brooks.

I's maternal grandfather was born in Texas of ancestry half French-Huguenot and the rest German-English. He was a high school graduate. He was in later life a merchant and real estate operator and active in community affairs.

I's maternal grandmother was born in Oklahoma, her ancestry being French-Huguenot, Welsh, and Irish. In education she lacked a half year of completing the work for her B.A. in the University of New Mexico. After her marriage she devoted herself to her home and family. She was talented in dramatics and was active in local church, club, and lodge affairs.

Father. I's father was born March 21, 1909, in South Dakota. He is mainly of English descent. He has the degree of B.A. and also of M.A. from Stanford University, and he was a candidate for the degree of Ph.D. in Public Law in an Eastern university at the time of this inquiry. He was for eight years a college instructor, and later was connected with a government department at Washington, D. C. He has been active in his profession, has written in the field of government, and is a member of various academic societies. He was one of the 1000 children described by Terman in *Genetic Studies in Genius*. He has been self-supporting since the age of 19.

Mother. I's mother was graduated from high school in New Mexico and attended the University of Kansas for one year. She then transferred to the University of New Mexico, receiving her B.A. degree in 1930. Two years before (1928), when she was 20 years old, she married I's father, and continued her college course. After graduation she managed her home and also took some graduate courses. In high school she was class poet and in the Honor Society four years. In her college years she was active in sorority life and on publications. Her major interests were debating, dramatics, and student government. At the University of Kansas she was on the Dean's Honor Roll (1925–1926). At New Mexico she held various scholastic offices and was awarded several honors.

In more recent years I's mother has taken an active part in the League of Women Voters and in the Faculty Wives' Club in the college where her husband has been teaching.

PRESCHOOL HISTORY

The following data have been supplied by Child I's parents, who kept a baby-book record of her development:

Length of pregnancy, 8.5 months. Weight at birth, 8 pounds. Breast fed to 2.5 months, then bottle fed to 18 months. First teeth appeared at 5 months and first permanent teeth at 5 years. Walked alone (several steps) at 10.5 months. Talked in short sentences at from 18 months to 2 years.

Childhood illnesses — measles, whooping cough, mumps, chicken pox, colds.

EARLY EDUCATIONAL HISTORY

At the age of about 2 years Child I had been observed in the Institute of Child Development (Teachers College, Columbia University) and reported as being hyperactive and of high intelligence.

At the age of 3 or 4 years she was used as a demonstration case before a class in psychology in the University and the Mental Age of 7 was assigned to her at that time.

Shortly after, she attended a kindergarten in the neighborhood of her home where "they gave her extra work — French and dancing." She liked this school. At the age of 5 years she entered kindergarten at P.S. 193, Manhattan, for half-day sessions only, although she wished to go all day.

At the age of 6 years she was entered in the first grade at P.S. 186, Manhattan, and in the second term was "skipped" to Grade 2A. "She spent her spare time aimlessly drawing, and was allowed to bring library books to school. Some of the time she sat with folded hands when her work was finished, and she resented this."

MENTAL MEASUREMENTS

January 14, 1937, was the date of I's first examination, at the age of 7 years 7 months, and her Stanford-Binet IQ was 184.

In September, 1937, at the age of 8 years 3 months, she was given Intelligence Examination CAVD, Levels H-M. Her score was 361 points. The comment recorded by the examiner (Leta S. Hollingworth) is: "Median seventh-grade child is close to this mark." Child I had at this time just come from a school in which she had been placed in the third grade.

Records are available of several achievement tests Child I took at different dates. Representative results are to be found in two Stanford Achievement tests given in December, 1937, and in June, 1938. In the first of these she averaged an age rating of 12–3 and a grade of 6.3; in the second, her age rating was 13–5 and her grade 7.6. In six months she had advanced a year and two months in Educational Age and had made a similar advance in grade status. The following table gives the detailed results of these two examinations.

SUBJECT	AGE DECEMBER, 1937	AGE JUNE, 1938	GRADE DECEMBER, 1937	GRADE JUNE, 1938
Paragraph Meaning	13–7	15–8	7.8	9.7
Word Meaning	12–11	15–4	7.2	9.3
Dictation	9–11	11–7	4.1	5.7
Language Usage	14–4	15–4	8.4	9.3
Literature	11–11	15–6	6.1	9.5
History and Civics	13–1	13–7	7.4	7.8
Geography	12–4	14–8	6.6	8.7
Physiology and Hygiene . .	12–11	13–5	7.2	7.6
Arithmetic Reasoning. . . .	11–8	11–3	5.8	5.4
Arithmetic Computation . .	10–5	11–0	4.4	5.1
Average score	12–2	13–5	6.5	7.8

Child I left this experimental school a year after admission, when her father was appointed to a position in another state, to which the family moved. In the new school she was placed in the fifth grade, on the ground that she might make better social adjustments there, although her achievements were clearly already better than those of average sixth-grade pupils. It is unfortunate that no follow-up of this child has been possible. Her record and the variety of her abilities were striking. She was one of the most outstanding and best-liked pupils in the group at Speyer School. In addition to her remarkable intelligence she possessed desirable supporting traits which led the teachers to predict that she might "go farther" than any other child in the selected group of fifty "rapid learners."

The fairly complete account of I's background and early development has been here provided in the hope that it may be made use of by investigators at some later time.

PHYSICAL MEASUREMENTS AND HEALTH

Measurements, as of January 16, 1939, age 9 years 6 months, were as follows:

	Child I	Norm
Height	58.5 inches	52
Weight	96 pounds	61.5
Chest circumference	29 inches	
Head circumference	21.1 inches	
Eye color	brown	
Hair color	dark brown	

Tonsils and adenoids caused trouble in 1933 and were removed in 1934. No visual defects noted. Occasional headaches "usually from reading or remaining long periods indoors." Hearing excellent. Nutrition excellent. No symptoms of general weakness.

Parents report I to be "at least very excitable," and that she shows "impulsive actions and extreme eagerness."

No sleep difficulties; no muscular twitching; no special fears. Sleeps nine hours, fairly soundly.

MISCELLANEOUS CHARACTERISTICS

Her superior ability was first noticed by people from the University, at 15 months, because of "comprehension beyond that expected at such an age."

She is interested in music and wrote the school song at Speyer. She has been very much interested in nature study and science since her second or third year, and "in her relationship to the world and the cosmos." Has asked questions frequently concerning origins and creation.

She has shown no special interests in mechanics, drawing, or painting, but from her second year she has had active interests in recitation and in the dramatization of nursery rhymes, etc.

She has played with imaginary companions. She began making up rhymes at an early age. "She reasons logically and has a strong sense of justice."

A neatly bound volume of typed pages, prepared by I as a Christmas present, 1937, for Leta S. Hollingworth, is entitled "First Poems." There are in the collection a dozen short verses or longer poems, each dated by I's age at the time of composition. The ages range from 4.5 to 8 years. A few samples follow.

STARS

The stars are shining bright tonight
I wonder why they shine so bright
I guess to make it light at night.
Age 5 years

THE CAVE MAN

The cave man was a hunter,
  A hunter brave and bold.
He wore the skins of those he killed
  To keep him from the cold.
And many ages later, when he had passed away,
  Men found in caves the sharpened stones
That he used every day.

Age 7 years 5 months

FLOWERS

Red and yellow tulips blooming on the lawn,
Blooming in the woodland, trampled by the fawn,
Little yellow dandelions hiding in the meadows,
Given to the cow to eat every time she bellows.
Pretty red roses upon a bush
Like a little lady bursting with a blush.
White and purple lilacs on a bush of olive green
As a birthday present were given to the Queen.

Age 7 years 5 months

SEARCHING

A wandering stranger am I
I believe in nothing but the great powers of the gods,
The whole world have I searched for their wisdom.
But such wisdom found have I not.

Though I have searched the world over
  Not a trace of such can be found.

I have searched on the hilltops, in the valleys —
  I wonder if such things there are in this wide world of wonder.

The rocks have I broken
  To find this great wisdom
But the wonderous marvels are not to be found.

Age 8 years

Chapter Thirteen

CHILD J

EARLY in 1937 the principal of P.S. 107, The Bronx, New York City, referred one of her pupils to the Bureau of Educational Guidance of Teachers College, Columbia University.[1] This child was J, a girl then about 7 years 6 months old, born May 18, 1929. She was at this time in Grade 5A, and the principal and teachers had concluded that she was so superior in mental level that the ordinary school program could offer her no challenge.

Examinations by the psychologists of the Bureau showed clearly enough the correctness of this judgment. At the age of 7 years 10 months, March 22, 1937, her Mental Age by Stanford-Binet was 15–5. Since she met with success on the Superior Adult Level, no actual upper limit of her ability was established. She was reported, therefore, as having an IQ of 197 or better, and was recommended for admission to the experimental class for quick learners in Speyer School, P.S. 500, Manhattan, which she entered.

In connection with these tests at the Bureau of Child Guidance a most instructive and detailed report was made by the psychologist (Edna Mann). Most of the items of the following description of J at this age are drawn from this report, which fills three single-spaced typewritten pages.

[1] This chapter was written by H. L. H.

FAMILY BACKGROUND

Both parents graduated from college. The father is an instructor in English in a large Eastern university. In the interests of educational research he took, on April 20, 1939, IER Intelligence Scale CAVD, Levels M-Q. His score was 445 points, which the examiner, Leta S. Hollingworth, reports "is included in the top 1 per cent of college graduates and indicates an IQ of not less than 180 in childhood."

The mother of J is a graduate of a large Midwestern university and a former schoolteacher. She also took the CAVD test at the same time that her husband did, making a score of 436 points. This, the examiner reported, "is included in the top 5 per cent of college graduates and indicates an IQ of not less than 170 in childhood."

J has one sister, four years younger than herself, born May 1, 1933. This sister was given a Stanford-Binet test under distracting conditions following a trolley-car accident. Of the outcome, the examiner (Dr. M. C. Pritchard) notes: "This was not a good test and perhaps should not even be included. . . . Several times she asked to leave the room to see how her mother was. She was obviously distracted throughout." Nevertheless, the Mental Age found was 9–2 at Chronological Age 7–0 (IQ 131). In "the routine test given to pupils in 1A grades of the public schools" this sister is reported to have had a score of 143 (presumably IQ, by some group test).

CHILDHOOD CHARACTERISTICS

At the age of 7 years 10 months J is described as poised, competent, self-controlled, and with social and intellectual maturity strikingly advanced. She had clear speech, excellent diction, fertile and pointedly expressed ideas. She was a rather thin child, with clear complexion and very bright blue eyes, and was neatly dressed. Teeth were described as "slightly protruding."

In the test she was interested and coöperative. Her conversation revealed a rich cultural background. She disliked the necessity in school of repeated drill in things she already knew, and she did not need or wish repeated instructions for the tests, even when standard practice called for them.

She was well-read, and discussed with discrimination plays, books, and radio programs. At 3 years of age she had been reading books. At 5 she learned to write her name so that she could take out a library card. At 7 years 10 months she had read six Shakespearean plays. She read all kinds of books, and used dictionaries and encyclopedias independently. She was at that time composing, with a playmate, a "Jingles Book."

At this age she liked to play with children two or three years older than herself. She played vigorously and for several hours a day at many outdoor sports; she did not need to do school homework.

Her manner was natural, free from conceit and from exhibitionism of her abilities. She had good habits of work and enjoyed the challenge of the mental tests. Her vocabulary, language responses, and abstract thinking were clearly on an adult level. She is credited by the examiner with remarkable degrees of mental control, concentration, constructive visual imagery, and manipulation of mathematical and verbal concepts, rote memory, and inductive reasoning.

On a standardized test of reading ability she exhibited a

Reading Age of 14 years 5 months at this time (7 years 10 months).   Her writing was reported as excellent.

Her earlier educational progress reflects her extraordinary ability.   In her first six months at school she completed four terms of work.   She was one term in Grade 3A, and then in one term passed through 3B, 4A, and 4B.

J's parents had from the beginning given intelligent attention to her adjustments in school and to her friendships. She had been wisely guided, motivated to make friends rather than to be in constant leadership, and she was well liked and accepted by her classmates.

At this early age the psychological examiner was able confidently to predict: "In view of her exceptional intelligence, her apparently good health, her apparently excellent social adjustment, she can be expected to attain distinction and to win leadership in higher educational and professional fields."

LATER MENTAL TESTS

J was given a second Stanford-Binet test by Dr. M. C. Pritchard within three days of her tenth birthday, on May 15, 1939, using the 1937 Revision, Form L. A Mental Age of 20 years was achieved which, if her limit had been reached, would have meant an IQ of 200 — very like the 197 plus attained at the earlier Chronological Age.

On February 17, 1938, at the age of 9 years 9 months, J had also taken IER Intelligence Scale CAVD, Levels I to M, making a score of 384 points.

Several records are available on the New Stanford Achievement Tests given, a different form each time, to the pupils in the experimental class at Speyer School at intervals of six months.   Annual tests at the close of each school year, for a period of three years, may be used here to show J's ability and progress in these respects. Such scores are as follows:

FUNCTION	EDUCATIONAL AGE			Form W May 18, 1940
	Form W June 16, 1937	Form Y June 1, 1938	Form X May 31, 1939	
Paragraph Meaning	17–0	18–5	Unmeasured	Unmeasured
Word Meaning. . .	15–9	16–10	17–2	17–8
Dictation	16–6	17–8	18–2	Unmeasured
Language Usage . .	16–5	19–2	18–11	Unmeasured
Literature	16–0	16–2	18–8	17–4
History and Civics .	12–6	12–10	15–11	16–3
Geography	11–11	16–2	17–4	18–5
Physiology and Hygiene	12–6	14–6	16–10	18–5
Arithmetic Reasoning	13–1	16–6	17–4	17–6
Arithmetic Computation	11–10	14–6	17–6	17–6
Average score . .	14–4	16–3	17–8	18–5
Grade status . .	8.4	Unmeasured	Unmeasured	Unmeasured

The first of these achievement tests was given shortly after J entered the experimental class, from the fifth grade in a public school, at the age of about 7 years 6 months. At that time her school achievement scores show her to have been between eighth- and ninth-grade status, with an Educational Age just about twice her Chronological Age. So far as Educational Age is concerned, although the experimental program was half concerned with enrichment activities rather than with the conventional fundamentals, J advanced one year and eleven months during the first school year there, one year and five months during the second year, and nine months during the last year. By this time progress was practically impossible because after the first year most of her scores were unmeasured in grade status, being above the standards for tenth grade.

As a matter of mere achievement scores, J was ready for high school work at the age of being received from the fifth grade into the experimental classes at Speyer School.

There are in the files several poems written by J while she was in Speyer School, before May, 1939; that is, before her tenth birthday. The following may be given as a representative sample of these compositions.

A MARCH SNOWFALL

It's March, yet snow is falling fast,
And one may hear the wintry blast.
A budding tree, a sign of spring,
Will to me great gladness bring.
When crocuses have put their heads,
Above the softened garden beds,
And when in all the fields around
Lively little lambkins bound,
And green creeps up across the lawn
I'll be glad the snow has gone.

Chapter Fourteen

CHILD K

CHILD K is a boy, born December 19, 1922.   He first came to the attention of this series of researches in 1929 when his grandmother sought advice concerning his education from Leta S. Hollingworth.[1]

FAMILY BACKGROUND

K's paternal grandparents are English and Scotch-Irish. The grandfather is said to write poetry and the grandmother to compose music for the verses.

K's maternal grandparents are of Jewish origin, both born in America.   The grandfather was a teacher, the grandmother was "in business."   This grandmother was the seventh of twelve children.   The youngest of these is said to be "a brilliant woman of executive ability."   The eldest, at the age of 79, "reads all the papers, compares notes, etc." One of the brothers in this group was a physician, another a lawyer.   A cousin of K teaches in Massachusetts Institute of Technology and was called during the First World War for special work in mathematics.   This man's sister is an archeologist married to an archaeologist.   Three of K's grandmother's sisters are teachers; another is an artist.

---

[1] This chapter was written by H. L. H.

No mentally deficient or totally incompetent persons are known among the ancestors.

K has two siblings, brothers younger than himself.   Both are reported to be "bright."

Father.   K's father is an electrician, a graduate of high school and of Cooper Union.   He was born in Antigua and was 32 or 34 years old when K was born.   One of his sisters is a high school teacher in Brooklyn; another is a nurse; another, a stenographer.

Mother.   K's mother is recorded as of American-Jewish origin.   She was 30 or 31 years old when K was born.   She is a graduate of high school and of Hunter College (A.B.), New York City, and holds a license to teach music in the New York City schools.   At the date of record she was actively in service, teaching general subjects.   She had taken three maternity leaves of absence.

EARLY DEVELOPMENT

K's parents rate him as a child with excellent health, sturdy but nervous.   He may have had measles, but there were no other childhood illnesses except occasional colds. When tiny, he would wake up with "great imaginings." At a little older age he would cry "with high tension"; "he no longer does this."

According to the parents, K cut his first tooth at 6 months. He began to walk at about 20 months and to talk at about 2 years.   He learned to read at about 3 years.   "While still a baby in his carriage he could read 'ice' and he would read the billboards.   Before 3 he would sit down with a book and read."

At 5 years of age K wanted to discriminate in meaning between "bluff," "joke," and "fake."   He is "untiring in his attention to books. He will sit with an American history, an English history, and Godey's *History of American Beginnings in Europe* (which goes into Greece and Rome) and the dictionary around him, and will work at these for hours."

At the age here reported K had no playmates. His younger brothers played by themselves. K did not like to play. His favorite recreations were reading and transferring pictures, and consulting almanacs and dictionaries.

He has a passion for accuracy. He has as yet made no collections, and has no pets. He has no imaginary companions and no imaginary lands.

MENTAL MEASUREMENTS

On April 10, 1929, K was brought to Teachers College, Columbia University, for mental testing. The Stanford-Binet and other methods were employed. He was then 6 years 4 months old and had not yet entered school. On the Stanford-Binet his Mental Age at that date was 9–1, giving an IQ of 143. But the examiner added a note to the record to the effect that: "It is predicted that this child will test much higher later, when examined under standard conditions, alone with the examiner." The conditions under which this test was taken are not recorded, but it was probably a class demonstration.

On March 26, 1931, at the age of 8 years 3 months, K was again given a Stanford-Binet test by the same examiner. He was then in Grade 5A, although only two years before he had not yet entered school. This time his Mental Age was 14–8, giving him an IQ of close to 180. The earlier prediction of an increase in IQ at a later age was fulfilled, under standardized conditions.

Although K was in Grade 5A at this time, it is noted that "Writing is only about third-grade ability." In this manual coördination K's score was nearer to his Chronological Age than was his mental level. He was also given Trabue Language Completion Scale A on this date, with a score of Grade 6.5, a full year ahead of his actual, though advanced, school placement.

Of such cases the examiner commented as follows:

> The little boy scored a Mental Age of 14 years 8 months. Only one or two eight-year-olds in a hundred thousand reach such a score. These children are so far beyond the average that schools are not equipped to handle them adequately. Experts in education do not know what the best procedure is in regard to their placement in school, but we hope to find out as time goes on. . . . I asked you to bring the little boy again for purely professional reasons — to learn how he is developing, how he conducts himself, and what his interests are. We want to find out how to educate these children. . . . Tell him I am sure he is going to have a good future if he learns to get self-control. (I mention this last because you spoke of his having emotional upsets.)

PHYSICAL MEASUREMENTS

At the age of 6 years 4 months, K's standing height was 48.2 inches and his weight was 50.5 pounds. (Norms 46.0 inches, and 44 pounds.)

At the age of 8 years 3 months, K's standing height was 53 inches; sitting height, 28.2 inches; weight, 62 pounds. In the two-year interval K had gained 5 inches in height and 12 pounds in weight. (Age norms 49.8 inches, and 54.6 pounds.)

LATER EDUCATIONAL PROGRESS

There is little record in the files of the subsequent career of this boy and no follow-up has been made possible. A letter from his mother, dated December 30, 1933, reports that K "is now just eleven (birthday this month) and will graduate from public school next month."

This would mean completion of the eighth grade at the age of 11 years.

There is also a letter from his mother dated December 10, 1937, at which time K was 15 years old. In the following month he was to be graduated from Theodore Roosevelt High School, New York City. Plans were being made and advice sought concerning college. K had "gone through high school an honor student. . . . His high school record is outstanding. Regents marks, etc., exceptionally high."

Chapter Fifteen

CHILD L

THIS exceptionally gifted boy, born May 5, 1927, was a member from the beginning of the experimental group for "rapid learners" established February, 1936, in Speyer School by Leta S. Hollingworth.[1] In achievement as measured by standard tests from time to time he led that group of highly selected children, his IQ being 200. At the request of his parents he had been recommended for admission to the project by the principal of the public school he was then attending in Brooklyn (P.S. 35).

FAMILY BACKGROUND

Child L's ancestry is Austrian-Hebrew. Of his paternal relatives, an uncle and a cousin are rabbis, and at the time this record was made a cousin was professor of mathematics in the University of Krakow.

L's maternal grandfather was an Austrian merchant and also a learned man, who is said to have written several books. The maternal grandmother of L was active in local circles to which she belonged. At her death she left money for L's college education. A maternal uncle is an architect. L's mother's cousin is a physician.

No mentally defective or totally incompetent persons among L's ancestors are known.

[1] This chapter was written by H. L. H.

Father. Child L's father is a high school graduate. He was 33 years of age when L was born. His trade is that of jeweler, but being unable to find work in this line he has taken employment in a factory making airplane precision instruments.

Mother. L's mother is a high school graduate. She was 29 years of age when L, her only child, was born. She was a dressmaker before her marriage.

EARLY HISTORY

L is rated by his parents as having "good health" and as being "well-balanced." He cut his first tooth at 9 months, began to talk at 9 months, according to his parents, and to walk at 15 months. He learned to read at 4 years. His playmates are several years older than he (10–12 years). L likes to play. His favorite recreations are reading, chess, and checkers.

In January, 1935, at the age of 8 years 5 months, he was in Grade 5A1. His school ratings had been A for every term and he had accomplished four years' work in two years. The Otis Self-Administering Tests had been used in the school and L had been credited with an IQ of 153 — much lower than that subsequently found to characterize him. It was at this time that he was recommended for the group of "rapid learners" at Speyer School.

On September 28, 1936, at age 9 years 5 months, a Stanford-Binet test given L by Donald MacMurray, a graduate student, showed him to have a Mental Age of between 17–10 and 18–4, and an IQ of from 189 to 195.

On January 18, 1939, a Revised Stanford-Binet (1937

form) given L by another graduate student showed him to have a Mental Age of 19–6, his Chronological Age then being 10–8. The IQ thus determined was 183.

More dependable is a similar measure made May 5, 1937, by an expert in the Guidance Laboratory at Teachers College (Rosalind Blum). At Chronological Age 10–0, with the Revised Stanford-Binet (1937 Form 1) L's score was Mental Age 19–11, IQ 199. Certain details in the report of this test are worth reproduction here.

GUIDANCE LABORATORY REPORT OF L

Date of birth:	May 6, 1927	CA	10–0
Date of test:	May 5, 1937	MA	19–11
Test: Revised Binet, Form L		IQ	199

L earned a basal age at Superior Adult I Level. At Superior Adult II Level he successfully completed all the items except interpretation of one of the proverbs. At Superior Adult III Level one more test was passed — Orientation.

L was friendly and coöperative throughout the test. Although he had never seen the examiner before, he made an excellent adjustment to the testing situation. Throughout the test he indicated a genuine desire to be as accurate as possible. All his responses were given in great detail and he always told much more than was necessary in order to earn credit.

Psychometrically L ranks in the top tenth of one per cent of the population. His intellectual development is very superior. His level of comprehension, vocabulary, memory, and verbal ability are outstanding. He displayed excellent insight into his work and spontaneously criticized his own performance. When difficult items were presented, he frankly admitted that he could not respond accurately. He was persistent in his efforts and devoted excellent attention at all times. He has a good understanding of the limits of his ability. . . .

It is impossible to recommend appropriate school placement

for this boy, since such ability as he possesses appears in about one out of every million individuals. . . . His emotional, educational, and social adjustments will always be difficult because of his advanced intellectual development. . . .

L has acquired a wealth of information. We can be sure of one thing — no matter where this boy attends school, no matter what the teaching devices are, he will always learn new facts and instruct himself. Such intellectual curiosity as this boy possesses will always be satisfied because of his own drive to acquire both information and skills.

A further picture of L's ability at an early age is given by his scores in two CAVD Intelligence Scale records, made under the supervision of Leta S. Hollingworth. The first of these was made by L in November-December, 1936, at the age of 9 years 6 months. His score (Levels M-Q) was 392 points, which is noted as "equivalent to a good score for tenth-grade pupils who plan and are encouraged to go to a first-rate college."

The second CAVD score (Levels M-Q) was made in the spring of 1939, at the age of 11 years 10 months. His score was 416 points — a score which is median for Teachers College M.A. candidates and also for Yale Law School freshmen. Such a score is at the 3d decile of scores made by Ph.D. candidates at Teachers College, Columbia University. It was made by L while he was still in the elementary grades.

ACHIEVEMENT AT SPEYER SCHOOL

A few records of scores on the New Stanford Achievement Test will show the remarkable academic work of this boy from the age of 9 years 6 months to 12 years 6 months.

At the time of the first of these achievement examinations, age 9 years 6 months, L's achievement already exceeded the

Subject	December 4, 1936		December 6, 1937		December 12, 1938		December 4, 1939	
	Age	Grade	Age	Grade	Age	Grade	Age	Grade
Paragraph Meaning	17–8	11.7	18–5	UM	UM	UM	UM	UM
Word Meaning. . .	15–8	9.7	17–11	UM	17–8	UM	18–8	UM
Dictation	15–6	9.5	17–6	UM	17–8	UM	18–2	UM
Language Usage . .	15–9	9.8	16–10	UM	18–8	UM	19–2	UM
Literature	13–9	7.9	16–2	UM	16–6	UM	16–8	UM
History and Civics .	14–4	8.4	15–0	9.0	16–5	UM	UM	UM
Geography	17–6	11.6	19–2	UM	17–8	UM	UM	UM
Physiology and Hygiene	15–4	9.3	19–2	UM	UM	UM	UM	UM
Arithmetic Reasoning	14–1	8.2	19–2	UM	17–8	UM	UM	UM
Arithmetic Computation	14–10	8.9	17–4	UM	17–11	UM	UM	UM
Average.	15–6	9.5	17–6	UM	18–2	UM	UM	UM

status of high school freshmen. After this his work could not be measured (UM) by grade standards. Progress was still possible, however, in the subject in which his initial scores were relatively lower. All but one of these were brought up to an "unmeasurable" point during the second year. For such a child the time spent on drill in the fundamentals would be sheer waste — and yet he is too young to go to high school with children half again as old as he. In Speyer School he entered actively into the enrichment program and was intellectually easily the leader of the group.

The following chart shows, through scores in Modern School Achievement Tests as of February 13, 1936, L's comparative status with respect to normal expectations for his age and also with respect to the average status of the class of gifted children which he had just joined in the experimental school at Speyer.

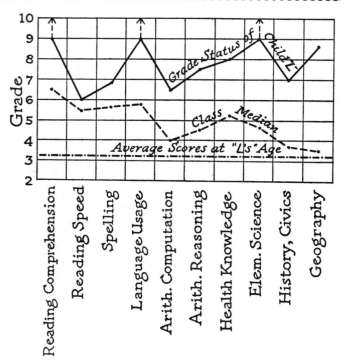

Fig. 13. Comparative Educational Achievement.

Young L's erudition was astonishing. His passion for scholarly accuracy and thoroughness set a high standard for accomplishment. He was relatively large, robust, and impressive, and was fondly dubbed "Professor." His attitudes and abilities were appreciated by both pupils and teachers. He was often allowed to lecture (for as long as an hour) on some special topic, such as the history of timepieces, ancient theories of engine construction, mathematics, and history. He constructed out of odds and ends (typewriter ribbon spools, for example) a homemade clock of the pendular type to illustrate some of the principles of chronometry, and this clock was set up before the class during the enrichment unit on "Time and Time Keeping," to demonstrate some of the principles of chronometry.   His notebooks were marvels of masterly exposition.

Being discontented with what he considered the inadequate treatment of land travel in a class unit on "Transportation," he agreed that time was too limited to do justice to everything.   But he insisted that "at least they should have covered ancient theory."   As an extra and voluntary project "he brought in elaborate drawings and accounts of the ancient theories of engines, locomotives, etc."

Subsequent to a visit to the school by an assistant superintendent associated with its work, L addressed to this dignitary the following communication.   He was at that time 10 years of age.

November 30, 1939

Dr. ——— ———
Assistant Superintendent
500 Park Avenue
New York, N. Y.

Dear Dr. ———:
Several of my classmates have informed me that you questioned them as to the relationship of Archimides to our unit on "Music, Art, and Literature."   We are not confining ourselves to Music, Art, and Literature, but are also studying the background that helped to produce this culture.   We feel that the only way that we can acquire a full view of this is to study contemporary contributors to the advance of civilization.   I, being greatly interested in mathematics, volunteered to deliver a report on Archimides who was famous for his mathematical research.

But this is not the only way Archimides is related to our unit on "Music, Art, and Literature." In the act of writing any great piece of music a knowledge of mathematics is essential. Also in any good work of art it enters in the form of perspective without which a drawing is apt to be void and lifeless. Therefore Archimides has been included in our unit.

I hope that you will soon visit our classroom again for all the children enjoy the talks you often give them.

Respectfully yours
(Signed)

HIGH SCHOOL RECORD TO DATE OF WRITING

L entered Bronx Science High School in February, 1940. This high school selects its students on the basis of a competitive examination. No classification on the basis of ability is made after entrance to the school.

L's final grades for the first term, closing June, 1940, are: English, 95; Social Studies, 99; Mathematics, 100; Science, 99; Average, 98.25.

The judgment of his supervisors and teachers is shown by the following quotations from comments about him, as of June, 1940.[2]

He is an excellent student. My only criticism of the boy is that he is too mature. He should be more of a nuisance. As I see it, our problem of adjustment here for L is to make him more of a real boy. *Dr. M., Administrative Assistant.*

He is a wonderful boy, and that covers everything. *Mr. C., Social Studies.*

L is the best boy I have had in all of my teaching experience, and I have taught in the New York City schools since 1913. He is the only boy I ever gave 100 to as a final mark.

[2] This section is an abbreviation of an account courteously provided by Dr. Miriam C. Pritchard, who made a follow-up study of L's first-term adjustments in high school.

He knows rules of trigonometry that he never has had in school. *Mr. W., Mathematics.*

I first became acquainted with L when he walked into my office last term and introduced himself. He said he was trying to make up his mind between Science High School and Townsend Harris. He had decided the most sensible way was for him to visit both schools and then make his decision.

He is a most unusual youngster. We found he surpassed any child in the class. I am going to discuss with his next term's teacher what modifications can be made of the required work. It won't be a matter of skipping anything. L needs to cover all the subject matter taught. He can profit from experience in manipulative situations in the laboratory. We may be able to arrange additional laboratory periods which will give him an opportunity to work out his own problems. His classmates look upon L as something of a genius. *Mr. Z., Head of Science Department.*

L feels that the school he chose is a good one and is well suited to his purposes, because the teachers are very good, the school teaches the subjects he wants to learn, and he is not hampered by the excessive size of the school. By way of improvement he suggests "More mathematics equipment and class formed according to students' ratings, smartest ten, say, in first class, etc."

In addition to his work in this school, and to his earlier school work, L has gone to Hebrew school about nine hours a week for four years, and has just been graduated therefrom with first honors. He reports many hobbies and outside interests — such as making model airplanes, doing science experiments at home, reading, using the microscope, collecting early American money and stamps. He does not do much outdoor playing — "Not because I do not want to play outdoors but because I lack the time and the companions. My favorite sport is swimming because it is both enjoyable and good exercise. . . . I very seldom take part in any organized athletic games except baseball for two reasons: first, I don't like to be disciplined and, second, I do not like games where a person's brawn is more important than a person's wit."

L and a friend have started a supply service in the high school, buying at wholesale and selling to students at retail prices. For this privilege, 20 per cent of the profits they turn into the General Organization carfare fund for needy students.

L's chief criterion in choosing his outside activities is their educational value. "By making model airplanes I can find out more about scientific principles of flying. . . . Any experiments in science I make may help me to advance my scientific knowledge. . . . I am doing some experimenting in soilless gardening as a scientific hobby. . . . I believe that stamps should have real interest behind them and not money value alone. . . . I do not play any musical instruments although I was drafted into the high school glee club by the music teacher. I would rather work on amateur radio if I had the money. I like music but I can't make it." L wants to take stenography and typing in night school. "It will come in handy in high school and when I get to college I may be able to get a job with some professor."

LATER TESTS AND INVENTORIES

In connection with the inquiry into L's adjustments upon entering high school, Dr. Pritchard has also given him several further tests and inventories, the results of which are as follows.

On CAVD (Levels (M-Q) his score is now 427 points,

which is in the 7th decile of the Ph.D. Matriculants at Teachers College.

On the Strong Vocational Interest Blank L's A (high) interests coincided with those of physicians, mathematicians, chemists, psychologists, and teachers of mathematics and physical science. His C (low) interests were on "most occupations dealing with large groups of people: personnel manager, social science high school teacher, purchasing agent, accountant, sales manager, real estate salesman, life insurance salesman, office worker, Y.M.C.A. secretary." His first choice for an occupation is mathematics teacher on the college level. He dislikes any occupation where there is "little opportunity to discover new facts."

On the Bernreuter "Personality Inventory" the following characteristics were indicated: Emotional adjustment better than average, tends to be alone, rarely asks for sympathy or encouragement, tends to ignore advice of others, seldom worries, rarely substitutes daydreaming for action, tends to dominate in face-to-face situations, to be wholesomely self-confident, well adjusted to environment, solitary, independent, and non-social. The following records were made on the Sones-Harry High School Achievement Test:

Language and Literature, 83
> The 99th-percentile score for students completing first-term high school English is 75. A score of 83 falls at the 88th percentile on norms based on 943 graduates from a large cosmopolitan city high school.

Mathematics, 64
> The score at the 99th percentile for first-term mathematics students is given as 36. A score of 64 exceeds the scores of 98 per cent of the 943 high school graduates cited above, and 99 per cent of 1156 college entrants.

Natural Science, 61

>   The 99th-percentile score for students who have had one term of high school science is 42. A score of 61 exceeds the scores of 96 per cent of the high school graduates.

Social Studies, 64

>   The 99th-percentile score for students completing one term's work in social science is 65. A score of 64 exceeds 90 per cent of the scores of the high school graduates.

Total Score, 272 points

>   A total score of 272 points exceeds the score of 95 per cent of the group of high school graduates from a cosmopolitan city high school.

On his own initiative, L is investigating the possibilities of scholarships with college work in mind. He says: "I spend between two or three hours a night on homework. I don't need to do this, but I am aiming for a scholarship and taking it very seriously."

Chapter Sixteen

SUMMARIES OF HEREDITY AND EARLY BEHAVIOR

I T IS of course obvious that no very general conclusions can be drawn from data relating to a dozen instances of exceptional mental endowment such as those reported in this monograph. Such data may, however, be added to information in process of accumulation from similar studies, the whole providing a respectable basis for judgment. The facts concerning the group of individuals presented in this book are, therefore, summarized in the form of the following brief review.[1]

FAMILY HISTORY AND BACKGROUND

The racial and national ancestry of the twelve children whose records have been presented in preceding pages may be chiefly a condition arising from the population in which they were found. Comparison with results from other population areas may serve to check certain implications suggested herein. All these cases were found and studied in New York City and about half of them in the public schools.

Among the ancestors whose origins are mentioned, in the endeavor to go behind the simple statement of "American

[1] This chapter was written by H. L. H.

parents," the nationalities are given as Jewish, 13; British, 9; German, 2; French, 2. In most cases the ancestors are individually compound — as Austrian-Jew, German-American, etc.

The activities of the more remote ancestors cover a wide range, from farming and small-town storekeeping to the learned professions, large business, and political activity. On the whole, the remote ancestors appear to have been fairly successful people, with the majority of them in the professions. No cases of mental deficiency or total incompetence are recorded among them.

A few of these children were from families in economic distress. These cases were largely instances in which the father was dead or incapacitated and the mother was struggling to carry on with slender resources. But on the whole, as in earlier cases cited from the literature of gifted children, the socio-economic status was moderate.

The fathers' occupations are in 10 of the 12 cases in the professions. They may be classified as:

Engineer	1	Lawyer	1
Army officer	1	College teacher	2
Accountant	2	Electrician	1
Journalist	2	Jeweler	1
Insurance	1		

The occupations of the mothers, either before or after marriage, when stated, were:

Advertising	1	Teacher	2
Housewife	3	Secretary	2
Statistician	1	Dressmaker	1
Scientist (M.D.)	1		

All but 2 of the fathers are known to be high school graduates; 5 went beyond this point in business or trade school; 4 are college graduates.

As for the mothers, all but 2 are high school graduates, and 5 hold college degrees.

Ages of parents at time of birth of child, when given, are as follows:

	Father	Mother
Below 25	2	1
From 25–30	3	4
30–35	2	2
35–40	3	1

Median age of fathers, 31; of mothers, 28.5.

Of the 11 cases where the facts are known, 5 are only children; 4 have one sibling; 1 has 2 siblings and 1 has more than this. In 5 cases where the child in question is not an only child, he or she is the eldest sibling. That is, in 10 of the 12 cases the child is a first-born, so far as the records show.

In a few cases the IQ of the sibling (or siblings) is known. Such IQ's are invariably above 130, in most cases much higher but in no case so high as the 180 that would have been required to admit them to the group here considered. Otherwise, of course, they would have been included in the study.

Of the 12 cases here described, 4 are girls. It has already been noted that among the 19 cases cited from the literature of gifted children there were 12 girls and 7 boys. The total of 31 cases which this study now makes available comprises 16 girls and 15 boys — as equitable a division of the honors as an odd number makes possible.

PHYSICAL AND BEHAVIORAL DEVELOPMENT

No single item indicative of early developmental pace in physique and movement is given for all the 12 cases. For most of them records are given on walking, talking, reading, first tooth, height, and weight. Grip is recorded in 5 cases, weight at birth in 3 only. These data are summarized in the following table. Since height, weight, and grip were taken at varying ages on the different children, all that is indicated in these columns is "above normal" ($\sharp$) or "below normal" (—).

Child	Age of Walking (Months)	Age of Talking (Months)	Age of Reading (Years)	First Tooth (Months)	Height	Weight	Grip
A		11	3	7	$\sharp$	$\sharp$	$\sharp$
B	15	9	3	7	$\sharp$	$\sharp$	$\sharp$
C	15	16	3	9	—	—	
D	12	11	1.5	4	$\sharp$	—	
E	13	24	8	8	$\sharp$	Normal	—
F	14	12	4.5	10			
G					$\sharp$	$\sharp$	—
H	14	16	4	9.5	$\sharp$	—	
I	10.5	21	3	5	$\sharp$	$\sharp$	
J							
K	20	24	3	6	$\sharp$	$\sharp$	
L	15	9	4	9	$\sharp$	$\sharp$	

Median age of walking, for the cases recorded, is 14 months — a wholly normal age for children in general. Median age of talking is 14 months — considerably earlier than the norm usually recognized. The range, too, is wide — from 9 to 24 months. First teeth normally begin to appear in the sixth to seventh month, and the median here is close to that. Median age of reading here reported — 3 years — is earlier even than that found in the 19 cases cited

from previous literature (3.5 to 4 years). All but one of
the 10 cases for which stature is reported exceed the norms
in this respect. Six are heavier than the age norm, 1 just
at it, and 3 are lighter in weight. The records of grip tests
show nothing unusual. In 3 cases where weight at birth was
recorded, this was from 7 to 10 pounds. Health is generally reported good.

Talking and reading are the two developmental indices
that most clearly differentiate these records from the norms.
These activities, both involving the use and understanding
of symbols, are the earliest clear expressions of mental liveli-
ness. After they have appeared, the gifted child's characteristics appear in those traits called understanding, judgment, learning, discrimination, and in the interest in and
capacity for such linguistic and abstract activities as are provided by schoolwork. It is, therefore, in the earlier scholastic activities and in social relations that these children most
notably declare their quality under our prevailing system of
child management.

Chapter Seventeen

SCHOLASTIC ACHIEVEMENT AND CREATIVE ACTIVITY

T HE following brief summaries of the achievement and adjustment of these twelve children may serve to suggest a few general principles that are applicable to other cases as well.[1]

SCHOLASTIC ACHIEVEMENT AND EDUCATIONAL ADJUSTMENT

Child A. This boy showed signs of precocity before his second year, reciting, classifying, and playing with words and letters; and before the age of 3 years showing interest in rhymes and stories. From first school entrance suitable placement was a recognized problem, and by the time A was 6 years old he was brought to a college clinic for educational guidance.

Throughout elementary school A was a trying problem, lacking interest in the routine program. He was behind his mental level in handwork and was not motivated to do his best work; he fitted poorly into social activities. Character traits were highly approved, except perhaps for independence and obstinacy. He resorted to imaginary lands, reading, and science and mathematics as forms of play.

The case was not followed far enough to show his final

[1] This chapter was written by H. L. H.

educational achievement, although it is known that he went through high school and entered college.

Child B. This girl was occupied with words by the time of her second year. Her ability was not early recognized by the schools she attended, although she passed seventh-grade standards while still in the fourth grade and her marks were always high. As she had marked social interests and aptitudes, this educational misplacement caused no serious trouble. When eventually "skipped," her size and poise kept her from being conspicuous, although the youngest in the class. She was apparently a natural leader, and in addition to the usual preoccupation with reading she had as an outlet the groups and clubs she organized.

Since she was followed only to high school, her final educational adjustment is not known.

Child C. This boy learned to read "almost as soon as he talked," and read fluently before beginning school. He was at once recognized as "odd," but in spite of perfect work he was not advanced and his ability was unappreciated by his teachers. At 9 years 6 months, with a mental age of 18, he was still in the fifth grade. He was very unhappy until the principal sought educational advice on his case and he was admitted to a segregated experimental class for rapid learners, where he quickly became adjusted and was an enthusiastic scholar.

Personal traits made social adjustment faulty, but he persisted in his educational career against heavy economic handicaps, finished high school and college with honors, and completed the medical training that admitted him to the profession that had been his ambition since childhood.

Child D. This boy was reading before he was 2 years of age, and was also interested in numbers and relationships. He made social contacts even before entering school by publishing a playground newspaper. As an exception to the prevailing rule, this boy's ability was early appreciated by his parents and it was recognized by his teachers as early as kindergarten.

His educationally interested parents supervised his instruction and sought expert advice. Various side talents in which he was versatile were also cultivated. Mathematical and scientific interests appeared early and were encouraged. Progress through school was facilitated and he entered college at 12 years 6 months of age, graduating with honors at just over 16.

In the following twelve years he became a proficient and well-trained industrial chemist, holding an important position in this field at the time of his death at the age of 28.

Child E. This child's ability also was recognized by teachers and parents at an early age, and this appreciation led to diligent supervision of his subsequent education. When he began to talk he was equally conversant with four languages. He was always accelerated in school and his superior size made this procedure feasible, at least in childhood. His whole bent was toward scholarly pursuits, and much of his study was privately conducted.

E entered college at 12 years and his precocity was widely exploited on the campus and in the press. His devotion to his work and his good sense and humor preserved him from social difficulties. He even impersonated himself in a class play.

His subsequent intellectual progress was phenomenal and he speedily became a scholarly contributor and an influential and active leader in the field of his boyhood choice.

Child F. This boy was an educational problem even in

his first years in an ungraded school. Afterward teachers refused to place him in grades high enough to keep him occupied. A benign form of truancy that led him to the public library and to chess tournaments was his way out of his predicament. But in this process he developed an aversion to educational processes and to authorities of all kinds.

He was appreciated neither by his parents nor by his teachers until he was discovered in a survey that sought for just such minds for an experimental project in the education of the gifted. Traits other than intellectual made his subsequent educational history take the form of spurts, with intervening debacles. He died before the outcome of this group of circumstances could materialize.

Child G. This is a third case of early recognition by teachers and of guidance by parents, which led in childhood to an educational clinic for advice. Early interests in reading were fostered and directed, and more extrovert and social activities were devised by his parents.

G was rapidly promoted, and after entering an individual progress class he was a contented scholar. In spite of the facilitation of his progress through the grades he was not through high school until 15, and there is every evidence of satisfactory personal and social adjustment. The case record ends with his admission to college, on a scholarship, with definite and clearly defined aims and interests.

Child H. This girl's interest in words, stories, and relationships was noticed before her third year, and early recognition of her gifts appears to have come through an aunt who had special educational insight. Although H resorted to imaginary companions, she was socially minded enough to enjoy playmates.

Since the record terminates with her tenth year, there are

no data on her later educational career. But her story thus far appears placid and marked by good adjustment and intelligent guidance.

Child I. This case had the advantage of a parent who also had been studied by educational experts interested in the gifted. Also her parents were themselves teachers. As early as 2 years she had been identified as exceptional and her subsequent career appears to have been guided throughout with wisdom.

I's discontent with aimless activity in the first two school grades was solved by placing her in the special experimental class for rapid learners. Her excellent progress and adaptation here constitute a clear demonstration of the advantages of early identification and intelligent educational placement.

Child J. This child's ability was recognized by her teachers from the beginning. She was accorded very rapid advancement, which was probably the only solution available under the circumstances. The parents, themselves educators, also contributed intelligent care and guidance in her development.

This favorable conjunction led to her prompt admission to an experimental group for children of her quality as soon as the regular teachers realized their inability to provide further stimulation for her. The definite service provided in this case by the Bureau of Educational Guidance is also an instructive part of the picture.

Child K. This boy's history is meagerly recorded. His picture is the usual one of early reading and native interest in learning. By his seventh year he had been appreciated by relatives who sought expert advice and guidance in his education. Such advice was then sought from time to time by his parents, and the brief record shows no untoward developments in his subsequent education up to the end of high school.

Child L. Achievement was so conspicuous in this case that as soon as L entered school he was given rapid promotion. His recommendation to the special class for rapid learners was due to the joint action of his parents and the school principal.

Once in this group, L's educational problems vanished. Expert guidance also attended his entrance to high school. As a result of these circumstances his further career appears to be propitiously launched.

The observations that seem most obviously to emerge from these brief summaries of educational history are as follows:

1. Such children as are here presented constitute difficult educational problems from their entrance in school. The problems are not only those of the teachers and educational authorities, but they are chiefly, perhaps, the problems of the children themselves.

2. Depending on the solution of these problems, such children may either be well articulated to the work of school and society and thus their remarkable talents be socially capitalized, or they may, on the other hand, develop distaste for such activities, negativism toward social projects, and personal obstinacy and recalcitrance, perhaps accompanied by bitterness.

3. The advantages of early recognition, appreciation and, if possible, measurement are apparent in the study of this small group of exceptionally intelligent children. Although all were identified fairly early in their lives, there are very different degrees of adaptation to school and society, ranging from opposition and truancy, through indifference, to

rapt and enthusiastic preoccupation. To a considerable extent these variations appear to have depended on the earliness of identification of the child's intellectual quality. The valuable services of surveys, guidance clinics, and school psychologists are clearly manifested in this group of cases.

4. The cases that have achieved most contented and socially useful adaptation are those in which parents, teachers, and principals have made prompt use of special gift identification, have sought educational guidance, have personally fostered and supervised the child's development and the solution of his adjustment problems, or have taken advantage of such experimental classes for exceptional children as the schools have offered at the time.

5. Among the cases herein reported the clearest ones of easy and useful adjustment occurred when the exceptional child became a member of an experimental group comprised of others of his approximate kind. In the dozen cases cited, four different projects of this kind in the New York City schools have been referred to.

CREATIVE WORK

Is it true that children such as those herein described differ from those of less intelligence merely in having a readier and more tenacious memory? Are their distinctive achievements only the phenomenal reproduction of things they have learned — the recitation of answers they have been taught? Or do they also exhibit signs of originality and creativeness? Of their superior capacity for learning there is of course ample evidence. Is it this feature of their endowment that accounts for their high scores in conventionally standardized measures such as tests and examinations?

Ordinary records and histories are perhaps not well suited to disclose originality in childhood unless it is obtrusive. The child who devises a new way of tying his shoes, of arranging his books, of managing his pets, of sharpening his skates, may very easily get no clinical credit for these inventions. No one, indeed, except the child himself may ever know of them, and it may never occur to him that they are "creative." A boy who writes a poem, draws a steamboat, or devises a new game of checkers may immediately get credit for originality, while one who invents a technique of his own for shaving the back of his own neck may remain unheralded as a creator.

Our concept of "creativeness" has become standardized so as to suggest chiefly contributions to the conventional arts. It may nevertheless be instructive to review these case histories, looking in each for signs of activity that might in one way or another be construed as creative.

Child A. At 12 months he was classifying his blocks according to letter shapes. Before 16 months of age A tired of saying the letters of the alphabet forward and "guessed he would say them backward." He "made rhymes" of his own by the third year. He developed arithmetical principles unsuspected by either parents or teachers. He had an elaborate "imaginary land." He did not play well with other children because he always wanted to introduce new methods of playing the games. He devised elaborate schemes of his own for classifying events and objects. There is very little of the conventional interest in drawing, painting, poetry, mechanics, or music in this account, but it is clear enough that in his own way A had originality.

Child B. This child's early acquisition of the art of reading appears to have been untutored, and her passion for organizing clubs showed at least a certain type of initiative. But the record gives little evidence of other creative activity. Her chief distinction so far as noted was in the fields of excellent schoolwork and social adaptability.

Child C. This boy's earliest recognition was on the basis of what the teachers called his "phenomenal memory." But from early years his chief passion was for science, and his main interest therein was the possibility of discovering new things. There is, however, little evidence of ingenuity in the record, and C was chiefly distinguished by the mass and facility of his knowledge, learned chiefly from others.

Child D. The very curiosity of this boy might be said to have a creative or original character. "He was always asking unexpected questions." His playground newspaper was an original project in spite of its conventional character. So also was his passion for tabulation and calculation. His imaginary land was a complicated creation, as was the elaborate dictionary of its unique language. Musical composition was one of his pastimes, and he had active native talent for drawing and design. The invention of new words and new games was creative, and he had original classifications for many varieties of natural objects. His interest in science, which became uppermost, led to original experiments such as those on "the path of a tack." His final adoption of scientific work as a career is in keeping with this, and the position held at the end of his brief life was one concerned with chemical research in a relatively new industry. In a very real sense this boy's creative interests are fundamental in the picture of his development.

Child E. Originality appears among E's characteristics even in his definitions of words in the vocabulary tests. His life was, however, so harnessed to the organized pursuit

of degrees that conventional fields of learning came to pre-
occupy him and there was little originality in his choice of
an occupation, to which he appears to have been guided by
solicitous elders.   Such originality as he had appeared ab-
stractly and verbally.   Thus his "constructive ability" was
good but his "manual dexterity" poor.   He had an imaginary country.   After his escape from the hierarchy of organized education he became an active and productive scholar
in his field, although it may be that theology is not a field
in which creativeness is encouraged.

Child F.   There is little evidence in the career of F of
anything that could be called creative.   He was in many
ways ingenious, and he was socially nonconforming.   He
was a storehouse of information but not sagacious in the
use of his knowledge.   His ingenuity was not along original
lines but in such conventionalized fields as chess, bridge, and
dialectic.   His capacity for intellectual work was phenomenal, but for the most part such activities were in
prescribed fields, and a temporary interest in science was
deflected to law — like theology, a field in which creativeness is not always an asset.

Child G.   This boy's education was so scrupulously supervised and so sedulously recorded that he had little time for
original projects.   His questions and remarks evince a lively
curiosity, and his abiding interests in chemistry and mathematics, with a research turn, perhaps point to creative trends
that are poorly reflected in more elementary years.   There
is little evidence of unusual proficiency in any of the creative
arts.

Child H.   The chief interests of H as a child were in
"drawing, painting, and mosaic blocks."   She developed
imaginary companions.   She showed at an early age pro-

nounced interests and aptitudes in stories and in versification. She was a composer of creditable childhood songs, poetry, and plays. She was followed only to her eleventh year and up to this point seems to have shown definite signs of constructive imagination.

Child I. This girl was versatile in many creative ways. She developed imaginary companions, wrote music and songs, produced dramatizations, wrote effective verses and longer poems. So far as the brief record shows, her creative interests remained close to the conventionalized arts, except for the native curiosity characteristic of most very bright children.

Child J. The data on J are so scant that little assurance as to her originality can be felt. At 7 she was in many ways an independent thinker. She composed "jingles" at the same time that she was reading Shakespearean plays, and the examiner commented on her "constructive imagery." She wrote acceptable poems before her tenth birthday. But for the most part she had been so occupied by rapid educational promotion that this is the most conspicuous feature in her description.

Child K. This boy has without doubt an enthusiasm for scholarly inquiry. He made no spontaneous collections, had no pets, no imaginary companions or lands. In a sense these traits which are lacking in K's personality are usually counted as originalities in children of such high intelligence. But data are not at hand to enable a judgment to be made of the presence or absence of creativeness in this child.

Child L. This is the case of a boy who showed such independent zeal for acquiring information that this curiosity had itself a creative tone. He is inventive and constructive even in mechanical ways — an exception in this par-

ticular group of cases. His teachers find him possessed of
knowledge in mathematics which he must have derived from
his own reflection. He also has marked initiative in using
his knowledge, is full of constructive suggestions, makes
many scientific experiments of his own, has many hobbies,
and wants to do things "to advance scientific knowledge."
Although he shows no unusual proficiency in the conventional
arts, there can be no doubt that in affairs intellectual and
scientific his mind is not only creative but also fertile.

GENERAL STATEMENT

If a general statement be attempted on the basis of such
data as the descriptions and these summaries afford, it might
be to the effect that one third of these highly intelligent children (A, D, H, L) show notable signs of creativeness. Another third (C, E, I, J) show such indications to a moderate
degree. In the remaining third (B, F, G, K) there is at
least no indication of marked constructive originality provided
by these descriptions.

Certainly these creative dispositions are more conspicuous
in these cases than in the general population of children.
How these very rare intelligences compare in this respect
with those ranging from, say, 130 to 175 IQ we cannot
know. Creativeness even at best is infrequent enough. In
experiences of daily life of course such creativeness might
be more often found in children in the middle range of high
intelligences because there are so many more of these in
the population.

On the other hand, it may be that creativeness in marked
degree appears in these higher ranges only. Under any
circumstances it is not an all-or-none phenomenon, and the
problem of the correlation of originality with intelligence

scores perhaps deserves more careful study than it has received. It seems suggested at least by these few cases that very high intelligence may in some instances become directed along wholly conventional channels, showing itself in the amount of work or the rate of progress, with little or no manifestation of creative originality. If this is the case, it should be important to discover to what extent this is a reflection of the regimentation of the occupation of such children by organized educational projects and close parental supervision, and to what extent it is a characteristic that is native in the individual. If it should be true that creativeness is closely dependent on such a high range of intelligence as that shown by this group of twelve children, a social order that esteems creativeness should give serious thought to the conditions of its cultivation and its development.

In this connection it is of some significance that so far as these cases are concerned, the best adjustments appear to have been made in educational arrangements that required the devotion of only one part of the child's time to established curricula, thus leaving time and providing encouragement for individual initiative and enrichment.

PART III

GENERAL PRINCIPLES AND IMPLICATIONS

Chapter Eighteen

ADULT STATUS AND PERSONALITY RATINGS

OBSERVATION of such cases as those described in the foregoing chapters suggests that children of exceptionally high intelligence do not regress toward mediocrity as they mature but maintain their initial distinguished status. Studies by other workers (Kuhlmann, Baldwin and Stecher, Terman) confirm such a conclusion. A further study of this point was reported by Hollingworth and Lorge in 1936, in which the following questions were investigated:

1. To what extent is status in IER Intelligence Scale CAVD at maturity predictable from childhood scores in Stanford-Binet?

2. How do those who tested above 180 IQ in childhood differ at maturity from those at lower levels in measures of general culture and of scientific information?

3. Is there discernible any consistent specialization in mental abilities from childhood to maturity?

4. At what degree of intelligence in terms of IQ (Stanford-Binet) is the word "genius" justifiable, if at all?

5. At what point on the scale of IQ (Stanford-Binet) obtained in childhood will individuals later prove "unmeasurable" by available tests of adult intelligence?

In 1934–1935 a group of eighteen persons whose high IQ's had been measured twelve or thirteen years earlier (at ages 7 to 9 years) were measured in these respects and to these were added three others whose childhood IQ's were known to have been over 170. The tests used, to be reported here, were: CAVD Intelligence Scale, Levels N–Q; the Coöperative General Culture Test (Form 1933 or 1934); and the Coöperative General Science Test (Form 1933). There were also available data on most of the individuals from Army Alpha tests taken at ages 16 to 19. Of the 21 cases thus studied, nine had a childhood IQ over 170; eight over 150; the remaining four ranged down to 133.

ADULT STATUS OF HIGHLY INTELLIGENT CHILDREN [1]

The detailed data have been reported elsewhere and only the general results need be recited here:

"For these gifted individuals (albeit there are so few studied) superior status on the Stanford-Binet at or near ages 7 to 9 years of age is highly predictive of status on Army Alpha at or near 16 to 19 years of age, and of status on CAVD at or near maturity. . . .

"It is clear that CAVD is more closely associated with General Culture than with General Science. . . . There obviously is a specificity of success for Science as compared with General Culture. . . .

"The results for the CAVD as interpreted through norms obtained on selected populations show that highly intelligent children (of IQ 140 or above) fall within the upper quartile

[1] For a more detailed account see Lorge and Hollingworth's "The Adult Status of Highly Intelligent Children," in *Journal of Genetic Psychology.* (1936), Vol. 49, pages 215–226.

of the college graduate population of the United States, when they are at or near maturity."

Such results are confirmed also by a study reported two years earlier, in which over 100 children had been remeasured with Army Alpha 10 to 12 years after their initial Stanford-Binet measurements at ages 7 to 9 years.[2] All these children had IQ's over 130, and half of them were over 150, ranging up to 190. From this study the following conclusions had been drawn:

"Of 116 children testing in the top centile of the distribution of school children by Stanford-Binet, 82 per cent were found when near maturity, ten years later, to rate in the top centile of the military draft by Army Alpha. The remainder rated in high centiles. No individual of either sex regressed to or nearly to the average. . . . Girls regressed from the top centile somewhat more frequently than boys, this regression being in part but not fully accounted for by the known sex difference between medians on Army Alpha.

"This result affords a validation, by means of elapsed time, of the predictive power of available mental tests on the one hand; and on the other, a proof of the constancy of the intellectual development of gifted children in terms of centile status."

CRITIQUE OF THE CONCEPT OF "GENIUS" AS APPLIED
IN TERMS OF IQ

The term "genius" has been used by Terman — and following him by many others — to denote children testing at or above 140 IQ (S–B). In the light of the developmental data herein presented, it would appear that the term "genius"

[2] Hollingworth and Kaunitz. "The Centile Status of Gifted Children at Maturity." *Journal of Genetic Psychology* (September, 1934), pages 106–120.

is thus misapplied, unless we wish to define as "geniuses" persons who represent approximately the best fourth of all students being graduated from American colleges.

Of individuals here followed to early maturity, those who test at about 140 IQ (S–B) are found to define approximately the 75th percentile of college graduates, taking the country over. They are far from "genius," if by that term is to be meant the degree of mental ability that is capable of outstanding original intellectual achievement. It is only when we have an IQ (S–B) of at least 160 in a child, that we may begin to expect mildly noteworthy accomplishments, such as winning "honors" in a first-class college. Very rarely are "honors" won in first-class colleges by those who test below this status in childhood. The small sample of college graduates here presented is truly representative of the much larger sample in our files (not tested by our end tests) in this respect.

Of primary interest to the present investigators is the subsequent history of those who in childhood have achieved the extremely infrequent rating of 180 IQ or higher. At maturity will these persons still stand out from their contemporaries in mental tests and in achievement?

This question is answered affirmatively by our data. The five children here included,[3] who achieved IQ's (S–B) on *first* test in childhood of more than 180, are they who "find the tops" on CAVD, at maturity. Every one of these top-rank persons is noteworthy among contemporaries. Before the age of 22 in all cases, one had prosecuted research in history, one in mathematics, one in chess, and two had become established in learned professions. One stood high in the national ranking for chess. A long list of medals and prizes

[3] Study made by Leta S. Hollingworth in previous years.

had been won by them. All but one of those graduated from college had been elected to Phi Beta Kappa.

These unusual achievements show how children testing above 180 IQ rise above the generality of the college populations in adolescence and in early maturity. None of those who tested in childhood around 140, 150, or 160 IQ (S–B) approaches these others at maturity in honors and prizes won, or in test scores.

This is, perhaps, the most significant fact to be derived from our data: that the children who test at and above 180 IQ constitute the "top" among college graduates. They are the students of whom one may confidently predict that they will win honors and prizes for intellectual work.

Furthermore, it is shown that at approximately 190 IQ (S–B) individuals "go through the ceiling" of available tests for adult intelligence by the time they are 21 years old. We cannot at present distribute these persons at maturity.

Perhaps this is the point at which the term "genius" begins to apply — i.e., at or near IQ 180 (S–B) — if we adhere to the dictionary definition of the word, "Exalted intellectual power, marked by an extraordinary faculty for original creation, expression, or achievement" which is beyond the reach of available modes of measurement in its maturity.

APPLICATION OF BERNREUTER INVENTORY OF PERSON-
ALITY TO HIGHLY INTELLIGENT ADOLESCENTS [4]

The data of the present study were obtained early in 1933, the subjects being 36 boys and 19 girls, of the average age of 18 years 6 months. The IQ's (S–B) of all had been taken in early childhood. The group ranged from 135–190 IQ

---

[4] For detailed results see the paper by this title, by Hollingworth and Rust, *Journal of Psychology* (1937), Vol. 4, pages 287–293.

SHOWS GROUP RESULTS FOR HIGHLY INTELLIGENT BOYS AND GIRLS, GIVING EVIDENCE THAT SUCH GROUPS ARE MUCH LESS NEUROTIC, MUCH MORE SELF-SUFFICIENT, AND MUCH LESS SUBMISSIVE IN ATTITUDE THAN COLLEGE STUDENTS OR ADULTS IN GENERAL ARE, ACCORDING TO THE CATEGORIES AND NORMS SET UP BY BERNREUTER

Statistical categories	B1-N Neurotic Tendency			B2-S Self-Sufficiency			B4-D Dominance-Submission		
	Highly intelligent boys	College norm group	Adult norm group	Highly intelligent boys	College norm group	Adult norm group	Highly intelligent boys	College norm group	Adult norm group
Number	36	427	86	36	427	99	36	427	100
Mean	− 104.9	− 52.9	− 69.3	54.5	24.9	38.8	87.4	46.3	52.7
σ	56.7	85.2	76.3	42.3	54.0	52.4	44.6	67.4	61.8
σ Mean	9.4	4.1	8.2	7.0	2.6	5.3	7.4	3.3	6.2
σσ	6.7	2.9	5.8	5.0	1.8	3.7	5.2	2.3	4.4
σ diff. ms. D		10.2	12.5		7.5	8.8		8.1	9.6
σ diff.		5.1	2.8		3.9	2.1		5.1	3.6
Median	− 112.0	− 70.0	− 75.0	54.5	25.0	35.0	98.1	45.0	55.0
Girls									
Number	19	317	123	19	317	126	19	317	130
Mean	− 45.0	− 39.6	− 34.2	52.0	6.9	16.8	46.5	33.1	19.2
σ	65.7	78.9	80.6	51.7	55.7	55.6	55.5	63.5	65.5
σ Mean	15.1	4.4	7.3	11.9	3.1	5.0	12.7	3.6	5.7
σσ	10.7	3.1	5.1	8.4	2.2	3.5	9.0	2.5	4.1
σ diff. ms. D		15.7	16.8		12.3	12.9		13.2	13.9
σ diff.		.04	.64		3.7	2.7		1.0	1.96
Median	− 42.6	− 40.0	− 30.0	52.0	5.0	0.0	40.7	33.0	15.0

(S–B), with a median at about 153 IQ (S–B). All but four of these young persons were Jewish, a factor which must be considered as of possible consequence, but which cannot be evaluated properly from any data at present in scientific literature.

The inventories were taken and scored by the investigators in person. All subjects had been personally known since childhood to the senior investigator.

The method of scoring follows Bernreuter, three categories only being found of sufficient independence to warrant recording.

The summary of results shows that the highly intelligent are less neurotic, more self-sufficient, and less submissive, as a group, than are the populations with which they are comparable. This divergence from the norms is found both for boys and for girls of the highly intelligent group, but it is much more pronounced for boys.

To one who has been familiar with the characteristics and the careers of these persons for fifteen years, the correspondence between what is found on the inventory and what is found in the actual lives is interestingly close. Boy 13, for instance (extremely high score for self-sufficiency and dominance), took ship on his own initiative as soon as he was twenty-one years old and sailed around the world as an ordinary seaman, returning to his post in the financial district of New York City when the journey was completed. Boy 35 is a well-known player in metropolitan and sectional chess tournaments, and was able to meet seasoned players when he was fifteen to seventeen years old (high scores for self-sufficiency and dominance). Boy 29 entered college at 14 years of age, "held his own" with the older students, earned money throughout his course, graduated at eighteen years of age with Phi Beta Kappa, and won a prize for research, in competition, in his junior year at medical school. Girl H won and held an appointment in public service, against heavy odds of sex, age, and general economic depression.

The indication from these data is that adolescents who as children tested from 135–190 IQ (S–B) are *much less neurotic, much more self-sufficient* and *much less submissive* than college students in general, or than adults of the mental caliber represented in the Bernreuter norms. It is to be noted in this comparison with the generality of college students that from data so far collected, the median intelligence of the group here presented reaches about Q_3 for college students, taking them the country over.

Chapter Nineteen

THE DEVELOPMENT OF PERSONALITY IN HIGHLY INTELLIGENT CHILDREN [1]

THE children included in the term "highly intelligent children" cover a very wide range in intellectual variation — from an IQ of 130 (S–B) to the topmost limit of human diversity. This topmost limit seems to define itself at approximately 200 IQ. The most extreme deviates reported in the literature as fully measured fall at or near this point. A considerable number falling above 180 IQ have been reported, many of them not fully measured by Stanford-Binet because of the limitations of the test. It is therefore clear that children in the upper 1 per cent are not all alike. On the contrary, the child at the top of this group exceeds the child who barely reaches the group by much more than the latter exceeds the average child. The most able child in the upper 1 per cent surpasses the least able in this group by as much as the average child surpasses a moron (in terms of IQ). The really difficult problems of adjustment to life and to people come to those who test above 170 IQ. As there are so very few of these children, parents and teachers are

[1] For the original discussion of this topic see the paper by this title, by Leta S. Hollingworth, in the Fifteenth *Yearbook* of the Department of Elementary School Principals, National Education Association (July, 1936), pages 272–281.

seldom called upon to consider their needs. Thus when one does appear, he or she is the more likely to be misunderstood.

GENERAL CONSIDERATIONS

Obviously, it is not possible to discuss every aspect of personality in the limited number of pages of this book. We shall confine ourselves, therefore, to a few of the more important phases of development which are unique in the case of gifted children; particularly to such complexities as arise from the combination of immaturity and deviation, these continuing for approximately twenty-one years. This is the period when development is taking place, as distinguished from the period of maturity.

It should be stated emphatically at the outset that children of very superior intelligence are not, as a group, socially annoying. The problems of personality adjustment are those of the child, not those of society as ordinarily understood. If the gifted child should annoy society, society would pay more attention to him. Society builds splendid institutions and provides expert care and guidance for vicious and feeble-minded children. That society does not pay such attention to the gifted is in itself evidence of social acceptability. The researches of Terman,[2] of Hartshorne and May,[3] and of Haggerty,[4] among others, have shown that highly intelligent children are more stable emotionally than are children in general, are much more resistant to childish temptations, and exhibit far less of undesirable behavior than is exhibited by

[2] Terman, Lewis M. *Genetic Studies of Genius:* Vol. I. Stanford University Press, Stanford University, California; 1925.

[3] Hartshorne, H., and May, M. A. *Studies in Deceit.* The Macmillan Company, New York; 1927.

[4] Haggerty, Melvin E. *Evaluation of Higher Institutions.* University of Chicago Press, Chicago, Illinois; 1937.

the dull. Teachers do, however, report them for "restlessness" and "lack of interest" somewhat more often than they report children of 100 IQ for these behaviorisms. The researches of Burt [5] and of Healy and Bronner [6] show few children testing above 130 IQ among delinquents, in proportion to their frequency in the population as a whole.

With these facts as to generally superior adjustment before us, let us inquire whether there are, nevertheless, special perplexities in the life of a gifted child, and at what point in the range of intellect these perplexities begin. Is it possible that a child who varies as far *above* his contemporaries as an imbecile or an idiot varies *below* them, will find only advantages and no special difficulties of development created for him by the fact of his wide deviation from the norm?

Observation and measurement of gifted children as they have grown from early childhood to maturity have made it possible to formulate definitely some of the special problems of development which arise from being an extreme and infrequently occurring deviate. The more intelligent the child, the more likely he or she is to become involved in these puzzling difficulties. Let us consider some of these problems.

THE PART PLAYED BY PHYSIQUE

The "looks" of a person has much to do with his social adjustment. If highly intelligent children really resembled the cartoonist's idea of them, there would be little chance of excellent development. Fortunately, the researches of the past twenty years have proved that the popular notions about

[5] Burt, C. *The Young Delinquent*. D. Appleton-Century Company, Inc., New York; 1924.
[6] Healy, W., and Bronner, A. F. *Criminals and Delinquents: Their Making and Unmaking*. The Macmillan Company, New York; 1928.

the poor physiques of the gifted and the weird ugliness of their physiognomies are not only erroneous but the exact opposite of the truth. These are superstitions, founded perhaps on the unconscious longing for "a just nature" which will distribute gifts somewhat equally instead of bestowing everything upon a few persons.

It has been amply proved, by measurements, that highly intelligent children are tall, heavy, strong, healthy, and fine looking as a group, exceeding the generality of children in all these respects. This does not mean that every individual among the gifted is physically superior, but it does mean that a gifted child is more likely to have a fine body than is a child taken from the general population.

As for beauty of face, in two separate series of photographs in which the faces of highly intelligent adolescents were compared with the faces of adolescents of ordinary mentality, the faces of the former were found to be more beautiful. This was the impression made upon "naïve" judges who knew nothing concerning the comparative intelligence of those judged. It may be that one reason why teachers often do not identify gifted children accurately, is that they are looking for pupils who correspond to the cartoonist's picture, and thus are led away from consideration of the beautiful and the well grown!

As gifted children approach and reach maturity, they reap the benefits of superior vitality, size, and beauty. However, many of them suffer, while growing up, from feelings of inferiority connected with size and strength, for typically they are somewhat accelerated in school status and they naturally choose children older than themselves as chums. Thus in physical competitions they are at a disadvantage. Observation shows that they tend to develop sedentary forms of play, or forms of physical enjoyment that do not depend upon being included in a group; such as swimming, skating, horseback riding, and walking.

PROBLEM OF LEADERSHIP

Also, in all matters pertaining to leadership, the competition with older classmates and friends exerts an influence, particularly during adolescence. The very young boy (or girl) in high school is not so likely to be elected to a post of leadership because of his comparative size, his voice, and the juvenility of his clothes. Thus a feeling may be engendered in him that he cannot gain the confidence of contemporaries; and this, in turn, may impair his self-confidence.

If long continued, this state of affairs may lead to emotional straining after social recognition. In social gatherings, size and physical maturity are important as *absolute* quantities and qualities, and not in relation to age. Thus a child should not be placed too far out of his age-group. A very gifted boy, reaching at twenty years a stature of five feet nine inches, remarked, "It is very odd to be as large as the people you're with!" Being always the smallest member of a social group may develop attitudes which are hard to revise when eventually the boy or girl achieves adult stature and is "as large as the people you're with."

This difficulty in assuming a normal place among more mature schoolmates arises especially in adolescence, when association with members of the opposite sex makes its introduction. Being in high school or in college with much older classmates, the boy of thirteen to sixteen finds himself at a disadvantage with the girls whom he meets. The girls brought to parties by the older boys are "too old" for him, and he feels unable to claim their attention. Many of these young boys show sufficient insight and sufficient management of their disadvantage to take care of it. They know that the trouble lies in being "too young," and that later they will achieve standing with the girls. In a few cases, however, this difficulty may lead to an unfortunate avoidance of girls, even in more mature years. In the case of girls, adjustment to the society of older boys in high school and college seems to present no special difficulties, since girls develop earlier than boys do, and are taken seriously by boys who are older than themselves.

The "inferiority complexes" of gifted persons have been little studied, but it is certain that many such persons do feel socially inferior and shy. Some of this may be due to the physical comparisons just suggested, arising from prolonged association with older persons.

PROBLEMS OF ADJUSTMENT TO OCCUPATION

Where the gifted child drifts in the school unrecognized, working chronically far below his capacity (even though young for his grade), he receives daily practice in habits of idleness and daydreaming. His abilities never receive the stimulus of genuine challenge, and the situation tends to form in him the expectation of an effortless existence. Children with IQ's up to 150 get along in the ordinary course of school life quite well, achieving excellent marks without serious effort. But children above this mental status become almost intolerably bored with school work if kept in lockstep with unselected pupils of their own age. Children who rise above 170 IQ are liable to regard school with indifference or with positive dislike, for they find nothing in the work to absorb their interest. This condition of affairs, coupled with the supervision of unseeing and unsympathetic teachers, has sometimes led even to truancy on the part of gifted children.

On the other hand, if a very gifted child is placed in the regular grades as far ahead of his age as his learning capacity warrants, the evils of social dislocation may result, as previously described. Experimental education is at present trying to solve the problem of how to secure right habits of work for the highly intelligent child, and some progress has been made in recent years.

Another problem of development with reference to occupation grows out of the versatility of these children. So far from being one-sided in ability and interest, they are typically capable of so many different kinds of success that they may have difficulty in confining themselves to a reasonable number of enterprises. Some of them are lost to usefulness through spreading their available time and energy over such a wide array of projects that nothing can be finished or done perfectly. After all, time and space are as limited for the gifted as for others, and the life-span is probably not much longer for them than for others. A choice must be made among the numerous possibilities, since modern life calls for specialization.

The dangers in development with respect to work habits are, therefore, that the child may not develop any habits of sustained effort, and that he may fail of success as a worker through being interested in too many things ever to accomplish very much at any one of them. His problem as he goes into adolescence is to make a definite choice, and to form the habit of effort.

LEARNING TO "SUFFER FOOLS GLADLY"

A lesson which many gifted persons never learn as long as they live is that human beings in general are inherently very different from themselves in thought, in action, in general intention, and in interests. Many a reformer has died at the hands of a mob which he was trying to improve in the belief that other human beings can and should enjoy what he enjoys. This is one of the most painful and difficult lessons that each gifted child must learn, if personal development is to proceed successfully. It is more necessary that this be learned than that any school subject be mastered. Failure to learn how to tolerate in a reasonable fashion the foolishness of others leads to bitterness, disillusionment, and misanthropy.

This point may be illustrated by the behavior of a seven-year-old boy with an IQ of 178. He was not sent to school until the age of seven because of his advanced interest in reading. At seven, however, the compulsory attendance law took effect and the child was placed in the third grade at school. After about four weeks of attendance, he came home from school weeping bitterly. "Oh, Grandmother, Grandmother," he cried, "they don't know what's *good!* They just *won't* read!"

The fact then came to light that he had taken book after book to school — all his favorites from his grandfather's library — and had tried to show the other third-grade pupils what treasures these were, but the boys and girls only resisted his efforts, made fun of him, threw the treasures on the floor, and finally pulled his hair.

Such struggles as these, if they continue without directing the child's insight, may lead to complete alienation from his contemporaries in childhood, and to misanthropy in adolescence and adulthood. Particularly deplorable are the struggles of these children against dull or otherwise unworthy adults in authority. The very gifted child or adolescent, perceiving the illogical conduct of those in charge of his affairs, may turn rebellious against all authority and fall into a condition of negative suggestibility — a most unfortunate trend of personality, since the person is then unable to take a coöperative attitude toward authority.

A person who is highly suggestible in a negative direction is as much in bondage to others around him as is the person who is positively suggestible. The social value of the person is seriously impaired in either case. The gifted are not likely to fall victims to positive suggestion but many of them develop negativism to a conspicuous degree.

The highly intelligent child will be intellectually capable of self-determination, and his greatest value to society can be realized only if he is truly self-possessed and detached from the influences of both positive and negative suggestion. The more intelligent the child, the truer this statement is. It is especially unfortunate, therefore, that so many gifted children have in authority over them persons of no special fitness for the task, who cannot gain or keep the respect of these good thinkers. Such unworthy guardians arouse, by the process of "redintegration," contempt for authority wherever it is found, and the inability to yield gracefully to command.

Thus some gifted persons, mishandled in youth, become contentious, aggressive, and stubborn to an extent which renders them difficult and disagreeable in all human relationships involving subordination. Since subordination must precede posts of command in the ordinary course of life, this is an unfortunate trend of personality. Cynicism and negativism are likely to interfere seriously with a life career. Happily, gifted children are typically endowed with a keen sense of humor, and are apparently able to mature beyond cynicism eventually in a majority of cases.

THE TENDENCY TO BECOME ISOLATED

Yoder [7] noticed, in studying the boyhood of great men, that although play interests were keen among them, the play was often of a solitary kind. The same is true of children who "test high." The majority of children testing above 160 IQ play little with other children unless special conditions are provided, such as those found in a special class. The difficulties are too great, in the ordinary course of events, in finding playmates who are appropriate in size and congenial in mentality. This fact was noted some years ago by the present writer. Terman [8] in 1930 made a special study of the play of those in his group of children who tested above 170 IQ and found them generally more solitary in work and play than children clustering around 140 IQ.

These superior children are not unfriendly or ungregarious by nature. Typically they strive to play with others but their efforts are defeated by the difficulties of the case. These difficulties are illustrated in the efforts of the seven-year-old boy already mentioned. Other children do not share their interests, their vocabulary, or their desire to organize activities. They try to reform their contemporaries but finally give up the struggle and play alone, since older children regard them as "babies," and adults seldom play during the hours when children are awake. As a result, forms of solitary play develop, and these, becoming fixed as habits, may explain the fact that many highly intellectual adults are shy, ungregarious, and unmindful of human relationships, or are even misanthropic and uncomfortable in ordinary social intercourse.

[7] Yoder, G. F. "A Study of the Boyhood of Great Men." *Pedagogical Seminary* (1894).
[8] *Op. cit.*

This difficulty of the gifted child in forming friendships is largely a result of the infrequency of persons who are like-minded. The more intelligent a person is, regardless of age, the less often can he find a truly congenial companion. The average child finds playmates in abundance who can think and act on a level congenial to him because there are so many average children.

Adding to the conditions which make for isolation is the fact that gifted children are often "only" children, or they have brothers and sisters who differ widely from them in age. Thus playmates in the home are less numerous for them than for children generally.

The imaginary playmate as a solution of the problem of loneliness is fairly frequent. We know but little at present of the psychology of this invention of the unreal to fill real needs. Reasoning from the general principles of mental hygiene, one would say that the pattern of companionship represented in the imaginary playmate is less valuable for personal development than a pattern founded on reality, and that effort should be made to fill the real need with genuine persons, if possible.

Also, the deep interest in reading which typifies the gifted child may further his isolation. Irwin believes that reading should be deferred in the education of the highly intelligent. "I believe it is especially important that intellectual children get a grasp on reality through real experiences in making and doing things before they are ever introduced to the wonders that lie within books." From this point of view, the development of the physical, social, and emotional aspects of personality would have first attention in the education of a gifted child, the intellectual being fostered last of all because it comes of itself and is too likely to run away with the other three and lead to isolation.

This tendency to become isolated is one of the most important factors to be considered in guiding the development of personality in highly intelligent children, but it does not become a serious problem except at the very extreme degrees of intelligence. The majority of children between 130 and 150 IQ find fairly easy adjustment, because neighborhoods and schools are selective, so that like-minded children tend to be located in the same schools and districts. Furthermore, the gifted child, being large and strong for his age, is acceptable to playmates a year or two older. Great difficulty arises only when a young child is above 160 IQ. At the extremely high levels of 180 and 190 IQ, the problem of friendships is difficult indeed, and the younger the person, the more difficult it is. The trouble decreases with age because as persons become adult, they naturally seek and find on their own initiative groups who are like-minded, such as learned societies.

THE CONCEPT OF "OPTIMUM INTELLIGENCE"

All things considered, the psychologist who has observed the development of gifted children over a long period of time from early childhood to maturity, evolves the idea that there is a certain restricted portion of the total range of intelligence which is most favorable to the development of successful and well-rounded personality in the world as it now exists. This limited range appears to be somewhere between 125 and 155 IQ. Children and adolescents in this area are enough more intelligent than the average to win the confidence of large numbers of their fellows, which brings about leadership, and to manage their own lives with superior efficiency. Moreover, there are enough of them to afford mutual esteem and understanding. But those of 170 IQ and beyond are too intelligent to be understood by the general run of persons with whom they make contact. They are too infrequent to find many congenial companions. They have to contend with loneliness and with personal isolation from their contemporaries throughout the period of immaturity. To what extent these patterns become permanently fixed, we cannot yet tell.

There is thus an "optimum" intelligence, from the viewpoint of personal happiness and adjustment to society, which is well below the maximum. The exploration of this concept should yield truths of value for education, and for social science as well. The few children who test at the very top of the juvenile population have a unique value for society. On them depends in large measure the advancement of learning. If they fail of personal happiness and human contact, their work for society as a whole may be impaired or lost.

CONCLUSION

As far as observations go at present, intellectually gifted children between 130 and 150 IQ seem to find the world well suited to their development. As a group, they enjoy the advantages of superior size, strength, health, and beauty; they are emotionally well balanced and controlled; they are of good character; and they tend to win the confidence of their contemporaries, which gives them leadership. This is the "optimum" range of intelligence, if personal happiness is being considered. If a parent would want his child to enjoy "every advantage," he could not do better than wish the child to be endowed with an IQ not lower than 130 or higher than 150.

Above this limit, however — surely above 160 IQ — the deviation is so great that it leads to special problems of development which are correlated with personal isolation. As one boy with an IQ of 190 has said: "It isn't good to be in college so awfully young (twelve years of age). It produces a feeling of alienation."

How to provide against alienation from contemporaries of both sexes, and how to prevent the negativism that results from continuous living under inefficient or unreasonable authority, are two of the important problems for education in its attempt to insure good adjustment of personality for children of extremely high intelligence.

Chapter Twenty

THE CHILD OF VERY SUPERIOR INTELLI-
GENCE AS A SPECIAL PROBLEM IN
SOCIAL ADJUSTMENT [1]

THIS discussion is limited to the problems that arise from *the combination of immaturity and superiority*. Thus the problems considered pertain chiefly to the period in the life of the gifted child before he is twenty years of age; for the problems of the person of superior intellect tend to be less numerous as he grows older and can use his intelligence independently in gaining control of his own life.

It should be stated emphatically at the outset that children of very superior intelligence are not, as a group, socially annoying. The problems presented are *those of the child*, not those of society, as ordinarily understood. That this is so is sufficiently proved by the scant attention that organized society has bestowed upon the study of gifted children. Society studies that which is socially annoying. The school attends to those who give it trouble. Thus feeble-minded children ("minus deviates," as they are called in modern laboratories) have long been studied. Millions of dollars have been spent in considering them, and a volumi-

[1] Reprinted from *Mental Hygiene:* Vol. XI, No. 1, pages 3–16 (January, 1931). Read by Leta S. Hollingworth at the First International Congress of Mental Hygiene, Washington, D. C., May 8, 1930.

nous literature has grown up through prolonged investigation of their maladjustments. Gifted children, on the other hand, have been studied hardly at all. Such investigations as we have are the result of intellectual interest on the part of a few educators and psychologists, who in the course of mental surveys became interested in those children who test always at the top.

THE QUALITY OF GIFTED CHILDREN

Such data as we now possess, from the scientific study of the gifted as organisms, show us that children of very superior intelligence are typically superior in other qualities also. They are superior in emotional stability and control. The old idea that the very bright "child prodigy" is likely to be nervous has been widespread, and popular fallacy inclines to mention "bright and high-strung" in the same breath. In fact, we not infrequently hear people claiming to be "high-strung" as a kind of compliment to themselves, implying that they are therefore also bright. Psychological researches of recent years have shown these ideas to be merely superstitions, founded on nothing more substantial than the human craving for a just nature that will somehow penalize the lucky and equalize biological wealth.

The researches of Terman,[2] particularly, and of Hartshorne and May [3] have shown that highly intelligent children are more stable emotionally than are unselected "controls" age for age, and are superior to "controls" in their resistance to temptation. The researches of Burt,[4] and of

[2] Terman, Lewis M. *Genetic Studies of Genius:* Vol. I. Stanford University Press, Stanford University, California; 1925.

[3] Hartshorne, H., and May, M. A. *Studies in Deceit.* The Macmillan Company, New York; 1927.

[4] Burt, C. *The Young Delinquent.* D. Appleton-Century Company, Inc., New York; 1924.

Healy and Bronner,[5] show among delinquents few children of the high degree of intelligence with which this paper deals.

The studies cited do not, of course, exhaust the recent scientific literature, but they do fairly exemplify the results of concrete, impersonal investigation, as distinguished from the results of popular "wishful thinking." The child who tests above 130 IQ [6] is *typically* (though of course not invariably) large and strong for his age, healthier than the average, contributes far less than his quota to juvenile misbehavior as socially defined, and is emotionally stable in superior degree.

Starting with these facts as to generally superior adjustment, let us inquire whether there are, therefore, no special perplexities in the life of a gifted child. Is it possible that a child may vary as far in a "plus" direction from the average performance of his contemporaries as an imbecile varies in a "minus" direction, and find no special problems created for him by this wide difference in mental power between himself and the average child of his age?

The psychologist who is professionally acquainted with children who test above 130 IQ will be able to formulate clearly certain special problems of adjustment, observed in the case study of these children, which arise primarily from the very fact that they are gifted. Let us attempt to state some of these problems. The more intelligent the child, the more likely he is to become involved in these puzzling situations.

[5] Healy, W., and Bronner, A. F. *Criminals and Delinquents: Their Making and Unmaking.* The Macmillan Company, New York; 1928.

[6] The intelligence quotient is the ratio between the status achieved on tests by an individual and that achieved by the generality.

THE PROBLEM OF WORK

Where the gifted child drifts in the school unrecognized, held to the lock step which is determined by the capacities of the average, he has little to do. He receives daily practice in habits of idleness and daydreaming. His abilities are never genuinely challenged, and the situation is contrived to build in him expectations of an effortless existence. Children up to about 140 IQ tolerate the ordinary school routine quite well, being usually a little young for grade through an extra promotion or two, and achieving excellent marks without serious effort. But above this status, children become increasingly bored with school work, if kept in or nearly in the lock step. Children at or above 180 IQ, for instance, are likely to regard school with indifference, or with positive distaste, for they find nothing interesting to do there.

On the other hand, if the child be greatly accelerated in grade status, so that he is able to function intellectually with real interest, he will be misplaced in other important respects. A child of eight years graded with twelve-year-olds is out of his depth socially and physically, though able to do intellectual work as well as they can. These problems come out clearly when we consider that the seats and desks planned for twelve-year-olds will not fit him; that he will always be the last one chosen in athletic contests; that no one will know how to treat him at class parties; that the teacher will be prone to complain of his manual work, such as handwriting; and that he will be emotionally immature in comparison with older classmates. When he jumps up and down, clapping his hands and shouting, "Goody! goody!" at an announcement from the teacher, the older children will laugh at him, and later may hang paper tails and other tokens of ignominy upon him; whereas his childish glee would have constituted no violation of taste among eight-year-olds.

A thousand concrete instances might be described to show what these problems of adjustment are. Experimental education is trying to solve them. At present, the special class is being tried in populous centers, wherein a whole group of the young gifted can be brought together (as has long been done for the dull and slow).

In less populous communities, a moderate degree of acceleration, combined with enrichment of the curriculum for the individual, is being tried. We do not yet know how the problem of adjustment to school work can best be solved. Indeed, we have just learned how to define this problem.

THE PROBLEM OF ADJUSTMENT TO CLASSMATES

Typically, where there is no scientific recognition of the presence of the gifted, these children, by the time they are eight or nine years old, are more or less accelerated in scholastic status and appear as the youngest in the class. Such a child is thus youngest in the fourth or fifth grade, in a heterogeneous group in which the oldest are retardates, thirteen or fourteen years old. Now, in the case of boys especially, it may happen that these dull adolescents lie in wait to bully and tease the young gifted boy, whose "booklearning" they detest and whose immaturity suggests the term "baby." The present writer knows of instances in which these young children have valiantly suffered at the hands of dull, bullying classmates, protecting themselves as best they might by agility and wit, since, of course, they could not possibly compete in size and strength. The gross indignities and tortures thus suffered are directly a penalty of being gifted; for little boys of like age, in the grade proper to their age, do not come into classroom contact with these over-age bullies to anything like the same extent, and hence do not become targets for the latter.

One young gifted boy thus bullied said, "I rigged up a sling and was going to hit him [the bully] with a marble, but got afraid I might shoot his eye out." This simple statement tells volumes.

It would seem that the school should somehow take effective cognizance of this problem of the bully, which is created for the gifted child directly as a result of the contacts forced upon both of them by the school. Segregation of pupils on the basis of mentality would go far to obviate such problems, but except in cities, homogeneous grouping is difficult. At present, compulsory education, with heterogeneous classes, forces upon gifted children situations that would be analogous to those arising if teachers and superintendents were compelled to consort daily, unprotected, with giant thugs and gangsters. Gifted adults are free to segregate themselves from thugs and gangsters, and also to make explicit provision for police protection, but the American school forces the dull bully upon the gifted child, in daily contacts, out of which lasting problems of mental hygiene may arise.

THE PROBLEM OF PLAY

Reports by gifted children themselves show that they are, as a group, much interested in play, and that they have more "play knowledge" than has the average child. When their reports are compared item by item with reports similarly rendered by unselected children, it appears that the gifted know more games of intellectual skill, such as bridge and chess; that they care less, age for age, for play which involves predominantly simple sensori-motor activity which is aimless; and that gifted girls are far less interested in traditional girls' play, as with dolls and tea sets, than unselected girls are. The gifted enjoy more complicated and more highly competitive games than the generality do, age for age. Outdoor sports hold a high place with the gifted, being almost as popular among them as is reading.

But although they love play, and have much play knowledge, the play of the highly intelligent works out in practice as a somewhat difficult compromise among their various powers. They follow their intellectual interests as far as they can, but these are checked in many ways by age, by degree of physical immaturity, and by tradition. An eight-year-old of IQ 160 may, for example, be deeply interested in tennis, but he is likely to be more or less kept from playing because his physical development is not yet equal to the demands of the game. He may love to play bridge, but others of his age who are available as playmates do not, of course, know how to play bridge, and he is not allowed to sit up at night when his elders play.

By trial-and-error experience, the highly intelligent child has to work out an adjustment if he can, but there is likely to be noticeable difficulty if he tests above 170 IQ. In the ordinary course of events, it is hard for such a child to find playmates who are congenial both in size and in mental interests. Thus many of those who test very high are finally thrown back upon themselves, and tend strongly to work out forms of solitary, intellectual play.[7] The same situation is discovered in studies of the childhood of eminent persons. Yoder,[8] in his study of the juvenile history of fifty very

[7] Hollingworth, Leta S. *Gifted Children: Their Nature and Nurture.* The Macmillan Company, New York; 1926.

[8] Yoder, G. F. "A Study of the Boyhood of Great Men." *Pedagogical Seminary* (1894).

eminent persons, concluded that their play "was often of a solitary kind." Reading, calculation, designing, compiling collections, constructing an "imaginary land," evoking imaginary playmates — these forms of play stand out prominently among the recreational interests of such children. Since physical activity is hard to carry out interestingly alone, their play tends to become habitually sedentary. Nevertheless, they develop to a high degree swimming, skating, and other forms of athletic enjoyment which do not depend upon being included in a group.

Of six young children testing above 180 IQ, known to the present writer, only one [9] had no conspicuous difficulty in play, during early childhood.[10] The other five were all so divergent from the usual in play interests that parents and teachers noticed them. They were unpopular with children of their own age because they always *wanted to organize the play* into a complicated pattern, with some remote and definite climax as the goal. As the mother of one six-year-old said, "He can never be satisfied just to toss a ball around, or to run about pulling and shouting." Children of six years are ordinarily incapable of becoming interested in long-sustained, complicated games which lead to remote goals, but are, on the contrary, characteristically satisfied only by the kind of random activity which bored this child of 187 IQ. The playmates of ordinary intelligence naturally resented persistent efforts to reform them and to organize them for the attainment of remote goals. Furthermore, they did not have in their vocabulary words that the gifted child knew well, used habitually, and took for granted. Literally, they

[9] This child attended a private school where a number of the pupils tested above 140 IQ.
[10] This was written in 1931.

could not understand each other. The result was that the child of 187 IQ did not "get along" with those of his own age and size. But when he sought to join the play of children *of his own mental age* (above twelve years), the six-year-old was rejected by them also, as being "a baby" and "too little to play with us." The child, thus thrown back upon himself, developed elaborate mathematical calculation, collecting, reading, and games with imaginary playmates, as his chief forms of play.

These young children of extremely high intellectual acumen fail to be interested in "child's play" for the same reasons that in adulthood they will fail to patronize custard-pie movies or chute-the-chutes at amusement parks. It is futile, and probably wholly unsound psychologically, to strive to interest the child above 170 IQ in ring-around-the-rosy or blind-man's-buff. Many well-meaning persons speak of such efforts as "socializing the child," but it is probably not in this way that the very gifted can be socialized. The problem of how the play interests of these children can be realized is one that will depend largely on individual circumstances for solution. Often it can be solved only by the development of solitary play.

What, if any, effect the habitual evocation of imaginary playmates, and the elaboration of the imaginary land, may exert on character formation and habits of adjustment in adulthood is at present unknown. Psychologists should study the hygienic aspects of these methods of finding satisfaction outside of the real world. Since gifted children are, as has been stated, on the whole a stable and rational group, perhaps no effects, or good effects only, result from this play of the imagination.

SPECIAL PROBLEMS OF THE GIFTED GIRL

It has been mentioned that gifted girls are less interested in traditional girls' play than are unselected girls. They show a preference for boys' books and boys' play, and a greater community of interests with boys than the generality of girls display. This merely means that girls of a high degree of intelligence are, as a group, more competitive, aggressive, and active than girls are supposed to be.

An illustrative case is that of a seven-year-old girl of IQ 170, whose mother wished to learn from psychology how to break her child of being a "tomboy" and how to rear her to "be a lady." The mother complained that the girl had never cared for dolls, that she would not take an interest in her clothes, and that she wanted to do nothing after school but read or play "rough, outdoor games." "How," inquired the mother, "could I break her of the habit of climbing lamp-posts?" This child was active and competitive. When asked why she did not play with dolls, she replied, "They aren't *real*. The doll that is supposed to be a baby doll is twice as big as the one that is made like a mother doll."

Aside from their dissatisfaction with the play habits ordinarily associated with their sex, gifted girls have various other problems to face which arise directly from the facts that they are able and that they are girls. When they reach the stage of life-planning, as they do very early, they are confused in their self-seeking by the uncertainty in contemporary customs as to what a girl may become. This difficulty is growing less and less, to be sure, but it is still something to be reckoned with, especially in certain localities. The intelligent girl begins very early to perceive that she is, so to speak, of the wrong sex. From a thousand tiny cues, she learns that she is not expected to entertain the same ambitions as her brother. Her problem is to adjust her ambitions to a sense of sex inferiority without, on the one hand, losing self-respect and self-determination, and, on the other, without becoming morbidly aggressive. This is never an easy adjustment to achieve, and even superior intelligence does not always suffice to accomplish it. The special problem of gifted girls is that they have strong preferences for activities that are hard to follow on account of their sex, which is inescapable.

PROBLEMS OF CONFORMITY

Judgments of teachers and parents indicate that highly intelligent children are, on the whole, more easily disciplined than children generally are. Nevertheless, certain problems of discipline do arise, which grow out of their intelligence. First, in the case of the schoolroom situation almost the only respect in which discipline is especially troublesome with these children is in the matter of orderly discussion when they are together in special classes. It is hard for them to maintain silence when ideas press for utterance. The tendency is for many to speak at once, each striving to outspeak the others. An atmosphere of confusion is thus created unless discipline can be imposed. To hold his tongue, to listen quietly and respectfully to others, to speak according to some order of procedure, and to restrain disappointment at failure to be heard at all — these habits seem especially difficult for gifted children to form. Only gradually do these children learn self-government in this respect.

Also it has been noticed during the experimental education of the highly intelligent that they sometimes tend to slight routine drudgery in favor of more stimulating and more original projects. The sheer drudgery involved in learning the multiplication table, for example, is likely to be waived in order to follow some absorbing story or experiment, unless conformity be urged from without.

At home, a special problem of discipline may arise occasionally due to the circumstance that a child, while still very immature in years, has come to exceed one parent or both in intelligence. For the best discipline routine *the parent must be more intelligent than the child* or the child's respect for the opinions of the former will inevitably be lost. With the most gifted children this may quite early become a problem, since such children, by the age of ten years or before, are more intelligent than the average adult is. Very readily such a child perceives that in comparison with himself his parent is slow-witted and lacking in general information. Yet in self-control and in experience of life, the child is still very immature. Thus quite unfortunate developments may ensue in the parent-child relationship. The child may become the director of the parent's activities, reversing the socially acceptable condition of affairs. Fortunately, in the vast majority of cases at least one of the parents is a person of superior intelligence. We seldom find a very intelligent child in a home where *both* parents are average or below average in mental power.

Because he learns everything very quickly, the highly intelligent child is especially quick to discover what forms of conduct on his part bring him satisfactions. If the tantrum is rewarded by the parent with cookies, company, attention, or other childish delights, then the bright child may display even "bigger and better" tantrums than will those who are slower to learn. If illness brings coddling, release from undesired responsibility, and other pleasures, then the quick learner will readily perceive the value of "headaches" and other aches as means to ends. On the other hand, the very intelligent learn readily to refrain from undesirable behavior that is followed quickly and inevitably by punishment. Two or three experiences usually suffice for these excellent learners. Neglect and ostracism are good forms of punishment for them. Darwin tells us that he was cured of telling sensational fibs, as a child, simply by the chilling silence with which they were always received by his parents.

One more problem may be noted here. There is with intelligent children a stronger tendency to *argue* about what is required of them than is found with the average child. This tendency to argue as to the why and wherefore of a requirement is met both at home and at school, and calls for thought in proper handling on the part of parents and teachers. To find a golden mean between arbitrary abolition of all argument, on the one hand, and weak fostering of an intolerable habit of endless argumentation, on the other, is not always easy, but it is always worth while as a measure for retaining the respect of the child.

THE PROBLEMS OF ORIGIN AND OF DESTINY

Early interest in origins and in destinies is one of the conspicuous symptoms of intellectual acumen. "Where did the moon come from?" "Who made the world?" "What is the very end of autumn leaves?" "Where did I come from?" "What will become of me when I die?" "Why did I come into the world?"

Although these questions rise vaguely and intermittently in the minds of children in general, they do not begin to require logically coherent answers until about the mental age of twelve or thirteen years. Then they begin to press for more or less systematic accounts. From these circumstances of mental development, the erroneous idea has long been promulgated, even by psychologists, that *puberty* in some mysterious manner leads to the rise of religious needs and convictions. Since among the generality a "mental age" of thirteen years is, roughly, coincident with the age of pubescence, the two developments have been assumed to be casually related.

When we observe young gifted children, we discover that religious ideas and needs originate in them *whenever they develop to a mental level* past "twelve years mental age." Thus they show these needs when they are but eight or nine years old, or earlier. The higher the IQ the earlier does the pressing need for an explanation of the universe occur, the sooner does the demand for a concept of the origin and destiny of the self appear.

In the cases of children who test above 180 IQ observed by the present writer, definite demand for a systematic philosophy of life and death developed when they were but six or seven years old. Similar phenomena appear in the childhood histories of eminent persons where data of childhood are available. Goethe, for example, at the age of nine constructed an altar and devised a religion of his own, in which God could be worshiped without the help of priests.

Much could be said of the special problems of the young gifted child in this period of immaturity when his intellectual needs are those of an adolescent while his emotional control and physical powers are still but those of a child. It would be of great interest to study the reactions of older persons to the insistent questions and searchings of these young children. "You are too young to understand." "You can't know all that till you grow older." "You unnatural child!"

These are responses that have been heard incidentally, falling from the lips of undiscerning parents. A girl of eight years, of IQ 150, recently was heard to express a determination to join the "Agnostic Church," because she had asked, "What is it called when you can't make up your mind whether there is a God or not?" and had been told that this would be agnosticism.

Part and parcel of these questionings concerning origin and destiny are those concerning birth and reproduction. At a "tender" age these children ask for an account of sex and reproduction and suffer much at the hands of parents and guardians who are shocked at what thus emanates from the mouths of babes. Lifelong problems of mental hygiene may be thus engendered by parents who cannot understand why a child should be "so unnatural" as to weep over questions of birth and death at six or seven years of age.

In the same way problems of right and wrong become troublesome for these young children in a way that does not happen except for the very able. For instance, a six-year-old boy of IQ 187 wept bitterly after reading "how the North taxed the South after the Civil War." The problem of evil in the abstract thus comes to trouble these children almost in their cradles, at an age when they are ill-suited to grapple with it from the point of view of emotional maturity. Special problems of mental hygiene are perhaps inherent in this situation which do not arise with the generality of children.

GENERAL CONSIDERATIONS

The list of problems that we have suggested here does not by any means exhaust the subject under discussion. However, the present writer believes that these are some of the more important problems of childhood that originate directly from the circumstance of being very highly intelligent among official guardians who are ignorant or careless of the fact. These problems of adjustment do not arise unless a child is gifted intellectually. They are conspicuous to the psychologist who studies children with "test knowledge" of them.

It is especially to be noted that many of these problems are functions of immaturity. To have the intelligence of an adult and the emotions of a child combined in a childish body is to encounter certain difficulties. It follows that (after babyhood) the younger the child, the greater the difficulties, and that adjustment becomes easier with every additional year of age. The years between four and nine are probably the most likely to be beset with the problems mentioned.

The physical differences between a child of six whose IQ is 150 and children of nine years (whose mental age corresponds to his) are unbridgeable, and so are the differences of taste, due to differences in emotional maturity. The child of six graded with nine-year-olds is out of his element physically and socially, but the same thing is not true of a sixteen-year-old among nineteen-year-olds. The difference between six and nine is very great. The difference between sixteen and nineteen is small in terms of biological development.

Moreover, as the bright go forward in school, they find work increasingly adapted to their powers by the automatic developments of the established curriculum. Senior high schools are, we have discovered, adapted only to adolescents of superior intelligence. Classmates become automatically more congenial through being more highly selected. The dull bully, with his crude horseplay, has left school, and in any case the gifted, being older, can defend themselves physically.

By the time a gifted person is physically mature, many of the problems herein outlined automatically disappear as problems. What after-effects there may be of the poor solution of these childish problems we do not know. Apparently these superior organisms tolerate well the strains put upon them by reason of their deviation from the average. However, that an organism stands strain well is no reason for putting or leaving strain unnecessarily upon it.

As the gifted individual grows to maturity, he or she can achieve control of his or her own life, and can dispense to a relatively great extent with inadvertent cruelties and mistaken efforts of uninformed official guardians. It is *during childhood* that the gifted boy or girl is at the mercy of guardians whose duty it is to know his nature and his needs much more fully than they now do.

Chapter Twenty-One

THE ELEMENTARY SCHOOLING OF VERY BRIGHT CHILDREN

In this chapter are presented selected relevant paragraphs from two of the later papers by the author: "An Enrichment Curriculum for Rapid Learners" [1] and "What We Know about the Early Selection and Training of Leaders." [2]

THIS is neither the time nor the place for discussion of the techniques of mental measurement, but rather for the discussion of results. What, first, do we know about the selection of children who stand in the upper ranges of intelligence? Facts of much importance have been established since 1905.

In the first place, we have proved that children who rate in the top one per cent of the juvenile population in respect to "judgment," as Binet called it, also possess much more often than others those additional qualities which thinkers have most frequently named as desirable in leaders. There is a strong probability that a child who rates as only one in a hundred for intelligence will also be endowed in superior degree with "integrity, independence, originality,

[1] *Teachers College Record*, Vol. 39, No. 4 (1938), pages 296–306.
[2] *Teachers College Record*, Vol. 40 (1939). Also reprinted in *Public Addresses of Leta S. Hollingworth*, Science Press Printing Company, Lancaster, Pennsylvania; 1940.

creative imagination, vitality, forcefulness, warmth, poise, and stability."

These characteristics are identical with those set forth by Harvard College as the additional traits desired in boys, already proved by tests to be highly intelligent, who are to receive National Scholarships. I believe no one would wish to delete from the list any trait thus stipulated. I would, however, add to it audacity, capacity for nonconformity, love of beauty, and cold courage, as traits to cherish in leaders, although these are often uncongenial to teachers in the elementary school, and possibly to other educators.

We find all these qualities in superior measure among highly intelligent children, according to the ratings of those who know them. If one would call for a mathematical statement of the likelihood of finding these traits in combination with high intelligence, we could give it. I may say that the correlation coefficients hover around .50. This means that in selecting any child testing far up in the top one per cent — say at 160 IQ or above (100 IQ being par) — there is far more than an even chance of having thus automatically selected a tall, healthy, fine-looking, honest, and courageous child, with great love of adventure and of beauty in his makeup. With a correlation so far from unity as .50, however, we cannot be at all certain of such a happy combination. We shall find a minority of cases where fine judgment is combined with an unstable temper, a crippled body, an ugly face, a ruthless disregard for others, malign chicanery, cowardice. (I would say there cannot be a very high intelligence without the love of beauty.)

Educational psychology works constantly to find ways of knowing how to identify these additional elements. It will be a long time before we advance to a point where we can measure these as well as we can now measure intelligence. Some of these additional qualifications are undoubtedly as essential to leadership as intelligence is. A rascal, a coward, a liar, a tyrant, a panderer, a fanatic, an invalid, is not a desirable leader, no matter whether his IQ is 200. We must learn to select from among the highly intelligent those who have the greatest number of additional qualifications. We must learn what these additional qualifications are. One knows them when one sees them in action. For example, an eleven-year-old boy of IQ close to 180 decided to run for the office of class president in the senior high school to which he had been accelerated. His classmates were around sixteen years of age. During the electioneering a proponent of a rival candidate arose to speak against the eleven-year-old, and he said, among other things, "Fellows, we don't want a president in knee pants!"

In the midst of the applause following this remark, the eleven-year-old arose, and waving his hand casually in the direction of the full-length portrait of George Washington on the wall, he said, "Fellows, try to remember that when George got to be the Father of our country he was wearing knee pants." The eleven-year-old was elected by a large majority. He gave evidence not only of an IQ of 180, but also of the additional qualities of political leadership in highest degree: audacity, presence of mind, good humor, grace, and, above all, the genuine desire to be a popular leader. He knew how to bridge, by a debonair gesture, the great gap between him and those to be led.

This boy had qualities of *political* leadership. This limiting adjective opens the large subject of the different kinds of leaders. Leaders of whom, and for what ends? Observation of children suggests that there is a direct ratio between the intelligence of the leader and that of the led. To be a leader of his contemporaries, a child must be more intelligent, but *not too much more intelligent,* than those who are to be led. There are rare exceptions to this principle, as in the case we have cited. But, generally speaking, a leadership pattern will not form — or it will break up — when a discrepancy of more than about 30 points of IQ comes to exist between the leader and the led.

This concept of an optimum which is not a maximum difference between the leader and the led has very important implications for selection and training. We cannot do more than point to it here, in passing. Among school children — as among the peoples of all times — the great intellectual leaders are unrecognized, isolated, and even ridiculed by all but a few in the ordinary course of mass education. They can develop leadership of their sort only when placed in special classes.

Observation and investigation prove that in the matter of their intellectual work these children are customarily wasting much time in the elementary schools. We know from measurements made over a three-year period that a child of 140 IQ can master all the mental work provided in the elementary school, as established, in half the time allowed him. Therefore, one-half the time which he spends at school could be utilized in doing something more than the curriculum calls for. A child of 170 IQ can do all the studies that are at present required of him, with top "marks," in about one-fourth the time he is compelled to spend at school. What, then, are these pupils doing in the ordinary school setup while the teacher teaches the other children who need the lessons?

No exhaustive discussion of time-wasting can be undertaken

here, except to say briefly that these exceptional pupils are running errands, idling, engaging in "busy work," or devising childish tasks of their own, such as learning to read backward — since they can already read forward very fluently. Many are the devices invented by busy teachers to "take up" the extra time of these rapid learners, but few of these devices have the appropriate character that can be built only on psychological insight into the nature and the needs of gifted children.

Before education can discharge this most important task of all with economy and justice, it must become a science. The science which is fundamental to education is psychology. Psychology had to develop the methods of mental measurement before there could be accurate or humane dealing in a system of compulsory education. We must take "the measure of a man" before we can know how to educate him; and it remained for mental measurement to reveal the astonishing power of learning that is latent in an elementary school-child of IQ 170 or 180. How shall such pupils be taught? How shall we educate these rapid learners, these subtle thinkers, these children of potential genius in the elementary school?

CONSIDERATIONS IN PLANNING THE CURRICULUM [3]

At the outset we must realize and admit that no absolute criteria exist by which to select from all aspects of human experience those which are most valuable for a group of

[3] The curriculum here described is that organized by Leta S. Hollingworth and her collaborators in Speyer School, P.S. 500, Manhattan, for two experimental classes of "rapid learners." For an early account of this project see "The Founding of Public School 500," *Teachers College Record*, Vol. 38, No. 2 (November, 1936). Also "What Is Going On at Speyer School?" Chapter 21 of *Public Addresses of Leta S. Hollingworth*, Science Press Printing Company, Lancaster, Pennsylvania; 1940.

gifted children. There is no body of "revealed" wisdom about this matter. Nevertheless, we are not altogether at sea. Common sense, accompanied by scientific facts of psychology, comes to our assistance, and we may note first such negative considerations as occur to us under this guidance.

It is useless to undertake extensive work in classical languages or in mathematics as "general discipline" for the minds of these rapid learners. The education given should be such as will function specifically and uniquely in their lives. It should afford them a rich background of ideas, in terms of which they may *perceive the significant features of their own times.*

Another definitely negative consideration applies to the avoidance of all "subjects" which they will have occasion to encounter in high school and college in later years. These young children can learn algebra or Latin grammar or chemistry easily enough, but what is the use of having them do so? The opportunity and the prescribed necessity for this will come later.

Turning to positive considerations, we know that these pupils — they and no others — will possess as adults those mental powers on which the learned professions depend for conservation and advancement. Also, we know that they will be the literary interpreters of the world of their generation. And they will be the ones who can think deeply and clearly about abstractions like the state, the government, and economics. We know this because we have seen a group like this "grow up" over a period of fifteen years, and we know what "became" of every one of them. Below an IQ of 130 no very large amount of effective thinking about complex abstractions can be done at any age. That, we are learning, is about the median mental caliber of college students in first-class colleges, taking it our country over.   In many highly selected, first-class colleges, the boy or girl of IQ 140 finds himself or herself merely a good average student, steadily receiving "C's."   In such colleges one must be a very good thinker in order to survive the course, but no one would consider median students in our first-rate colleges to be geniuses.   The suggestion advanced about twenty years ago that 140 IQ represents "genius or near-genius" was premature.   And when we remember that 120 IQ and 115 IQ are well below these median students in mental power, it becomes clear that at and below those levels conservation and advancement of the abstractions underlying the learned professions will be very inadequately handled.   Really adequate *conservation* of the precious stores of knowledge laid up in medicine, law, theology, education, and the sciences depends on those not below 130 IQ.

As for *originations*, whereby one generation progresses beyond another in control of the physical environment and of preventable evils, we are learning that only a few in the topmost ranges can produce them in the realm of abstractions. Only a few in the top one per cent can contribute to actual *progress*.   As Franklin K. Lane has said, "Progress means the discovery of the capable.   They are our natural masters. They lead because they have the right.   And everything done to keep them from rising is a blow to what we call our civilization."   To develop each according to his ability: this is democracy at its ideal best.

The education of the best thinkers should be an education for initiative and originality.   Effective originality depends, first of all, upon sound and exhaustive knowledge of what the course of preceding events has been.   To take their unique places in civilized society, it would seem, therefore, that the intellectually gifted need especially to know what the evolution of culture has been. And since at eight or nine years of age they are not as yet ready for specialization, what they need to know is the evolution of culture as it has affected *common things*. At present, this is not taught to children or to adolescents, except in fragmentary and casual ways. Persons typically graduate from elementary school, high school, and college, and take postgraduate degrees without learning much, if anything, about the evolution of lighting, of refrigeration, of shipping, of clothing, of etiquette, of trains, of libraries, and of a thousand things which have been contributed to the common life by persons in past times and which distinguish the life of civilized man from the existence of the savage. These things are vaguely taken for granted even by the intelligent, educated person. No systematic knowledge of how they came into being enriches his understanding. Nor is he aware of the biographies of those who have made his comfort and his safety possible. No more does he understand how dangerous and destructive forces came to be in the world. Of these vast fields the college graduate is typically ignorant, as has frequently been proved.

The activities which make up the life of a civilized man may be variously organized and classified for purposes of study in the elementary school. A number of the progressive schools have undertaken projects in these fields. The pupils in such schools usually test at a median of about 118 IQ, and the work they have done, while it is helpful and suggestive, is not what is needed for pupils of the caliber with which we are here dealing.

Topical classifications which have suggested themselves as areas for study might be stated as follows: food; shelter;

clothing; transportation; sanitation and health; trade; time-keeping; illumination; tools and implements; communication; law; government; education; warfare; punishment; labor; recreation. Every one of these areas of human culture affords the opportunity and necessity for studying *the evolution of common things*, satisfying the intellectual curiosity, and challenging the power of learning of the children here considered.

ENRICHMENT UNITS AT SPEYER SCHOOL

Between the ages of seven and thirteen years, the minds of these children are occupied primarily with exploration of the world in which they have recently arrived. They are full of questions of fact, not yet being distracted by the emotional and dynamic interests that come with adolescence and adulthood. This is the golden age of the intellect. Why? How? When? Who? Where? What? are constantly on their tongues, as any parent of a child in our classes will testify.

Now, in accordance with the philosophy and psychology which we have tried all too briefly to indicate, a series of "enrichment units" is being worked out at Speyer School day by day in our classrooms. These are being published in the form of teachers' handbooks, in a series designated "The Evolution of Common Things," the first numbers of which have been published. It will take five years to complete the series, at the end of which time we shall know *from experience* how much knowledge along the lines indicated can be organized and learned by children above 130 IQ in the years of the elementary school.

The handbooks, as they appear in published form, will represent the actual work of *the pupils themselves*, guided by the teacher. The teachers did not discover and assemble the materials of instruction, and "give them out." The children did this work. In the end, the teacher organized the total work into an orderly sequence, and verbalized it in final form for presentation. But no teacher would have the time or energy to carry on the work of the school and also collect and compile the materials contained in one of these units.

When an area of knowledge has been circumscribed by the children as one chosen for study by class discussion, the teacher participating in the thinking but not leading it, the pupils (there are twenty-five in each class) divide themselves into "committees." These various groups of three to five children each bring special knowledge to the class periods, and all share in the sum total of facts and ideas thus assembled. Libraries are thoroughly utilized in this process. Ninety-five per cent of the pupils who were admitted to our classes in February, 1936 (they were then between the ages of seven and nine), had and were using "library cards" from the New York Public Library. They are taken by their teachers to the nearest branch of the Public Library on days arranged for, and they "look up" their own materials, following the topics listed.

Librarians were at first skeptical as to the wisdom of admitting these very young children to the card indices and other facilities of the library. But librarians are an openminded group, and they were persuaded to let the children try. No difficulty at all has been experienced. Stedman showed long ago that elementary school children of IQ above 140 can use a library and consult reference books as well as students in the normal school do.

In addition to work in the Public Library, the classes have the right to use books from the Teachers College Library; and to the librarians of Teachers College much credit is due for their effective coöperation. Also, the library facilities of the public schools are thoroughly utilized. Current periodical literature, coming to the homes of the pupils, makes a constant contribution. It is surprising how few of the books found most useful were written by professed educators.

Of the trips undertaken, the visual aids supplied, and other methods of instruction there is not space to tell here. These are described fully in the units as they appear.

"The Evolution of Common Things" is the chief enrichment project growing in our classes. However, much in addition to this work is incorporated in our curriculum. These additions may be described as follows.

First may be mentioned the study of Biography, because it is very closely allied to "The Evolution of Common Things." This is planned to continue for five years, though not being done in every term continuously. It is inevitable that it should become apparent to our pupils that all "common things" of the kind being studied have had their origins in the minds of *people*. Who these people were is answered by the study of biography. The question "Who?" is constantly in the air. During the year 1936–1937, about one hundred persons were "biografied" [4] by our pupils, most of them persons who have given us very important "common things."

The idea that biography is a study well suited to young gifted children was given trial experimentally fifteen years ago at Public School 165, Manhattan, and its suitability was there proved. At the Speyer School we are able to build upon the previous experiment and to extend and improve the work, mainly because of the astonishing improvement in

[4] A word coined by the pupils.

the writing of biography which has taken place in the recent past.

The French language and literature will be taught for the full five years. This is done for three reasons: (1) the pupils with whom we are dealing will, more than others, have occasion to meet foreign peoples, and to represent their country abroad in the realm of ideas; (2) it is thought that the earlier a language is studied, the more thoroughly it can be mastered, especially as regards pronunciation; (3) the teaching of a modern language enriches, without anticipating, the opportunities of the high school and college, since the pupils will have occasion to take *various* languages later, and may ultimately emerge with three, instead of the usual two, at their command. French rather than German, Spanish, or Italian was chosen because teachers of the French language were available on our staff, and we gladly adopted it.

Another of the important enrichment projects is the formulation of a curriculum in the Science of Nutrition. This, also, is a five-year plan, in the course of which a curriculum in nutrition will be set up in terms of the vocabulary, the concepts, and the capacity for thinking which are proper to these children.

SPECIAL WORK

Special work in general science has been carried on since the opening of the classes. For a time the "question-box" method was tried. A "question-box" dealing with science in any and all its aspects was opened once a week, and the children's questions found in it were discussed by a special teacher.

Through the courtesy of the Music and Arts High

School, special teachers of these subjects have been assigned, and many projects have been carried through. The pupils have made murals founded on their studies of common things. They have learned French songs, and have become familiar with many things in music.

Another teacher of the staff of the Speyer School is developing dramatics for our classes. It is evident that a large opportunity for the development of the creative abilities of our pupils lies here.

Handicrafts are taught at least once each week. The handwork of the rapid learners is very superior, contrary to the current superstition that highly intelligent children are "poor with their hands." During the year 1936–1937, the pupils made airplanes from blueprints, which involved very delicate operations with glue and small pieces of wood. They were then seven to nine years old.

One afternoon each week, the Games Club meets, and there the children learn games of intellectual skill. Chess and checkers are the favorites. It is believed that education for leisure time is a special responsibility of those who teach highly intelligent children. The most intelligent tend to become "isolates," through not finding in the ordinary course of life recreations congenial both to themselves and to contemporaries. A game like chess or checkers can be shared with pleasure, irrespective of age, by any two people who have a sufficient "mental nearness." Hence they help a very gifted child to "find company" and "enjoy himself" in all age groups — a very important factor in the social development of such a child. The interest in these games is kept within bounds by the restriction to one hour a week and to those pupils who are up to date in their school work.

Possibly more time should be allowed for the Games Club as the pupils grow older.

Having followed our description of the enriched curriculum to this point, readers who have no direct experience in the education of children of the caliber being considered may begin to be anxious for the welfare of "reading, writing, and arithmetic." Let them be reassured. Mornings are devoted to the established curriculum of the elementary school, the pupils working by "contracts." Achievement tests are given at regular intervals to determine conventional grade status in the various "subjects." In June, 1937, our pupils showed the "educational age" of pupils at the middle of the seventh grade of the elementary schools as measured by Stanford Achievement Tests. They were then nine years six months old, on the median. The "regular" grade status for them would have been the middle of the fourth grade. The most intelligent tenth of the pupils were already "through the ceiling" of Stanford Achievement and of other standard achievement tests in June, 1937.

At this point, it should be mentioned that our pupils do not have and never have had homework assigned to them.

The intellectual interest and capacity of young children who test from 160 to 200 IQ is incredible to those who have had no experience with the teaching of such children. We have in our classes about a dozen of such extreme deviates. They are the truly *original* thinkers and doers of their generation. A book could be made of the incidents constantly occurring which denote the qualities of their minds. It is these children who suffer most from ennui in the ordinary situation.

For instance, recently in the discussion of the biography of Madame Curie, the question was raised by a pupil as to what "radium *really* is." One suggested that "radium is a stone." Another said that "radium is a metal." The person in charge of the class then said, "What is the difference between a stone and a metal?" A pupil of an extremely high degree of intelligence rose and said, "The main difference is that a metal is malleable and ductile, and a stone is not." He then enlarged very precisely upon "what these properties are." At the moment of this discussion, this boy was nine years six months old. The others listened attentively, and understood the elucidation.

Such incidents, occurring daily, give some idea of the level of minds being dealt with in our classes. The boy who thought and said what is set forth above was placed in the sixth grade when his principal recommended him to our classes. He had then been "skipped" to a point well out of his age group, and yet he had nothing whatever to learn from the work of the sixth grade.

The pupils in the classes for rapid learners will go to senior high school when they are thirteen years old. In the meantime, they will be learning and thinking in the company of their contemporaries as regards age and social interests. They will have proper intellectual training, and will at no time idle their time away, be practiced in habits of laziness, or become the victims of boredom. They will emerge into high school with a background of knowledge richer and fuller by far than that of pupils of equal mentality, for whom no enrichment program has been provided.

EMOTIONAL EDUCATION

Much more might be said of the program of intellectual training, but I must pass on to consider what may be even more important — their training in attitudes, emotions, and drives; in other words, their emotional education. How shall we avoid the conditions which, under the prevailing system of mass education, tend to produce emotional habits destructive of leadership?

Of all the special problems of general conduct which the most intelligent children face, I will mention five, which beset them in early years and may lead to habits subversive of fine leadership: (1) to find enough hard and interesting work at school; (2) to suffer fools gladly; (3) to keep from becoming negativistic toward authority; (4) to keep from becoming hermits; (5) to avoid the formation of habits of extreme chicanery.

In the ordinary elementary school situation children of 140 IQ waste half of their time. Those above 170 IQ waste practically all of their time. With little to do, how can these children develop power of sustained effort, respect for the task, or habits of steady work? I could entertain you for some time telling you the various sorts of bizarre and wasteful activities that were taking up the time of the most intelligent elementary school children in this nation yesterday in their classrooms, but we must pass on to other things.

A lesson which many highly intelligent persons never learn as long as they live is that human beings in general are incorrigibly very different from themselves in thought, action, and desire. Many a reformer has died at the hands of a mob which he was trying to improve. The highly intelligent child must learn to suffer fools gladly — not sneeringly, not angrily, not despairingly, not weepingly — but *gladly*, if personal development is to proceed successfully in the world as it is. Failure to learn how to tolerate in a reasonable fashion the foolishness of others less gifted leads to bitterness, disillusionment, and misanthropy, which are the ruin of potential leaders.

Every day at school the opportunity presents itself to learn this lesson. Especially hard for these intelligent children to bear is the foolishness of accepted authority. For instance, our pupils found it stated in their encyclopedia that Mr. Orville Wright is dead. As is likely to be the case, a child in the group immediately identified error. "Mr. Orville Wright is as much alive as I am," declared this child. This was subsequently verified by the class as a whole. They wrote to Mr. Wright, fiercely protesting against the foolishness of the encyclopedia. They wanted to throw the false authority out at once.

The teacher discussed the incident on the basis of "glad suffering." I can't take time to describe the conversation that pivoted on this incident, but I can say that it was valuable as emotional education. The pupils still have the offending encyclopedia.

As a form of failure to suffer fools gladly, negativism may develop. The foolish teacher who hates to be corrected by a child is unsuited to these children. Too many children of IQ 170 are being taught by teachers of IQ 120. Into this important matter of the *selection of the teacher* we cannot enter, except to illustrate the difficulty from recent conversation with a ten-year-old boy of IQ 165. This boy was referred to us as a school problem: "Not interested in the school work. Very impudent. A liar." The following is a fragment of conversation with this boy:

> What seems to be your *main* problem in school?
> Several of them.
> Name *one*.
> Well, I will name the teachers. Oh, boy! It is bad

enough when the *pupils* make mistakes, but when the *teachers* make mistakes, oh, boy!

Mention a few mistakes the teachers made.

For instance I was sitting in 5A and the teacher was teaching 5B. She was telling those children that the Germans discovered printing, that Gutenberg was the first discoverer of it, mind you. After a few minutes I couldn't stand it. I am not supposed to recite in that class, you see, but I got up. I said, "No; the Chinese *invented*, not discovered, printing, before the time of Gutenberg — while the Germans were still barbarians."

Then the teacher said, "Sit down. You are entirely too fresh." Later on she gave me a raking-over before the whole class. Oh, boy! What teaching!

It seemed to me that one should begin at once in this case the lesson about suffering fools gladly. So I said, "Ned, that teacher is foolish, but one of the very first things to learn in the world is to suffer fools *gladly*." The child was so filled with resentment that he heard only the word "suffer."

"Yes, that's it. That's what *I* say! Make 'em suffer. Roll a rock on 'em."

I quote this to suggest how negativistic rebels may seize on the wrong idea. Before we finished the conversation Ned was straightened out on the subject of who was to do the suffering. He agreed to do it himself.

I will cite another conversation, this time with a nine-year-old, of IQ 183.

What seems to be the *main* trouble with you at school?

The teacher can't pronounce.

Can't pronounce *what?*

Oh, lots of things. The teacher said "Magdalen College" — at Oxford, you know. I said, "In England they call it

Môdlin College." The teacher wrote a note home to say I am rude and disorderly. She does not like me.

Just one more conversation, this time with an eight-year-old, of IQ 178, sent as a school problem:

> What is your *main* trouble at school?
> My really main trouble is *not* at school.
> Where is it, then?
> It is the *librarian.*
> How is *that?*
> Well, for instance, I go to the library to look for my books on mechanics. I am making a new way for engines to go into reverse gear. The librarian says, "Here, where are you going? You belong in the juvenile department." So I have to go where the children are all *supposed* to go. But I don't stay there long, because they don't have any real books there. Say, do you think you could get me a card to the other department?

This subject is inexhaustible, but we must go on to speak of the psychological isolation of these children when they drift unrecognized. The majority of children above 160 IQ play little with other children because the difficulties of social contact are almost insurmountable. Unless special facilities can be provided, these children tend to become isolates, a condition not conducive to leadership, except perhaps of a few rare sorts, later in life. Such children are ordinarily friendly and gregarious by nature, but their efforts at forming friendship tend to be defeated by the scarcity of like-minded contemporaries. The imaginary playmate as a solution of the problem of loneliness is fairly frequent, but far inferior to the real playmate, could one be found. Shaw makes Saint Joan say, "I was always alone." This danger of becoming an isolate and a hermit is one

that should be carefully studied in the interests of leadership. To combat it we must somehow supply the highly
intelligent in their early years with companions, especially
of their own age, who can understand what they say, and can
answer. This difficulty of communication is illustrated by
Voltaire's abortive attempt as an adult to get into contact
with the peasants around him. In *The Ignorant Philoso-
pher*, Voltaire says, "I discovered such a wide difference between thought and nourishment, without which I should
not think that I believed that there was a substance in me
that reasoned and another substance that digested. Nevertheless, by constantly endeavoring that we are two, I ma-
terially felt that I was only one: and this contradiction gave
me infinite pain. I have asked some of my own likenesses,
who cultivate the earth, our common mother, if they felt
that they were two? If they had discovered by their philosophy that they possessed within them an immortal substance . . . acting upon their nerves without touching
them, sent expressly into them six weeks after their con-
ception? They thought that I was jesting and pursued the
cultivation of their land without making me a reply."

Even so, the ten-year-old, of IQ 175, wishes to discuss
with his "own likenesses" the events of medieval history, but
he finds that they make him "no reply." And if he persists,
they become annoyed, hurling at him the dreadful epithet,
"Perfesser." If he still persists, they pull his hair, tear his
shirt from his back, and hit him with a beer bottle. (I am
speaking of *real* life.)

Turning now to habits of chicanery, it would be a question
for long and close debate, as to whether a highly gifted leader
can ever live and do his work among the mass of men without developing a technique of benign chicanery. Many of

the great political leaders have been past masters of benign chicanery, often exploiting the people for the good of the social order. Perhaps the arts of benign chicanery are absolutely necessary to a child of highest intelligence, compelled to find his spiritual way through mass education. Certain it is that these children learn all sorts of devious ways to self-preservation. For instance, two of our pupils of Public School 500 came to us followed by notes from teachers, saying they were hard-of-hearing. Both of them have very keen ears, but they had learned not to hear the insupportable drill on things they had known for years, and in self-defense they listened so little that their teachers thought them deaf. At Public School 500 their hearing is good — almost too good!

Guidance in regard to this matter of chicanery is absolutely necessary. Here we have one of the most delicate of all aspects of the training of a leader. By teaching these children that they should at all times act with complete candor and straightforwardness, in all sorts of company, shall we be educating them for self-destruction? We could spend hours in discussing this. We cannot do much more here than mention it.

MATTERS OF GENERAL POLICY

I am unwilling to close these remarks without touching upon some matters of general policy, which go beyond selection and training. What of those children, gifted for leadership, who through accidents of fate are without means for the development of their gifts? At our school we are compelled to witness daily the sight of children of fine quality, who do not have enough to eat or wear, to say nothing of having about them beauty or comfort. It is thought

by those who have given no precise attention to the matter that "bright children will take care of themselves." This is the routine answer given by foundations established to promote human welfare, when requests are made for grants to study and meet the need of such children. The concern of American philanthropy in the present state of public knowledge is for the chronic dependent, forever incapable of development. This criticism may be justly extended to include not only the leaders of philanthropy today, but political, educational, and other kinds of leaders, who would give all to the burdens of society and nothing to the burden-bearers. To such tendencies of those in power today some halt should be called. For a people to deny its natural aristocracy is a social error in the broader sense.

Now the truth is that children of great ability are virtually as helpless as any others under authorities blind to their exceptionality. It would be an impossibly strong and shrewd child who could today conduct his own education under the compulsory school laws; make money to live on and accumulate funds for his own higher education under the child-labor laws — all in the first eighteen years of his life. Yet this seems to be what elderly society has vaguely in mind, when reiterating that "the bright will take care of themselves."

It is common to refer in this connection to the fact that Mr. John D. Rockefeller had earned and saved a large sum of money by the time he was sixteen years old. However, in this day and age Mr. Rockefeller would have been arrested on the double charge of truancy and violation of the child-labor law, and would have had no savings whatsoever at sixteen years of age. It is shocking to think of Mr. Rockefeller standing at ten years of age before the Juvenile

Court, but such would be his situation were he a ten-year-old child *today* instead of having been such nearly a hundred years ago.   In our day a ten-year-old acquires no merit by staying out of school and engaging in the egg business. He acquires, instead, a court summons.

What is needed for the support and development of those children whom we see before us daily, and who represent scores of others in the same economic condition, is what we may call a revolving foundation.   By this is meant a fund from which the gifted young could draw at any age the means for their development, with the moral (not legal) obligation to repay according to ability to do so, after twenty years, without interest.   By this plan the superior could invest in themselves; very little money would actually be spent, because it would come back again, and the nation would benefit in ways not now fully foreseeable.   The establishment of a revolving fund for the development of tested children would be another "new thing under the sun."   It would be a great experiment in social science, now rendered possible for the first time by inventions and discoveries in the field of child psychology.

Chapter Twenty-Two

PROBLEMS OF RELATIONSHIP BETWEEN ELEMENTARY AND SECONDARY SCHOOLS IN THE CASE OF HIGHLY INTELLIGENT PUPILS

An address before the National Committee on Coördination of Secondary Education at a symposium on "The Education of Pupils of High Intelligence," Cleveland, February 27, 1939.[1]

I SHALL not dwell here upon the present knowledge of gifted children as organisms. Our findings in follow-up studies on tested children in New York City confirm in all particulars Professor Terman's researches on the Pacific coast. Since these several studies have been carried on in complete independence, one in the East, the other in the West, for nearly twenty years, we may certainly feel justified in the conclusion that we are arriving at truth about the mental and physical traits and development of highly intelligent persons, coming as we do to the same results.

My remarks here will deal, rather, with certain problems of the *education* of the highly intelligent. I may say at the outset that my direct contacts with the education of gifted pupils have all been on the level of the elementary school. I consider that the problems are most urgent on this level,

[1] Reprinted from *The Journal of Educational Sociology* (October, 1939), pages 90–102.

because it is in the primary and elementary school that the very intelligent child most especially needs a supplement to the standard curriculum. The program of progress through the elementary grades is based on what pupils at, or only very slightly above, the average can master at given ages, so that the extremely intelligent child has little or nothing to do there. His interest is not engaged, and his power is not challenged. The situation of such children has been well exemplified in a recent biography [2] which sets forth the sense of futility from which many of them suffer at school in the early years.

When the child reaches senior high school, however, the case is somewhat different. The college preparatory course of the secondary school was originated with and for pupils of college caliber. It is therefore based on what very intelligent adolescents, and they only, can learn. Hence it offers to the pupil at and above 130 IQ (S–B) tasks of sufficient interest and difficulty to engage his powers of learning.

Laying aside, for purposes of the moment, argument as to whether the content of the college preparatory course is what it should be from all angles, we maintain that it is sufficiently abstract, complex, and difficult to operate as an intellectual stimulus for quite highly intelligent adolescents. I shall return to this point later, raising it here merely to explain why it has seemed to me especially important to work in the elementary school.

One cannot work for long in the elementary school, however, without becoming involved in research which has to do with the secondary school. There are many problems of coördination that require for their adequate study the

---

[2] Bridgman, Amy S. *My Valuable Time: The Story of Paul Bridgman Boyd.* (109 pages.) Stephen Daye Press, Brattleboro, Vermont; 1938.

joint efforts of both elementary and secondary school. We are currently trying to find answers to these problems at Public School 500, Manhattan, for we shall begin sending pupils from there to the senior high schools in June, 1939.

THE ELEMENTARY SCHOOL

For some years, beginning about 1918, experimentation has been sporadically undertaken in New York City on the initiative of individual principals to find out what should be done in the elementary school for highly intelligent children. It was not, however, until January, 1936, that the Board of Education itself took official action in cognizance of the presence of these pupils in the school system. On January 28, 1936, Public School 500, Manhattan (Speyer School),[3] was founded by formal action of the Board of Education and Teachers College, jointly, for the study of intellectual deviates, other than the feeble-minded, in the elementary school.

Two classes for rapid learners were included in the setup of this school, to accommodate twenty-five pupils each. These classes have now (1939) been in progress for three years. Their chief purpose has been to find experimentally and to establish a curriculum that would provide a genuine education for children of mental calibers above 130 IQ (S–B); an education that would extend their minds and interest them in the interests of society during the years of the elementary school.

Pupils were selected for this experiment on the basis of three criteria: (1) they must test at or above 130 IQ (S–B); (2) they must be at least 7 years 0 month old, and at most

[3] Hollingworth, Leta S. "The Founding of Public School 500: Speyer School," *Teachers College Record*, Vol. 37 (November, 1936), pages 119–128.

9 years 6 months old; (3) they must be representative as a group of the various ethnic stocks composing the population of New York City. This constitutes what we consider a perfectly democratic selection. Nothing "counts" toward selection except the tested quality of the pupil himself.

The organization is that of an 8B elementary school, designed to run for five years as an experiment. Promotion to the ninth grade of the senior high schools at the age of 13 years was planned for our pupils. The school also includes seven classes for slow learners (IQ 75–90), the pupils of which mingle freely with those of the rapid learner classes except for purposes of classroom instruction.

The teachers were selected from a long list of applicants for the posts among licensed elementary-school teachers of New York City. Criteria for selection rested on personality, degree of education, and desire to undertake experimental work.

Enrichment of the curriculum has been going forward for three years. Pupils at and above 130 (S–B) need, on the average, about one half of their time in the elementary school for mastering the standard curriculum set up for "all the children." "Mastering" here means not "passing" with a mark of 65 per cent, but genuine *mastery* with marks of 90 per cent and above.

In the half day thus left to spare, an enrichment curriculum has been pursued, which has elsewhere been described in some detail.[4] The chief features of this enrichment curriculum are a series of units, one each term in each class, on "The Evolution of Common Things" and the French language and literature.

[4] Hollingworth, Leta S. "An Enrichment Curriculum for Rapid Learners at Public School 500: Speyer School," *Teachers College Record*, Vol. 39 (January, 1938), pages 296–306. See also Chapter 21 of this book.

TRANSITION FROM ELEMENTARY
TO SECONDARY SCHOOL

The time comes when pupils thus selected and educated are to pass to the ninth grade of the senior high school. At this point questions arise which call urgently for discussion as a joint responsibility of both elementary and secondary schools. Some of these questions are as follows:

1. Why is 13 years to be chosen as the optimum age for the transition?

2. Why is junior high school omitted from the picture?

3. What ceremony, if any, should mark the transition to senior high school?

4. What items of cumulative record should accompany the pupil as he or she enters high school?

5. What differences are there in the demands of high school, as compared with the elementary school, which would affect the minimum IQ at which enrichment is needed in the high school? Is enrichment needed in the high school at 130 IQ (S–B)?

6. The point at which enrichment begins to be needed having been determined experimentally, how should the secondary school organize to provide a genuine education for pupils at and above that level?

7. Assuming an enrichment program for pupils above 150 IQ (S–B) desirable or imperatively necessary in high schools, what matters shall be agreed upon to enter into the curriculum?

8. Shall we guide all of our highly intelligent elementary-school pupils into the college preparatory courses? Or shall some of them be so guided that they will end high school without the "credits" for college?

9. What can and should public schools do for those few pupils who test at or above 170 IQ (S–B), for whom no experimental work so far done is of much real effect, either in elementary or secondary school?

CONSIDERATION OF THE QUESTIONS ARISING

Not all the foregoing questions proposed can be fully discussed here. Whatever is said, however, is an outgrowth of our own professional observations, extending over the past seventeen years. In particular these observations result from the current obligation at Public School 500, Manhattan (Speyer School), to promote to senior high school our first group of children now reaching the thirteenth birthday.

It is obvious that we have to determine upon *an age* for promotion to the senior high school. This must take into consideration "the whole child." We cannot isolate the intellect for this purpose. "Body, mind, and soul" must pass as a unit to secondary school.

The brightest of our pupils were fully ready for the scholastic work of the ninth grade when they were 8 years old; several others, when they were 10 years old. Ability to "pass examinations" set for 8B pupils cannot, therefore, reasonably become our criterion for promoting these children, unless we wish to assume responsibility for placing prepubescent, 8-, 9- and 10-year-old children in a scholastic milieu that is determined by the physical size and social maturity of adolescents.

After much discussion, we fixed upon 13 years as the age for transition to senior high school. We came to this largely as a result of our pooled professional experience, but not wholly on that basis. We gave considerable weight to the follow-up study of pupils identified in 1922, and kept together for three years in special classes at Public School 165, Manhattan.[5] There were 56 of these children whom we promoted to the ninth grade at an average age of 11 years; and the high-school careers of all of them were followed through sixteen different high schools.[6] In the course of this follow-up, the question was repeatedly asked, "What would be the best age to enter the ninth grade?"

Sixty per cent of these pupils gave 13 years as the "best age" to enter high school, and twenty-six per cent gave 14 years or older. Only one child gave an age younger than 12 years as optimum for entering high school. This group, as a whole, would have preferred to enter the ninth grade at an age older than that at which they entered, and gave cogent reasons for the preference during their high-school careers.

These ideas persisted through the college careers, especially among the boys, many of whom felt they were misplaced in college at 15 years of age. Entering high school near the thirteenth birthday, a child saves time, and yet is not made subject to the tensions which may result from trying to meet social and physical requirements for which he is too immature.

Junior high school is omitted from the picture as ours was a five-year plan. Such a plan of curriculum enrichment as ours fits best into the 8B setup, for such a program cannot be supervised if the pupils are scattered and the situation made subject to the transition from 6B to junior high school. In the metropolitan situation it is not feasible to take the

[5] Lamson, E. E. "A Study of Young Gifted Children in Senior High School." *Contributions to Education* No. 424 (117 pages). Bureau of Publications, Teachers College, Columbia University, New York; 1930.

[6] Lamson, E. E. "High School Achievement of Fifty-Six Gifted Children." *Journal of Genetic Psychology,* Vol. 47 (1935), pages 233–238.

pupils for special classes until they are at least 7 years old. The infrequency of their occurrence makes it necessary to assemble them from several districts, and they are not mature enough to come from a distance when they are 6 years of age. Parents cannot assume the burden of accompanying them twice a day. Our pupils were 8 years old, on the median, when they entered our rapid learner classes.

We have found it feasible to organize classes for 8-year-olds, give them a five-year program of special studies, and have them fully ready for senior high school at 13 years of age. This plan has worked out well, whereas, if we had had to consider a transition to the junior high school in the midst of our work, difficulties would have arisen, and it is not clear how our program could have been carried out at all. However, a field for *experimentation* lies here for those who would be predisposed to favor the junior-high-school plan of school organization.

We decided that no ceremony of graduation should mark the promotion to senior high school. Our pupils will make the transition not in a body, but a few at a time at the end of each term. Some informal social event may take place, but no ceremony of graduation as such.

The question, "What items of cumulative record should accompany each child from the elementary school?" is one requiring much study. Here we are working quite experimentally. The public schools of Altoona, Elkins Park, and Fort Wayne, Pennsylvania, are reported to have formulated a cumulative record card for rapid learners, which we hope later to consult. The records of mental tests, the record of scholastic-achievement tests, and a statement of teachers' ratings on a variety of character traits should no doubt be included with the health record and attendance record in the elementary school.

Ideally, the secondary school should receive these pupils already tested mentally, with cumulative records; but, since in the existing state of affairs this is not possible, because such tests have not been generally made, the high schools are wondering what methods to use in selecting the highly intelligent as they arrive, in the ordinary course of events, for admission.

We must agree that we have, in fact, no method at present generally available of distributing the top percentile of the adolescent population. The Army Alpha, which strictly speaking pertains to adults, is no doubt the most nearly appropriate instrument we have for distributing the top one per cent of adolescents. No other group test has sufficient "top" for this purpose, and no individual test has a "ceiling" high enough to prevent the best from "going through." Two forms of Army Alpha combined will give as good an approximation as is at present available to a correct distribution of adolescents at and above 130 IQ (S–B).

There exist tests of scholastic aptitude which pertain to adolescents of college caliber, but these are not generally available, being limited to the organizations which make specific use of them.

From observations of the progress of highly intelligent children tested at an early age, I offer the hypothesis that pupils of 130 to 150 IQ (S–B) have quite enough to do in the truly efficient pursuit of the college preparatory curriculum of the senior high schools, and do not need any enrichment of this curriculum as far as challenge to ability is concerned. What these pupils need is merely freedom from the presence of great masses of classmates who are mentally unadapted to the college preparatory course, and the opportunity to work unhampered, in segregated groups, such as are now being formed in many secondary schools under the concept of *the honor school.*

Pupils above 150 IQ (S–B) are, however, probably in definite need of an enrichment of even the college preparatory course as it exists currently in senior high schools. If experimental observation should prove this hypothesis to be true, how should the secondary school set about it to provide for the genuine education of such pupils? Should the huge high schools of a great city, like New York, organize an enrichment curriculum within the honor schools for these extreme deviates? Should honor schools have faculties proper to them only? Assuming an enrichment program for pupils above 150 IQ (S–B) to be found desirable or necessary in secondary school, what matters shall find place in such a curriculum?

The answers to these questions cannot be stated from the swivel chair or the arm chair. Years of realistic hard and intelligent work will have to be done, by way of experiment with various groups of adolescents. As regards the question pertaining to enrichment of curriculum, I dare offer the suggestion that there are "common things" the evolution of which would be more properly worked out at the adolescent level than at the level of childhood by highly intelligent pupils. Thus at Public School 500, Manhattan (Speyer School), we often find ourselves wishing that we might have our pupils at adolescence in order to take up with them the evolution of common but rather abstract things, such as the evolution of law and order, of trade and money, of warfare, of punishment, and many other things concerning which no systematic instruction is ever given outside of professional schools.

One may suggest that in the elementary school the enrichment curriculum might proceed by covering the evolution of "common things" which are concrete, as we have been doing, leaving for the secondary school those "common things" which are relatively abstract and involve especially concepts of social-economic consequence.

It is to be considered, also, that each of these pupils, at and above 150 IQ (S–B), would have the capacity to master a manual trade, in addition to mastering a profession, if time were allowed during adolescence. At 13 years of age, the hand then being developed, such pupils might be trained for skilled trades, in their spare time, as an enrichment of curriculum. In a changing world it is perhaps a good thing for those who are capable of *both* profession and skilled manual craft to have *both* at their service as adults, and to be capable of serving society and themselves in more than one specialized vocation, as was and is actually the case with many able Americans, reared and educated under pioneering conditions of the nineteenth century and earlier.

To this point we have been speaking of enrichments accompanying and supplementing the college preparatory course for pupils testing above 150 IQ (S–B). But shall we guide *all* our highly intelligent pupils into college preparatory courses? Or shall some of them be positively guided so that they will end high school without the "credits" for college? Shall all whose circumstances tend to force them into vocational high schools be allowed to drift in that direction? Here is a question of fundamental importance for society, which at this moment we hardly know enough to raise, much less to answer. Only one in every hundred born tests at or above 130 IQ (S–B). What does society most *need* from this little handful of persons? These can perform socially desired functions which none of the other ninety and nine can possibly perform. They can be educated in ways which are forever out of the reach of all who test below them. What should we, as educators, the publicly appointed guardians of their intellectual lives, do with these children for their own and society's best interests?

There is no more serious question than this in all education: How shall a democracy educate the most educable? At present these children are to a great extent lost in the vast enterprises of mass education, and are left to handle their special problems as they may, by themselves, while the energies of teachers are bent upon the main business of dealing with the ninety-nine per cent who test below 130 IQ (S–B). Common sense would tell us that a child who tests as far above the average as a feeble-minded child tests below cannot escape having special problems under conditions of mass education. We cannot go into this matter in detail here. These problems have been set forth in another place.[7] It is for us to consider them carefully, for educators are the sole group appointed by society to guard the interests of children. We are their official guardians, adding our guidance to that of their natural guardians, parents, who are often helpless either to recognize these children's abilities or to develop them.

WHAT ABOUT GENIUS?

We come finally to what may be the most important point of all — the point where we inquire into the responsibility

[7] Hollingworth, Leta S. "The Child of Very Superior Intelligence as a Special Problem in Social Adjustment." *Proceedings* of the First Interna-

of the public schools for children who are as far above those of 130 IQ (S–B) as the latter are above 100 IQ (S–B). I refer to those very rarely occurring pupils who test at or above 170 IQ (S–B). These children are important for civilization in inverse ratio to their infrequency of occurrence. They are the ones who can not only *conserve* thought in its abstract reaches, but who can *originate* new thoughts, new inventions, new patterns, and who can solve problems.

When, about twenty years ago, Terman [8] began to attempt classifications of high deviates, on the basis of IQ, he called 140 IQ (S–B) "genius or near genius." The intervening years have proved that this idea must be revised. Seniors in many of our first-rate colleges test at a median of 140 IQ (S–B) or even higher, and about a quarter of *all* college graduates test at or above this level.

That point in the distribution of IQ where mental products suggestive of genius, as defined by lexicographers, begin to appear, seems to be as far above 140 IQ as 140 IQ is above average. Somewhere between 170 and 180 IQ (S–B) we begin to see merging in early adulthood that "highly unusual power of invention or origination," that "original creative power, frequently working through the imagination," which is ordinarily called "genius." [9]

This element in our juvenile population, so significant and so rarely found, passes unrecognized at present through the

tional Congress on Mental Hygiene, Vol. II, pages 47–69. The International Committee for Mental Hygiene, Inc., New York; 1932.

[8] Terman, Lewis M. *The Measurement of Intelligence* (362 pages). Houghton Mifflin Company, Boston; 1916. Also, Terman, Lewis M. *Genetic Studies of Genius*, Vol. I (663 pages). Stanford University Press, Stanford University, California; 1925.

[9] Webster's New International Dictionary, 1935.

public schools. We have not even commenced to evolve an education suitable for a child who at 9 or 10 years of age is able to think on a college level. The idea that such children exist at all is even laughed to scorn by teachers and principals who have a quarter of a century of "experience" behind them. These children have no way of making themselves known. The *mental tests* make them known. They become known only to those educators who "believe in" mental tests.

The most interesting problem in education is to discover how these children, testing above 170 IQ (S–B), can and should be educated; to devise ways and means whereby these far deviates may get the full use of their abilities in school and society, especially when they have no money. The concept of democracy on which the United States was founded is one of equality of opportunity. The intention of our educational policy is that every child should have a chance to develop as his natural abilities may entitle him to do, all artificial distinctions being eliminated. Now at last psychological science has provided an effective instrument for achieving this democracy in education, namely the mental test, by means of which a child may be recognized for his own ability, regardless of age, sex, race, creed, or economic condition.

How shall we as educators utilize this instrument of genuine democracy? How shall we proceed under conditions in which the founding fathers are now mistaken by many citizens to have proclaimed and promised biological equality! [10]

[10] Butler, Nicholas Murray. "Is Thomas Jefferson the Forgotten Man?" Address delivered at the Parrish Art Museum, Southampton, September 1, 1935. Published at 405 West 117th Street, New York.

Perhaps we should take another leaf from the book of the French Republic, where the delusion of biological equality has always been successfully avoided; where the State continually reviews its attempt to secure equality of opportunity by explicit efforts to find and foster the natural élite, and to know where the gifted are located in the French population.[11]

We may also consider the Belgian policies, with regard to subsidy of the gifted,[12] "Ce principe fondamental: Que chaque enfant, quelle que soit la situation de fortune des parents, soit mis en état d'acquérir par l'instruction tout le développement intellectuel et professionnel dont il est capable."

All the questions here raised call for definite answers *at the present time.* Such questions could not be effectively raised prior to the twentieth century, because psychologists had not previously advanced to a point of supplying a scientific method of determining intelligence in childhood. It is the most significant contribution of psychology to education, in this century — and perhaps in all centuries — that we are enabled to know the mental caliber of a human being in his early years.

More and more it becomes clear that human welfare on the whole is much more a matter of the activities of *deviates* than it is a matter of what the middle mass of persons does. Those educators who make a joke of the genius and regard the dullard as a mere figment of the imagination of psychologists, or who solve the educational problems which

---

[11] Bouglé, C. *Enquêtes sur le Baccalauréat.* (120 pages.) Librairie Hachette, Paris; 1935.

[12] Bauwens, Léon. *Fonds des mieux doués.* (Cinquième édition, 77 pages.) Librairie Albert Dewit, Bruxelles; 1927.

these children present by the simple device of "not believing in" them, fiddle while Rome burns. It is the deviate who takes the initiative and plays the primary part in social determination. How shall we, then, educate him in a democracy?

INDEX

Index

Ability, modern study of, 21 ff. *See also* Genius

Activity, physical, among eminent adults, 17. *See* Eminent adults.

Adjustment problems, 254 ff., 271–272

Adult status of intelligent children, 245 ff.

Alger, William, quoted on genius, 12

Altoona, Pa., rapid-learner classes in, 314

Argue, tendency to, 279

Art and music work, 295 ff.

Aunts' influence on gifted children, 17

B, case of, 57–59

Background summary, 224–226

Baldwin, Bird T., cited, 245

Beatrice, case of, 35–37

Beauty, prevalence of, among the gifted, 256

Behavioral development summary, 227–228, 269

Bernreuter Inventory, application of, 249–252

Binet, Alfred, xi, xiv, 21; method, 22; cited on "judgment," 284

Binet-Simon Tests, case ratings by, 32–35

Blum, Rosalind, Child L tested by, 214

Bronner, A. F., cited, 269

Bureau of Educational Guidance, Teachers College, Columbia University, Child J referred to, 201

Burke, Agnes, xi

Burt, Cyril, case reported by, 61; cited, 268

Bush's daughter, B, case of, 32–33

Carothers, F. E., 115

Carrel, Alexis, quoted on genius, 4

Cases recorded by author: Child A, 69–94; Child B, 95–103; Child C, 104–117; Child D, 118–133; Child E, 134–158; Child F, 159–173; Child G, 174–185; Child H, 186–192; Child I, 193–200; Child J, 201–206; Child K, 207–211; Child L, 212–223. *See also under* Child A, Child B, etc.

Cattell, J. McKeen, 15

Characteristics, physical, 16, 62, 255–257, 269

Child A, xv, 69–94; family background, 69–72; preschool history, 72–74; school history, 74–76; judgments of teachers, 77–81; mental measurements, 81–82; traits of character, 83–85; physical measurements and health, 85–87; diversions, 87–88; imaginary land, 88; re-

Classics In
Child Development

An Arno Press Collection

Baldwin, James Mark. **Thought and Things.** Four vols. in two. 1906-1915

Blatz, W[illiam] E[met], et al. **Collected Studies on the Dionne Quintuplets.** 1937

Bühler, Charlotte. **The First Year of Life.** 1930

Bühler, Karl. **The Mental Development of the Child.** 1930

Claparède, Ed[ouard]. **Experimental Pedagogy and the Psychology of the Child.** 1911

Factors Determining Intellectual Attainment. 1975

First Notes by Observant Parents. 1975

Freud, Anna. **Introduction to the Technic of Child Analysis.** 1928

Gesell, Arnold, et al. **Biographies of Child Development.** 1939

Goodenough, Florence L. **Measurement of Intelligence By Drawings.** 1926

Griffiths, Ruth. **A Study of Imagination in Early Childhood and Its Function in Mental Development.** 1918

Hall, G. Stanley and Some of His Pupils. **Aspects of Child Life and Education.** 1907

Hartshorne, Hugh and Mark May. **Studies in the Nature of Character. Vol. I: Studies in Deceit; Book One, General Methods and Results.** 1928

Hogan, Louise E. **A Study of a Child.** 1898

Hollingworth, Leta S. **Children Above 180 IQ, Stanford Binet:** Origins and Development. 1942

Kluver, Heinrich. **An Experimental Study of the Eidetic Type.** 1926

Lamson, Mary Swift. **Life and Education of Laura Dewey Bridgman, the Deaf, Dumb and Blind Girl.** 1881

Lewis, M[orris] M[ichael]. **Infant Speech:** A Study of the Beginnings of Language. 1936

McGraw, Myrtle B. **Growth: A Study of Johnny and Jimmy.** 1935

Monographs on Infancy. 1975

O'Shea, M. V., editor. **The Child: His Nature and His Needs.** 1925

Perez, Bernard. **The First Three Years of Childhood.** 1888

Romanes, George John. **Mental Evolution in Man:** Origin of Human Faculty. 1889

Shinn, Milicent Washburn. **The Biography of a Baby.** 1900

Stern, William. **Psychology of Early Childhood Up to the Sixth Year of Age.** 1924

Studies of Play. 1975

Terman, Lewis M. **Genius and Stupidity:** A Study of Some of the Intellectual Processes of Seven "Bright" and Seven "Stupid" Boys. 1906

Terman, Lewis M. **The Measurement of Intelligence.** 1916

Thorndike, Edward Lee. **Notes on Child Study.** 1901

Wilson, Louis N., compiler. **Bibliography of Child Study.** 1898-1912

[Witte, Karl Heinrich Gottfried]. **The Education of Karl Witte,** Or the Training of the Child. 1914